Psallite

Sacred Song for Liturgy and Life

Year A

Music by
The Collegeville Composers Group

LITURGICAL PRESS
Collegeville, Minnesota

www.litpress.org
800.858.5450

ACKNOWLEDGMENTS

Imprimatur: ✠ Most Reverend John F. Kinney, Diocese of Saint Cloud in Minnesota, May 29, 2007.

Music from *Psallite: Sacred Song for Liturgy and Life,* © 2005, 2006, 2007 by The Collegeville Composers Group (Carol Browning, Catherine Christmas, Cyprian Consiglio, O.S.B. Cam., Paul F. Ford, Ph.D., Paul Inwood). All rights reserved. Published and administered by Liturgical Press, Collegeville, Minnesota 56321.

The Psalm texts from The Grail (England), © 1963, 1986, 1993, 2000, The Grail. The Canticle texts from the Grail (England), © 1967, The Grail. All rights reserved. Licensed for *Psallite* and reprinted by permission of GIA Publications, Inc., 7404 South Mason Avenue, Chicago, IL 60638, North American agent for The Grail. *Imprimatur:* ✠ Most Reverend William Keeler, President, National Conference of Catholic Bishops, September 12, 1993.

The Canticle texts from the New Revised Standard Version (NRSV) Bible, © 1989, Division of Christian Education of the National Council of the Churches of Christ in the United States of America. All rights reserved. Used with permission. *Imprimatur:* ✠ Most Reverend Daniel E. Pilarczyk, President, National Conference of Catholic Bishops, September 12, 1991.

The cover design is by James Rhoades; photograph by Rob Fiocca, Botanica Images.

ISBN: 978-0-8146-3064-8

Contents

INTRODUCTORY NOTES

A new collection of liturgical songs inspired by the antiphons and psalms of the *Roman Missal, Psallite: Sacred Song for Liturgy and Life* includes music for each Sunday, Solemnity, and major feast day of the liturgical year.

For each liturgy, *Psallite* provides biblically based options for the entrance/opening song (the SONG FOR THE WEEK/DAY); the response song during the Liturgy of the Word (the SONG FOR THE WORD); and the song during the Communion procession (the SONG FOR THE TABLE). This collection contains a wealth of biblically based liturgical songs. While the music in this collection suggests specific Sundays or celebrations for its use, they have various, repeatable uses throughout the liturgical year.

The name *Psallite* (SAH-lee-tay) comes from the Latin version of Psalm 47:8, *psallite sapienter*, "sing praise with all your skill."

Psallite's music connects liturgy and life, church and home. The SONG FOR THE WEEK may be your theme tune for the entire week. The SONG FOR THE WORD may echo in your mind and keep the Word alive in your heart all day. The SONG FOR THE TABLE may be the one that you sing around your own dining table. All this is achieved by means of memorable music that will transform your life. Once this music gets under your skin, there's no turning back.

The **SONG FOR THE WEEK** opens the celebration, intensifies the unity of the assembly, leads their thoughts to the mystery of the liturgical season or festivity, and accompanies the procession of the presider and ministers. Another option is to use the SONG FOR THE WEEK at the end of the liturgy (with the addition of a doxology) to send forth the assembly into the world.

The **SONG FOR THE WORD**, an entirely new repertory of short, memorable antiphons, serves as the golden thread of the Liturgy of the Word.

The **SONG FOR THE TABLE**, which is the heart of *Psallite*, takes its texts and themes from the Liturgy of the Word, especially from the gospel of the day, transformed into processional music. People will now experience that the promises God made in his Word are fulfilled in the body and blood of Christ.

Psallite's music provides flexibility and allows leaders of music ministry to adapt the music for their assemblies. On the one hand, *Psallite* was designed for those parishes with the most limited musical resources: one well-trained cantor, no accompanist, but an assembly eager to sing the Mass. On the other hand, satisfying vocal, keyboard, and guitar arrangements will win the hearts of the most accomplished choirs and instrumentalists. Many of the descants not marked for a specific voice part may be sung in the alto/tenor range as well as the soprano range.

The style of music is eclectic—with influences ranging from chant to Afro-Caribbean to folk song but in all cases essentially vocal. The cantor calls to the assembly and the assembly responds. And every word they sing is biblically based.

The verse tones of *Psallite* can be used with any translation of the psalms, especially any Grail-based translation. Because *Psallite* models the use of moderately inclusive, horizontally inclusive language, it employs the 1993 Grail revision sponsored by the United States Conference of Catholic Bishops with the *imprimatur* of then-Bishop now Cardinal William H. Keeler, who was president at that time. The biblical canticles are mostly taken from the New Revised Standard Version, with some original translations for good measure.

Singing the antiphons and psalms of *Psallite* restores psalm-singing as our primary prayer language. Singing this kind of music helps our assemblies find their voices so that we all can sing the Mass, not just sing at Mass. Singing the same antiphons that our sisters and brothers sang at least a thousand years ago, and in some cases nearly two thousand years ago, connects us spiritually to the great communion of saints, a procession in which we are only the most recent walkers. Singing the various styles of music in *Psallite* will also help break down the cultural barriers that keep us from being "one body, one spirit, in Christ."

ABOUT THE COMPOSERS

The Collegeville Composers Group, a team of international musicians working collaboratively to create the collection, composed the music of *Psallite*. The composers group includes:

Carol Browning, the Director of Liturgy and Music at Saint Mary Magdalen Catholic Community in Camarillo, California and a music minister for almost twenty years. A member of the Religious Society of Friends (Quakers), Carol is a liturgical composer and an independently published inspirational songwriter.

Catherine Christmas, an accomplished organist and former cathedral director of music, currently working as Pastoral Coordinator for a group of parishes based in Winchester, England, and studying for a Master's in Pastoral Liturgy at Heythrop College, University of London.

Cyprian Consiglio, O.S.B. Cam., a musician, composer, author, and teacher who is a monk of the Camaldolese Congregation. He spends about half his time at home, writing and composing, and the other half of his time on the road, performing and teaching.

Paul F. Ford, Ph.D., a professor of systematic theology and liturgy, Saint John's Seminary, Camarillo, California. He is the author of *By Flowing Waters: Chant for the Liturgy*, published by Liturgical Press.

Paul Inwood, the Director of Liturgy and Director of Music for the Diocese of Portsmouth, England. He is an internationally known liturgist, composer, organist, choir director, and clinician. His liturgical music appears in numerous hymnals worldwide.

ADDITIONAL RESOURCES

Psallite: Sacred Song for Liturgy and Life

Published in three volumes, these editions include the full accompaniment and cantor/schola verses for all Sundays, Solemnities and major feast days of the liturgical cycle. Plastic coil binding, 8½" x 10⅞", over 320 pp.

Individual volumes: 1–4 copies, $24.95 each; 5 or more copies, $19.95* net each; please inquire for bulk purchases.

    978-0-8146-3064-8   Year A
    978-0-8146-3059-4   Year B
    978-0-8146-3065-5   Year C

Complete three-volume set (Years ABC): 1–4 sets, $59.95 per set; 5 or more sets, $49.95* net per set; please inquire for bulk purchases.

    978-0-8146-3060-0   Years ABC

Psallite Cantor/Choir Edition

This edition contains cantor/schola descants and harmonies for all Sundays and solemnities of the liturgical year and includes liturgical and Scriptural indices for various uses and planning. Titles are placed in alphabetical order. Single volume contains all titles in the Psallite collection.

    978-0-8146-3088-4

Kivar, 504 pp., 7 x 10, 1–4 copies $24.95; 5–9 copies $19.95 net; 10 or more copies $16.95* net

Psallite Antiphons on CD-ROM

Easy-to-use graphic files of all Psallite assembly antiphons (Years ABC) that can be used to select and insert music into desktop publishing documents, PowerPoint presentations, or other custom worship aids and programs. The parish or institution must purchase an annual reprint license in order to legally reproduce the antiphons.

    978-0-8146-7961-6 $39.95 CD-ROM
    978-0-8146-3061-7 $35.00 Annual license

Where Two or Three Are Gathered

A collection of twenty-six titles taken from Psallite: Sacred Song for Liturgy and Life (Year A). Titles include: Now Is the Hour • Be Patient, Beloved • Let the King of Glory Come In • Jesus, Mighty Lord, Come Save Us • Clothed in Christ, One in Christ (Rite of Baptism) • Clothed in Christ, One in Christ • Give Us Living Water • Give Thanks to the Lord, Alleluia • At Your Word Our Hearts Are Burning • I Am the Way: Follow Me • Here I Am • Light of the World • In God Alone Is My Soul at Rest • Keep These Words in Your Heart and Soul • Love Is My Desire • The Mercy of God Is for All • Everlasting Is Your Love • All Things Are from the Lord • Where Two or Three Are Gathered • Lord, You Are Close • Remember, Lord • All That Is True • I Shall Dwell in the House of the Lord • The Word of God at Work in Us • Come, All You Good and Faithful Servants • A River Flows

The music collection includes full accompaniment for cantor, schola, keyboard, and guitar plus reprintable antiphon graphics for assembly use. A CD recording of the collection is also available.

    Music collection: 978-0-8146-3077-8 • $11.95;
      5 or more copies $9.95* each
    CD recording: 978-0-8146-7965-4 • $16.95

Walk in My Ways

A collection of twenty-seven titles taken from Psallite: Sacred Song for Liturgy and Life (Year B). Titles include: To You, O Lord, I Lift My Soul • Rejoice in the Lord, Again, Rejoice • We Receive from Your Fullness • Here Is My Servant, Here Is My Son • Give, Your Father Sees • Those Who Love Me, I Will Deliver • My Shepherd Is the Lord • There Is Mercy in the Lord • This Is My Body • Send Out Your Spirit • Christ, Our Pasch • Live on In My Love • I Will See You Again • Walk in My Ways • Venite, adoremus • God Heals the Broken • Lead Me, Guide Me • Here in Your Presence • All You Nations • Don't Be Afraid • Those Who Do Justice • Let the Word Make a Home in Your Heart • I Loved Wisdom More than Health or Beauty • Courage! Get Up! • My Plans for You Are Peace • Rejoice in the Lord on This Feast of the Saints • May God Grant Us Joy of Heart

The music collection includes full accompaniment for cantor, schola, keyboard, and guitar plus reprintable antiphon graphics for assembly use. A CD recording of the collection is also available.

    Music collection: 978-0-8146-3058-7 • $11.95;
      5 or more copies $9.95* each
    CD recording: 978-0-8146-7960-9 • $16.95

We Will Follow You, Lord

A collection of twenty-eight titles taken from Psallite: Sacred Song for Liturgy and Life (Year C). Titles include: The Days Are Coming, Surely Coming • My Soul Rejoices in God • God's Love Is Revealed to Us • Not on Bread Alone Are We Nourished • You Are My Hiding-Place, O Lord • Lord, Cleanse My Heart, Make Me New • People of God, Flock of the Lord • A New Commandment • Joyfully You Will Draw Water • All Who Labor, Come to Me • This Day Is Holy to the Lord Our God • Love Bears All Things • Cast Out into the Deep • Forgive, and You Will Be Forgiven • Speak Your Word, O Lord, and We Shall Be Healed • For You My Soul Is Thirsting, O God, My God • We Will Follow You, Lord • Listen: I Stand at the Door and Knock • Do Not Store Up Earthly Treasures • From the East and West, from the North and South • In Every Age, O Lord, You Have Been Our Refuge • I Am Your Savior, My People • Seek the Lord! Long for the Lord! • Take Hold of Eternal Life • Worthy Is the Lamb Who Was Slain • Let Us Go Rejoicing to the House of the Lord • I Will Praise You, I Will Thank You • I Will Dwell with You, My House a House of Prayer

The music collection includes full accompaniment for cantor, schola, keyboard, and guitar plus reprintable antiphon graphics for assembly use. A CD recording of the collection is also available.

    Music collection: 978-0-8146-3075-4 • $11.95;
      5 or more copies $9.95* each
    CD recording: 978-0-8146-7964-7 • $16.95

To order or for further information contact:

Liturgical Press • www.litpress.org • 800.858.5450

*Asterisk indicates discount price available only on "no-returns" basis.

To You, O Lord, I Lift My Soul

First Sunday of Advent, Song for the Week

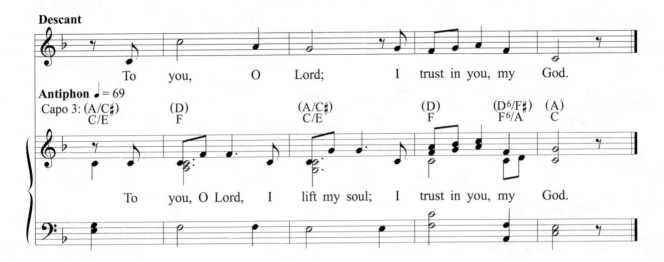

Descant

To you, O Lord; I trust in you, my God.

Antiphon ♩ = 69

Capo 3: (A/C♯)   (D)   (A/C♯)   (D)   (D⁶/F♯)   (A)
C/E   F   C/E   F   F⁶/A   C

To you, O Lord, I lift my soul; I trust in you, my God.

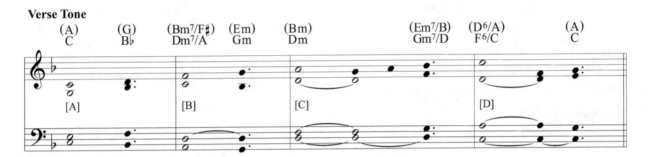

Verse Tone

(A)   (G)   (Bm⁷/F♯)   (Em)   (Bm)   (Em⁷/B)   (D⁶/A)   (A)
C   B♭   Dm⁷/A   Gm   Dm   Gm⁷/D   F⁶/C   C

[A]   [B]   [C]   [D]

Psalm 25:2-21

1. My God, I trust in you, let me not be disap<u>point</u>ed;
   do not let my enemies <u>tri</u>umph.
   Those who hope in you shall not be disap<u>point</u>ed,
   but only those who wantonly <u>break</u> faith.

2. LORD, make me know your <u>ways</u>.
   LORD, teach me your <u>paths</u>.
   Make me walk in your <u>truth</u>, and teach me,
   for you are God <u>my</u> savior.

3. In you I hope all the day <u>long</u>
   because of your goodness, O <u>LORD</u>.
   Remember your <u>mer</u>cy, LORD,
   and the love you have shown from <u>of</u> old.
   [repeat C-D)
   Do not remember the sins <u>of</u> my youth.
   In your love <u>remem</u>ber me.

4. The LORD is good and <u>up</u>right,
   showing the path to those who <u>stray</u>,
   guiding the humble <u>in</u> the right path,
   and teaching the way to <u>the</u> poor.

5. God's ways are steadfastness and <u>truth</u>
   for those faithful to the covenant de<u>crees</u>.
   LORD, for the sake <u>of</u> your name
   forgive my guilt, for it <u>is</u> great.

6. Those who revere the <u>LORD</u>
   will be shown the path they should <u>choose</u>.
   Their souls will <u>live</u> in happiness
   and their children will possess <u>the</u> land.
   [repeat C-D)
   The LORD's friendship is <u>for</u> the God-fearing;
   and the covenant is revealed <u>to</u> them.

Verse Tone

7. My eyes are always on the LORD,
   who will rescue my feet from the snare.
   Turn to me and have mercy
   for I am lonely and poor.

8. Relieve the anguish of my heart
   and set me free from my distress.
   See my affliction and my toil
   and take all my sins away.

9. See how many are my foes,
   how violent their hatred for me.
   Preserve my life and rescue me.
   Do not disappoint me, you are my refuge.
   [repeat C–D)
   May innocence and uprightness protect me,
   for my hope is in you, O LORD.

Let Us Go Rejoicing

First Sunday of Advent, Song for the Word
Anniversary of the Dedication of a Church, Song for the Word: Option III

Verse Tone

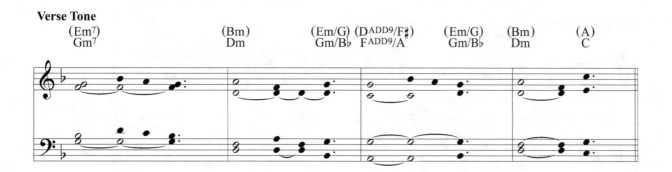

Psalm 122   *[The Lectionary selections for the Anniversary of the Dedication of a Church are indicated by an asterisk.]*

1. * I rejoiced when I <u>heard</u> them say:
   * "Let us go <u>to</u> God's house."
   * And now our <u>feet</u> are standing
   * within your gates, O Jeru<u>sa</u>lem.

2. * Jerusalem is built <u>as</u> a city
   * strong<u>ly</u> compact.
   * It is there that the <u>tribes</u> go up,
   * the tribes of <u>the</u> LORD.

3. For Israel's <u>law</u> it is,
   there to praise <u>the</u> LORD's name.
   There were set the <u>thrones</u> of judgement
   of the house <u>of</u> David.

4. For the peace of Jeru<u>sa</u>lem pray:
   "Peace be <u>to</u> your homes!
   May peace reign <u>in</u> your walls,
   in your pala<u>ces</u>, peace!"

5. * For love of my fam'<u>ly</u> and friends
   * I say: "Peace u<u>pon</u> you."
   * For love of the house <u>of</u> the LORD
   * I will ask for <u>your</u> good.

Now Is the Hour
First Sunday of Advent, Song for the Table

Antiphon ♩. = 56

Now is the hour to wake from sleep. All you na-tions, come to the feast: faith and mer-cy, just-ice and peace.

Verse Tone

Psalm 85:9, 11-14; Isaiah 2:2-5; Romans 13:11; Matthew 24:42, 44

1. I will hear what the LORD God <u>has</u> to say,
   a voice that <u>speaks</u> of peace,
   peace for his people <u>and</u> friends
   and those who turn to God <u>in</u> their hearts.

2. Mercy and faithful<u>ness</u> have met;
   justice and peace <u>have</u> embraced.
   Faithfulness shall spring from <u>the</u> earth
   and justice look <u>down</u> from heaven.

3. The LORD will <u>make</u> us prosper
   and our earth shall <u>yield</u> its fruit.
   Justice shall march in <u>the</u> forefront,
   and peace shall fol<u>low</u> the way.

4. In days to come
   the mountain <u>of</u> the LORD's house
   shall be established as the highest <u>of</u> the mountains,
   and shall be raised above <u>the</u> hills;
   all the <u>nations</u> shall stream to it.

5. Many peoples shall <u>come</u> and say,
   "Come, let us go up to the mountain of the LORD,
   to the house of the <u>God</u> of Jacob;
   that he may teach us <u>his</u> ways
   and that we may walk <u>in</u> his paths."

Verse Tone

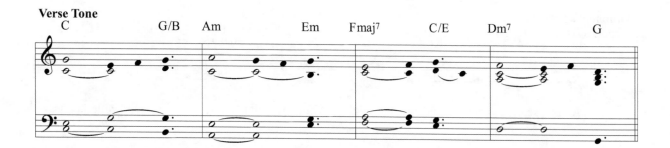

6. The Lord shall judge be<u>tween</u> the nations,
   and shall arbitrate for <u>many</u> peoples;
   they shall beat their swords in<u>to</u> plowshares,
   and their spears <u>into</u> pruning hooks.

7. Nation shall not lift up sword a<u>gainst</u> nation,
   neither shall they learn war <u>any</u> more.
   O house of Ja<u>cob</u>, come,
   let us walk in the light <u>of</u> the Lord!

8. You know what <u>time</u> it is,
   how it is now the moment for you to <u>wake</u> from sleep.
   For salvation is nearer to <u>us</u> now
   than when we be<u>came</u> believers.

9. Therefore <u>keep</u> awake,
   for you do not know on what day your <u>Lord</u> is coming.
   Therefore you also must <u>be</u> ready,
   for the Son of Man is coming at an unex<u>pect</u>ed hour.

Performance Notes

The Antiphon melody is derived from the old French carol tune "Shepherds, shake off your drowsy sleep."

Arise, Jerusalem, Stand on the Height

Second Sunday of Advent, Song for the Week

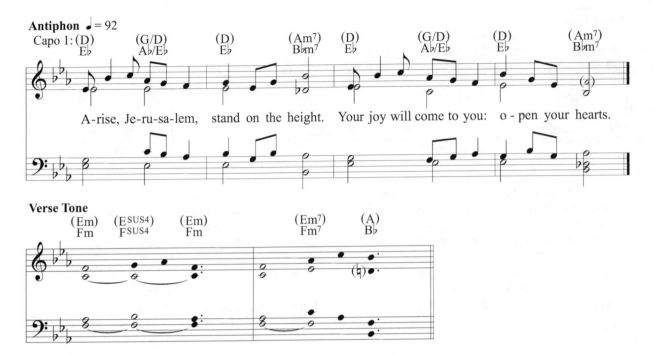

A-rise, Je-ru-sa-lem, stand on the height. Your joy will come to you: o - pen your hearts.

Baruch 5:1-2, 5-7, 9; Isaiah 12:3-6

1. Jerusalem, take off your robe of mourning and misery,
   put on forever the beauty of glory!

2. Wrapped in the robe of your justice and righteousness,
   put on your head the miter of majesty!

3. Jerusalem, arise, and look east from the highest heights!
   Your children are gathered at the word of your holy one.

4. Even though you went, led away by your enemies,
   God brings them back, borne aloft as if royalty.

5. God has ordered valleys and hills made into level ground
   so you can march safely in the light of God's glory.

6. God himself in joy will be the leader of Israel
   in glory, with mercy and justice for company.

7. You will draw water joyfully from the wellsprings of salvation.
   Give thanks to the LORD, give praise to his holy name.

8. Make the LORD's deeds known among the nations;
   proclaim the greatness of his name.

9. Sing a psalm to the LORD, for he has done glorious deeds;
   make known his works to all of the earth.

10. People of Zion, sing for joy,
    for great in your midst is the Holy One of Israel.

Justice Shall Flourish

Second Sunday of Advent, Song for the Word

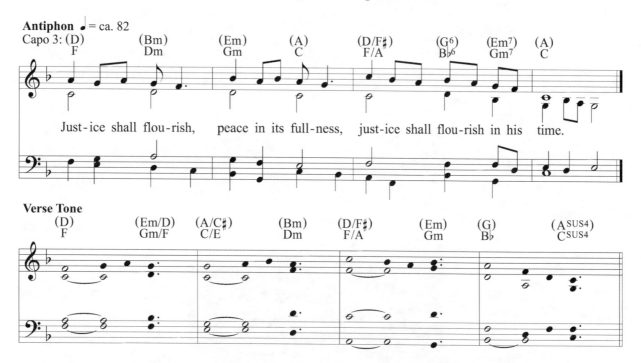

Psalm 72:1-4b, 5-14, 15c-19 [The Lectionary selections for the day are indicated by an asterisk.]

1. * O God, give your judgement to the king,
   * to a king's son your justice,
   * that he may judge your people in justice
   * and your poor in right judgement.

2. May the mountains bring forth peace for the people
   and the hills, justice.
   May he defend the poor of the people
   and save the children of the needy.

3. He shall endure like the sun and the moon
   from age to age.
   He shall descend like rain on the meadow,
   like raindrops on the earth.

4. * In his days justice shall flourish
   * and peace till the moon fails.
   * He shall rule from sea to sea,
   * from the Great River to earth's bounds.

5. Before him his enemies shall fall,
   his foes lick the dust.
   The kings of Tarshish and the seacoasts
   shall pay him tribute.

6. The kings of Sheba and Seba
   shall bring him gifts.
   Before him all rulers shall fall prostrate,
   all nations shall serve him.

7. * For he shall save the poor when they cry
   * and the needy who are helpless.
   * He will have pity on the weak
   * and save the lives of the poor.

8. From oppression he will rescue their lives,
   to him their blood is dear.
   They shall pray for him without ceasing
   and bless him all the day.

9. May corn be abundant in the land
   to the peaks of the mountains.
   May its fruit rustle like Lebanon;
   may people flourish in the cities
        like grass on the earth.

10. * May his name be blessed for ever
    * and endure like the sun.
    * Every tribe shall be blessed in him,
    * all nations bless his name.

11. Blessed be the LORD, the God of Israel,
    who alone works wonders,
    ever blessed God's glorious name.
    Let his glory fill the earth. Amen! Amen!

God's Tender Mercy

Second Sunday of Advent, Song for the Table
The Nativity of Saint John the Baptist (June 24), Song for the Table

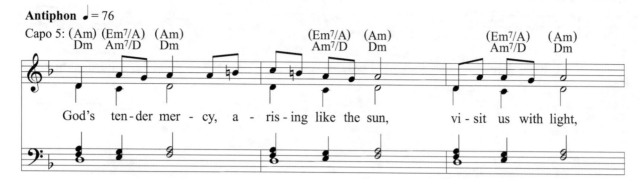

God's ten-der mer-cy, a-ris-ing like the sun, vi-sit us with light,

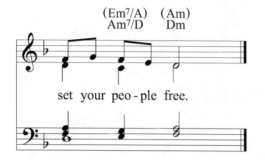

set your peo-ple free.

Verse Tone

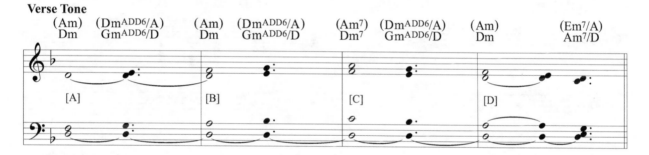

Psalm 92:2-6, 13-16

1. It is good to give thanks to the LORD,
   to make music to your name, O Most High,
   to proclaim your love in the morning
   and your truth in the watches of the night,
   [Repeat C-D]
   on the ten-stringed lyre and the lute,
   with the murmuring sound of the harp.

2. Your deeds, O LORD, have made me glad;
   for the work of your hands I shout with joy.
   O LORD, how great are your works!
   How deep are your designs!

3. The just will flourish like the palm tree
   and grow like a Lebanon cedar.
   Planted in the house of the LORD
   they will flourish in the courts of our God,

4. still bearing fruit when they are old,
   still full of sap, still green,
   to proclaim that the LORD is just,
   my rock, in whom there is no wrong.

Performance Notes
The Antiphon could be sung as a four-part round, if desired.

Rejoice in the Lord, Again Rejoice!

Third Sunday of Advent, Song for the Week

Verse Tone for Three-line Stanzas

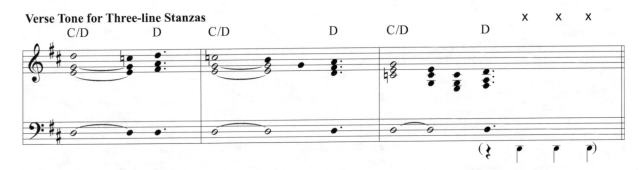

Psalm 96

1. O sing a new song to the LORD,
   sing to the LORD, all the earth.
   O sing to the LORD, bless his name.

2. Proclaim God's help day by day,
   tell among the nations his glory
   and his wonders among all the peoples.

3. The LORD is great and worthy of praise,
   to be feared above all gods;
   the gods of the heathens are naught.

4. It was the LORD who made the heavens,
   his are majesty and honor and power
   and splendor in the holy place.

5. Give the LORD, you families of peoples,
   give the LORD glory and power,
   give the LORD the glory of his name.

6. Bring an offering and enter God's courts,
   worship the LORD in the temple.
   O earth, stand in fear of the LORD.

7. Proclaim to the nations: "God is king."
   The world was made firm in its place;
   God will judge the people in fairness.

Verse Tone for Four-line Stanzas

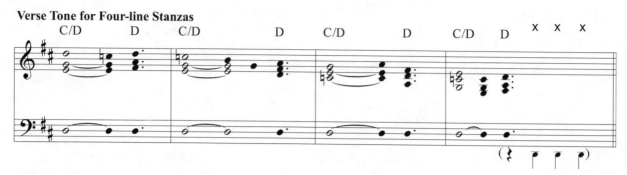

8. Let the heavens rejoice and earth <u>be</u> glad,
   let the sea and all within it <u>thunder</u> praise,
   let the land and all it bears <u>re</u>joice,
   all the trees of the wood shout <u>for</u> joy,

9. at the presence of the Lord <u>who</u> comes,
   who comes to <u>rule</u> the earth,
   comes with justice to rule <u>the</u> world,
   and to judge the peoples <u>with</u> truth.

Performance Notes
Both Antiphon and Verses are preferably sung unaccompanied. The Antiphon is sung twice every time.

x = *fingersnaps/handclaps/other percussion on the 2nd and 3rd beats of the measure within the Antiphon,*
   and three strong beats at the end of each verse to lead back into the Antiphon.

Come, Lord, and Save Us

Third Sunday of Advent, Song for the Word

Antiphon ♩ = ca. 72

Come, Lord, and save us.

Verse Tone *Psalm 146:6c-10b*

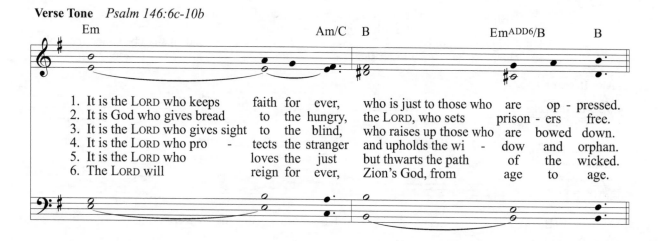

1. It is the LORD who keeps faith for ever, who is just to those who are op - pressed.
2. It is God who gives bread to the hungry, the LORD, who sets prison - ers free.
3. It is the LORD who gives sight to the blind, who raises up those who are bowed down.
4. It is the LORD who pro - tects the stranger and upholds the wi - dow and orphan.
5. It is the LORD who loves the just but thwarts the path of the wicked.
6. The LORD will reign for ever, Zion's God, from age to age.

Be Patient, Beloved

Third Sunday of Advent, Song for the Table

Verses Superimposed Tone *Psalm 85:9, 8, 10-14; Isaiah 35:1-7b, 8a-d, 10a-c, 10e*

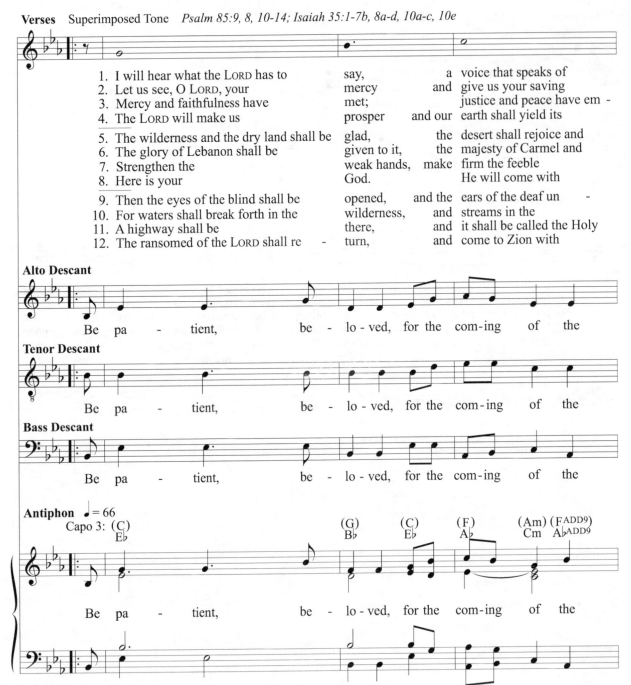

1. I will hear what the LORD has to say, a voice that speaks of
2. Let us see, O LORD, your mercy and give us your saving
3. Mercy and faithfulness have met; justice and peace have em -
4. The LORD will make us prosper and our earth shall yield its

5. The wilderness and the dry land shall be glad, the desert shall rejoice and
6. The glory of Lebanon shall be given to it, the majesty of Carmel and
7. Strengthen the weak hands, make firm the feeble
8. Here is your God. He will come with

9. Then the eyes of the blind shall be opened, and the ears of the deaf un -
10. For waters shall break forth in the wilderness, and streams in the
11. A highway shall be there, and it shall be called the Holy
12. The ransomed of the LORD shall re - turn, and come to Zion with

Alto Descant

Be pa - tient, be - lo - ved, for the com-ing of the

Tenor Descant

Be pa - tient, be - lo - ved, for the com-ing of the

Bass Descant

Be pa - tient, be - lo - ved, for the com-ing of the

Antiphon ♩ = 66

Capo 3: (C) (G) (C) (F) (Am) (F^ADD9)
Eb Bb Eb Ab Cm Ab^ADD9

Be pa - tient, be - lo - ved, for the com-ing of the

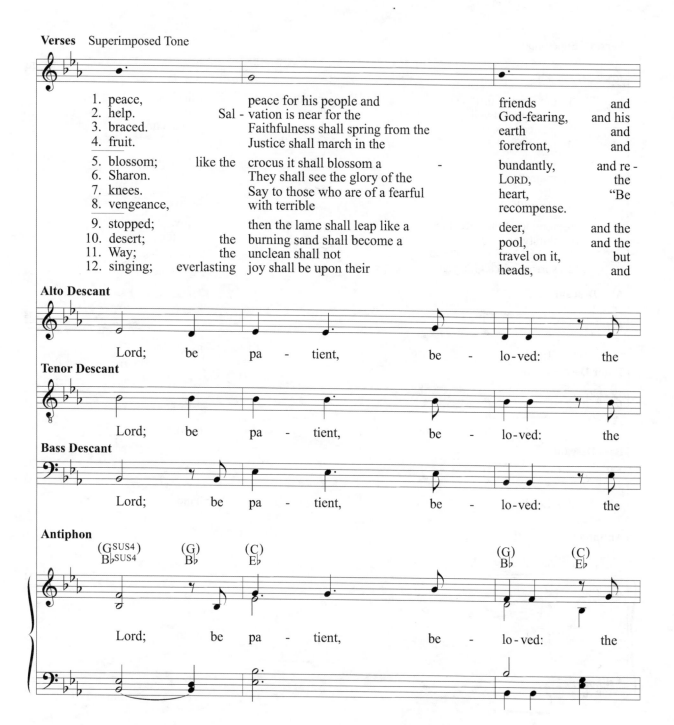

Verses Superimposed Tone

1. those who turn to God   in their   hearts.
2. glory will dwell   in our   land.
3. justice look   down from   heaven.
4. peace shall   follow the   way.

5. joice with   joy and   singing.
6. majesty   of our   God.
7. strong,   do not   fear!
8. He will   come and   save you."

9. tongue of the speechless   sing for   joy.
10. thirsty ground   springs of   water.
11. it shall be for   God's   people.
12. sorrow and sighing shall   flee a - way.

Alto Descant

Lord is close at hand.

Tenor Descant

Lord is close at hand.

Bass Descant

Lord is close at hand.

Antiphon

(F) Ab   (C) Eb

Lord is close at hand.

Open, You Skies: Rain Down the Just One

Fourth Sunday of Advent, Song for the Week

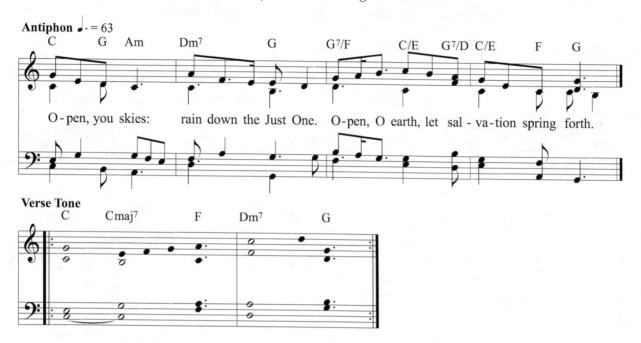

Psalm 72

1. O God, give your judgement to the king,
   to a king's son your justice,
   that he may judge your people in justice
   and your poor in right judgement.

2. May the mountains bring forth peace for the people
   and the hills, justice.
   May he defend the poor of the people
   and save the children of the needy.

3. He shall endure like the sun and the moon
   from age to age.
   He shall descend like rain on the meadow,
   like raindrops on the earth.

4. In his days justice shall flourish
   and peace till the moon fails.
   He shall rule from sea to sea,
   from the Great River to earth's bounds.

5. Before him his enemies shall fall,
   his foes lick the dust.
   The kings of Tarshish and the seacoasts
   shall pay him tribute.

6. The kings of Sheba and Seba
   shall bring him gifts.
   Before him all rulers shall fall prostrate,
   all nations shall serve him.

7. For he shall save the poor when they cry,
   and the needy who are helpless.
   He will have pity on the weak
   and save the lives of the poor.

8. From oppression he will rescue their lives,
   to him their blood is dear.
   They shall pray for him without ceasing
   and bless him all the day.

9. May corn be abundant in the land
   to the peaks of the mountains.
   May its fruit rustle like Lebanon;
   may people flourish in the cities
      like grass on the earth.

10. May his name be blessed for ever
    and endure like the sun.
    Every tribe shall be blessed in him,
    all nations bless his name.

11. Blessed be the LORD, the God of Israel,
    who alone works wonders,
    ever blessed God's glorious name.
    Let his glory fill the earth. Amen! Amen!

Let the King of Glory Come In

Fourth Sunday of Advent, Song for the Word
Presentation of the Lord (February 2), Song for the Word

Alto Descant

Let the king of glo-ry come in.

Tenor/Alto Descant

The Lord, the Lord is the king of glo-ry: let the king of glo-ry come in.

Antiphon ♩. = 65

Capo 1: (Bm⁷) (Em) (Am) (Bm) (Em) (Bm⁷) (Cmaj⁷) (Bm)
Cm⁷ Fm B♭m Cm Fm Cm⁷ D♭maj⁷ Cm

The Lord, the Lord is the king of glo-ry: let the king of glo-ry come in.

Verse Tone with Response *Psalm 24:7-10*

Cantor:

(Em) (Am/E) (Em) (Em/G) (Am/F♯) (Bm)
Fm B♭m/F Fm Fm/A♭ B♭m/G Cm

1. O gates, lift high your heads; grow higher, ancient doors.
4. O gates, lift high your heads; grow higher, ancient doors.

Alto Descant

Let the king of glo - ry come in.

Tenor/Alto Descant

Let the king of glo - ry come in.

Response *All:*

(Em/B) (Bm⁷) (Em/B) (Bm)
Fm/C Cm⁷ Fm/C Cm

Let the king of glo - ry come in.

Verse Tone with Response

Cantor:

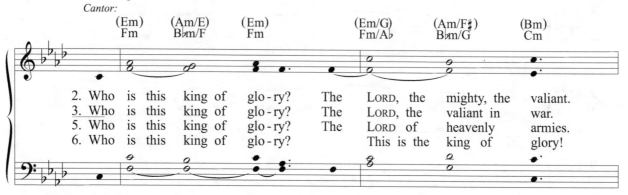

| (Em) | (Am/E) | (Em) | (Em/G) | (Am/F♯) | (Bm) |
| Fm | B♭m/F | Fm | Fm/A♭ | B♭m/G | Cm |

2. Who is this king of glo-ry? The LORD, the mighty, the valiant.
3. Who is this king of glo-ry? The LORD, the valiant in war.
5. Who is this king of glo-ry? The LORD of heavenly armies.
6. Who is this king of glo-ry? This is the king of glory!

Alto Descant

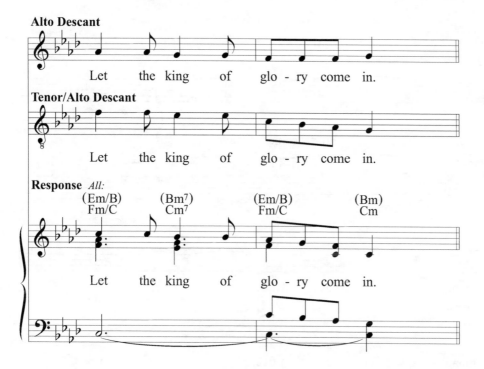

Let the king of glo-ry come in.

Tenor/Alto Descant

Let the king of glo-ry come in.

Response *All:*

| (Em/B) | (Bm⁷) | (Em/B) | (Bm) |
| Fm/C | Cm⁷ | Fm/C | Cm |

Let the king of glo-ry come in.

Psalm text: The Grail (England), © 1963, 1986, 1993, 2000, The Grail, GIA Publications, Inc., agent. All rights reserved. Used with permission.
Music and antiphon text: © 2005, The Collegeville Composers Group. All rights reserved. Published and administered by the Liturgical Press, Collegeville, MN 56321.

Jesus, Mighty Lord, Come Save Us

Fourth Sunday of Advent, Song for the Table

Verse Tone

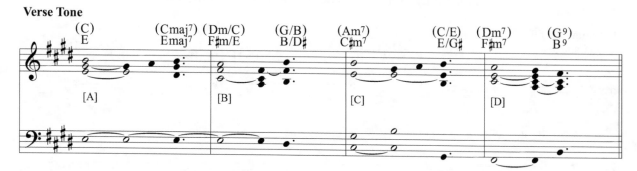

Psalm 19

1. The heavens proclaim the glo<u>ry</u> of God,
   and the firmament shows forth the work of <u>God's</u> hands.
   Day unto day takes <u>up</u> the story
   and night unto night makes known <u>the</u> message.

2. No speech, no word, no <u>voice</u> is heard
   yet their span extends through all <u>the</u> earth,
   [Omit C]
   their words to the utmost bounds of <u>the</u> world.

3. There God has placed a tent <u>for</u> the sun;
   it comes forth like a bridegroom coming from <u>his</u> tent,
   [Omit C]
   rejoices like a champion to run <u>its</u> course.

4. At the end of the sky is the rising <u>of</u> the sun;
   to the furthest end of the sky is <u>its</u> course.
   [Omit C]
   There is nothing concealed from its burn<u>ing</u> heat.

5. The law of the Lord is perfect,
   it revives <u>the</u> soul.
   The rule of the Lord is <u>to</u> be trusted,
   it gives wisdom to <u>the</u> simple.

6. The precepts of the Lord are right,
   they gladden <u>the</u> heart.

The command of the Lord is clear,
it gives light to <u>the</u> eyes.

7. The fear of the Lord is holy,
   abiding <u>for</u> ever.
   The decrees of the Lord are truth
   and all of <u>them</u> just.

8. They are more to be de<u>sired</u> than gold,
   than the purest <u>of</u> gold
   and sweeter are <u>they</u> than honey,
   than honey from <u>the</u> comb.

9. So in them your servant <u>finds</u> instruction;
   great reward is in <u>their</u> keeping.
   But can we discern <u>all</u> our errors?
   From hidden faults <u>acquit</u> us.

10. From presumption re<u>strain</u> your servant
    and let it <u>not</u> rule me.
    Then shall <u>I</u> be blameless,
    clean from <u>grave</u> sin.

11. May the spoken words <u>of</u> my mouth,
    the thoughts of <u>my</u> heart,
    win favor in your <u>sight</u>, O Lord,
    my rescuer, <u>my</u> rock!

Performance Notes

The Antiphon may be sung in unison, or as a round as indicated.

It is recommended that guitars are not used to accompany the Antiphon when sung as a round, since the chord-changes would be too rapid. For the purposes of giving the pitch only, the asterisked chord in square brackets at the beginning of the Antiphon may be used. Guitar chords are provided for the Verse Tone as usual.

The melody of the Antiphon is derived from the hymn tune Divinum Mysterium *("Of the Father's love begotten").*

A-13

A Light Will Shine on Us This Day

Christmas, Song for the Week
Solemnity of Mary, Mother of God, Song for the Week

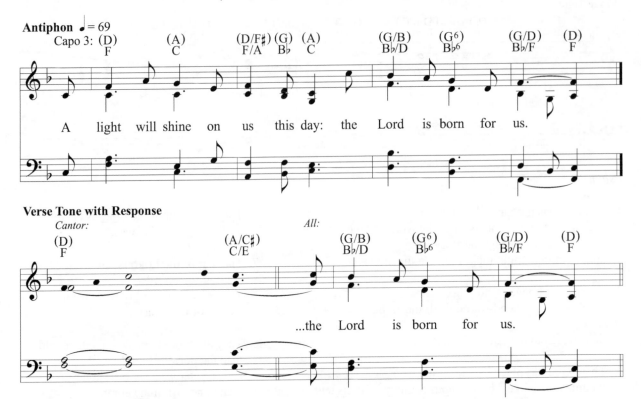

Isaiah 9:2-3, 6-7

1. The people who walked in darkness have seen a <u>great</u> light;   *the Lord is born . . .*

2. those who lived in a land of deep shadow, on them light <u>has</u> shone.   *the Lord is born . . .*

3. You have multiplied the nation, you have increased <u>its</u> joy;   *(simile)*

4. they rejoice before you as with joy at the harvest, as people exult when dividing <u>plun</u>der.

5. For a child has been born for us, a son <u>giv'n</u> to us;

6. authority rests upon his <u>shoul</u>ders;

7. and he is named Wonderful Counsellor, Mighty God, Everlasting Father, <u>Prince</u> of Peace.

8. His authority shall grow con<u>tin</u>ually,

9. and there shall be endless peace for the throne of David and his <u>king</u>dom.

10. He will establish and uphold it with justice and with righteousness
    from this time onward and for <u>ev</u>ermore.

11. The zeal of the LORD of hosts will <u>do</u> this.

All the Ends of the Earth

Christmas, Song for the Word: Option I

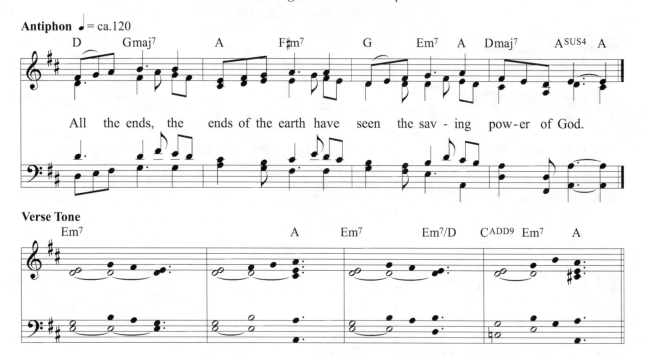

Psalm 98   *[The Lectionary selections for the day are indicated by an asterisk.]*

1. * Sing a new song to the LORD
   * who has worked wonders;
   * whose right hand and holy arm
   * have brought salvation.

2. * The LORD has made known salvation;
   * has shown justice to the nations;
   * has remembered truth and love
   * for the house of Israel.

3. * All the ends of the earth have seen
   * the salvation of our God.
   * Shout to the LORD, all the earth,
   * ring out your joy.

4. * Sing psalms to the LORD with the harp,
   * with the sound of music.
   * With trumpets and the sound of the horn
   * acclaim the King, the LORD.

5. Let the sea and all within it thunder;
   the world and all its peoples.
   Let the rivers clap their hands
   and the hills ring out their joy

6. at the presence of the LORD, who comes,
   who comes to rule the earth.
   God will rule the world with justice
   and the peoples with fairness.

Performance Notes

The Antiphon may be sung twice through each time.

God's Love Is Revealed to Us

Christmas, Song for the Word: Option II
Holy Family, Song for the Week

Antiphon *(1 John 4:9)* ♩ = 88

God's love is re-vealed to us, that we might have life through him.

God's love is re-vealed.

Verse Tone

Psalm 98 *[The Lectionary selections for Christmas Day are indicated by an asterisk.]*

1. * Sing a new song to the LORD
   * who has worked wonders;
   * whose right hand and holy arm
   * have brought salvation.

2. * The LORD has made known salvation;
   * has shown justice to the nations;
   * has remembered truth and love
   * for the house of Israel.

3. * All the ends of the earth have seen
   * the salvation of our God.
   * Shout to the LORD, all the earth,
   * ring out your joy.

4. * Sing psalms to the LORD with the harp,
   * with the sound of music.
   * With trumpets and the sound of the horn
   * acclaim the King, the LORD.

5. Let the sea and all within it thunder;
   the world and all its peoples.
   Let the rivers clap their hands
   and the hills ring out their joy

6. at the presence of the LORD, who comes,
   who comes to rule the earth.
   God will rule the world with justice
   and the peoples with fairness.

Optional Coda to the Final Antiphon

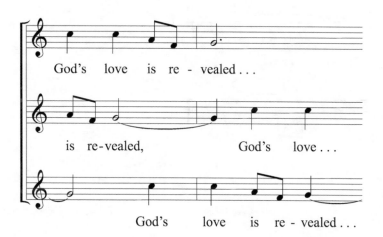

Performance Notes

Each two-measure phrase of the Antiphon is sung first by a cantor and then repeated by all.
Instead of repeating the last two measures of the final Antiphon, use the optional three-part coda above at a distance of two quarter-notes to create the effect of gently pealing bells, as shown. The top line is the Assembly, led by a cantor, the lower two lines being taken by other members of the choir.
The sustained accompaniment chord can easily be omitted if not required.
The canon may be repeated at any time as desired, gradually fading out.

We Receive from Your Fullness

Christmas, Song for the Table

Antiphon ♩ = 69
Capo 3: (A) (D) (G) (D)
C F B♭ F

We re-ceive from your full-ness light up-on light; we re-ceive from your full-ness

(G) (G/B) (A) (D) (Bm) (G) (Em) (A) (A7)
B♭ B♭/D C F Dm B♭ Gm C C7

truth up-on truth; we re-ceive from your full-ness grace up-on grace; we re-

(Bm) (G) (D/F♯) (Em7) (A)
Dm B♭ F/A♯ Gm7 C

ceive from your full-ness, O Lord.

Verse Tone

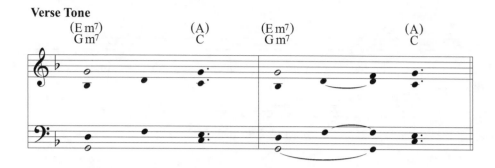

1 John 1:5-7; Isaiah 35:1-4

1. This is the message we have heard from him and proclaim to you,
   that God is light and in him there is no darkness <u>at</u> all.

2. If we say that we have fellowship with him while we are walking in darkness,
   we lie and do not do what <u>is</u> true;

3. but if we walk in the light as he himself is the light,
   we have fellowship with one another, and the blood of Jesus cleanses us from <u>all</u> sin.

4. The wilderness and the dry land shall be glad, the desert shall rejoice and blossom;
   like the crocus it shall blossom abundantly, and rejoice with joy <u>and</u> singing.

5. The glory of Lebanon shall be given to it, the majesty of Carmel and Sharon.
   They shall see the glory of the LORD, the majesty of <u>our</u> God.

6. Strengthen the weak hands, and make firm the feeble knees.
   Say to those who are of a fearful heart, "Be strong, do <u>not</u> fear!

7. Here is your God. He will come with vengeance, with terrible recompense.
   He will come <u>and</u> save you."

Holy Family, Song for the Week, *same as A-15* ← **A-17**

Holy Family, Song for the Word, *same as A-194* ← **A-18**

Let the Word Make a Home in Your Heart

Holy Family, Song for the Table

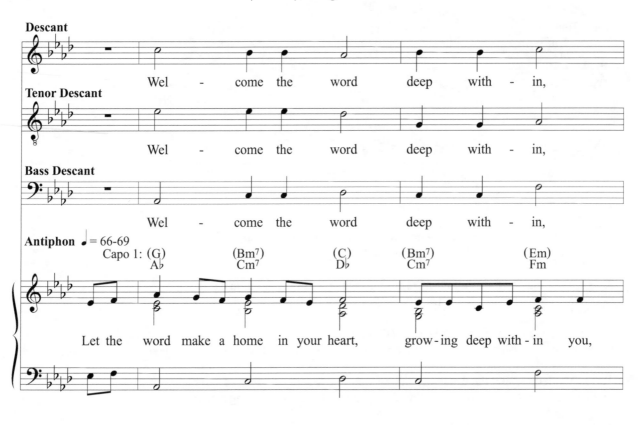

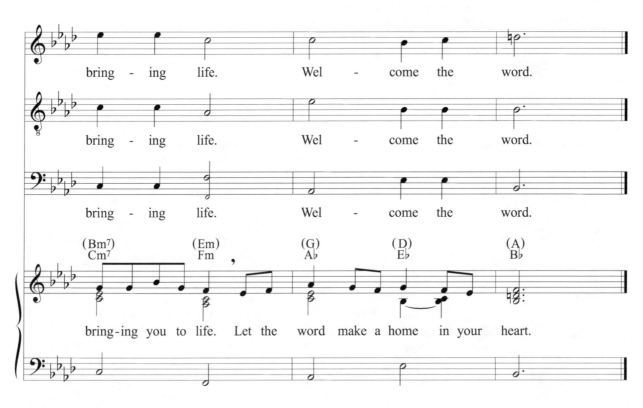

Verse Tone

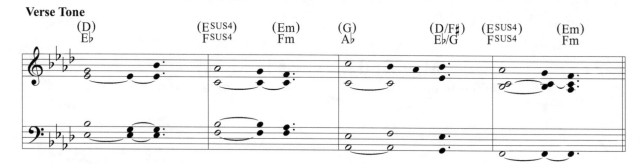

Psalms 146; 127; 45:17-18

1. Alleluia!
   My soul, give praise to the LORD;
   I will praise the LORD all my days,
   make music to my God while I live.

2. Put no trust in the powerful,
   mere mortals in whom there is no help.
   Take their breath, they return to clay
   and their plans that day come to nothing.

3. They are happy who are helped by Jacob's God,
   whose hope is in the LORD their God,
   who alone made heaven and earth,
   the seas and all they contain.

4. It is the LORD who keeps faith for ever,
   who is just to those who are oppressed.
   It is God who gives bread to the hungry,
   the LORD, who sets pris'ners free.

5. It is the LORD who gives sight to the blind,
   who raises up those who are bowed down,
   the LORD, who protects the stranger
   and upholds the widow and orphan.

6. It is the LORD who loves the just
   but thwarts the path of the wicked.
   The LORD will reign for ever,
   Zion's God, from age to age.

7. If the LORD does not build the house,
   in vain do its builders labor.
   If the LORD does not keep watch over the city,
   in vain do the watchers keep vigil.

8. In vain is your earlier rising,
   your going later to rest,
   you who toil for the bread you eat,
   when God pours gifts on the beloved
        while they slumber.

9. Yes, children are a gift from the LORD,
   a blessing, the fruit of the womb.
   The sons and daughters of youth
   are like arrows in the hand of a warrior.

10. O the happiness of those
    who have filled their quiver
        with these arrows!
    They will have no cause for shame
    when they dispute with their foes
        in the gateways.

11. Children shall be yours in place
        of your forebears;
    you will make them rulers over
        all the earth.
    May this song make your name
        for ever remembered
    May the peoples praise you from
        age to age.

Performance Notes
The Descant may be sung an octave lower as a Tenor part, the Tenor part being sung (at Tenor pitch) by Altos.

A-20 → Solemnity of Mary, Mother of God, Song for the Week, *same as A-13*

A-21   May God Bless Us in Mercy

Solemnity of Mary, Mother of God, Song for the Word

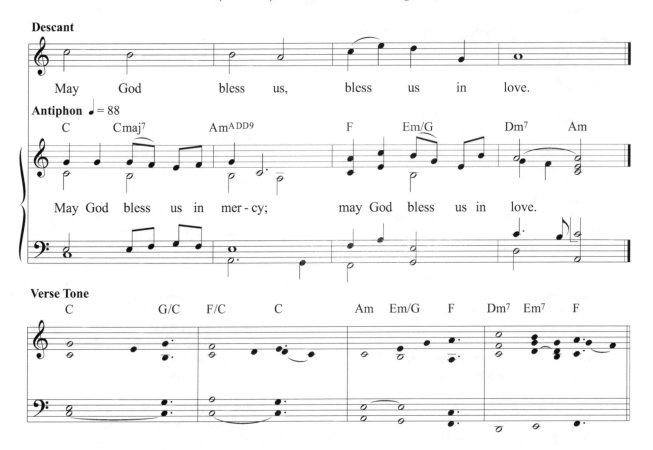

Psalm 67   *[The Lectionary selections for the day are indicated by an asterisk.]*

1. * O God, be gracious <u>and</u> bless us
   * and let your face shed its light u<u>pon</u> us.
   * So will your ways be known u<u>pon</u> earth
   * and all nations learn your <u>saving</u> help.

2. * Let the nations be glad and <u>exult</u>
   * for you rule the world <u>with</u> justice.
   * With fairness you <u>rule</u> the peoples,
   * you guide the <u>nations</u> on earth.

3. * The earth has yielded <u>its</u> fruit
   for God, our God, <u>has</u> blessed us.
   May God still <u>give</u> us blessing
   till the ends of the earth <u>stand</u> in awe.

4. * Let the peoples praise you, <u>O</u> God;
   * let all the <u>peoples</u> praise you.
   * Let the peoples praise <u>you</u>, O God,
   * let all the <u>peoples</u> praise you.

Jesus Christ, the Same Today, Yesterday and Evermore

Solemnity of Mary, Mother of God, Song for the Table

Colossians 1:11-20

1. May you be made strong with all the strength that comes from his glorious power,
   and may you be prepared to endure everything with patience,
   while joyfully giving thanks to the Father,
   who has enabled you to share in the inheritance of the saints in the light.

2. He has rescued us from the power of darkness
   and transferred us into the kingdom of his beloved Son,
   in whom we have redemption,
   the forgiveness of sins.

3. He is the image of the invisible God, the firstborn of all creation:
   for in him all things in heaven and on earth were created,
   things visible and invisible, whether thrones or dominions or rulers or powers—
   all things have been created through him and for him.

4. He himself is before all things, and in him all things hold together.
   He is the head of the body, the Church;
   he is the beginning, the firstborn from the dead,
   so that he might come to have first place in everything.

5. For in him all the fullness of God was pleased to dwell,
   and through him God was pleased to reconcile to himself all things,
   whether on earth or in heaven,
   by making peace through the blood of his cross.

Arise, Jerusalem, Look to the East

Epiphany, Song for the Week

Baruch 5:1-2, 5-7, 9; Isaiah 12:3-6

1. Jerusalem, take off your robe of mour<u>ning</u> and misery,
   put on forever the beau<u>ty</u> of glory!

2. Wrapped in the robe of your jus<u>tice</u> and righteousness,
   put on your head the mi<u>ter</u> of majesty!

3. Jerusalem, arise, and look east from the <u>high</u>est heights!
   Your children are gathered at the word <u>of</u> your holy one.

4. Even though you went, led away <u>by</u> your enemies,
   God brings them back, borne aloft <u>as</u> if royalty.

5. God has ordered valleys and hills made into <u>lev</u>el ground
   so you can march safely in the light <u>of</u> God's glory.

6. God himself in joy will be the lead<u>er</u> of Israel
   in glory, with mercy and jus<u>tice</u> for company.

7. You will draw water joyfully from the wellsprings <u>of</u> salvation.
   Give thanks to the LORD, give praise to his <u>ho</u>ly name.

8. Make the LORD's deeds known a<u>mong</u> the nations;
   proclaim the greatness <u>of</u> his name.

9. Sing a psalm to the LORD, for he has done <u>glo</u>rious deeds;
   make known his works to all <u>of</u> the earth.

10. People of Zion, <u>sing</u> for joy,
    for great in your midst is the Holy <u>One</u> of Israel.

They Shall Adore You

Epiphany, Song for the Word

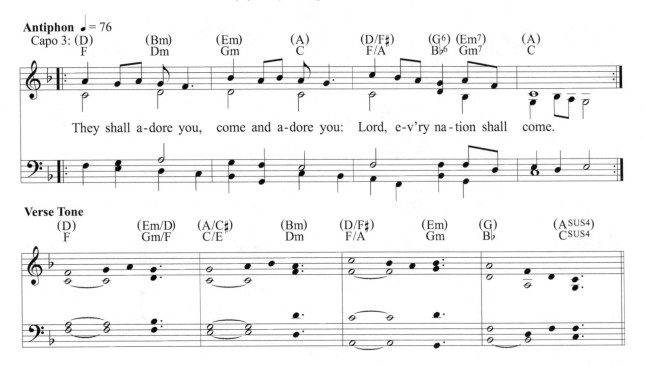

They shall a-dore you, come and a-dore you: Lord, e-v'ry na-tion shall come.

Psalm 72 [The Lectionary selections for the day are indicated by an asterisk.]

1. * O God, give your judgement <u>to</u> the king,
   * to a king's <u>son</u> your justice,
   * that he may judge your peo<u>ple</u> in justice
   * and your poor <u>in</u> right judgement.

2. May the mountains bring forth peace <u>for</u> the people
   and <u>the</u> hills justice.
   May he defend the poor <u>of</u> the people
   and save the children <u>of</u> the needy.

3. He shall endure like the sun <u>and</u> the moon
   from <u>age</u> to age.
   He shall descend like rain <u>on</u> the meadow,
   like raindrops <u>on</u> the earth.

4. * In his days just<u>ice</u> shall flourish
   * and peace <u>till</u> the moon fails.
   * He shall rule from <u>sea</u> to sea,
   * from the Great River <u>to</u> earth's bounds.

5. Before him his ene<u>mies</u> shall fall,
   his foes <u>lick</u> the dust.
   * The kings of Tarshish <u>and</u> the seacoasts
   * shall <u>pay</u> him tribute.

6. * The kings of She<u>ba</u> and Seba
   * shall <u>bring</u> him gifts.
   * Before him all rulers <u>shall</u> fall prostrate,
   * all na<u>tions</u> shall serve him.

7. * For he shall save the poor <u>when</u> they cry,
   * and the needy <u>who</u> are helpless.
   * He will have pity <u>on</u> the weak
   * and save the lives <u>of</u> the poor.

8. From oppression he will res<u>cue</u> their lives,
   to him their <u>blood</u> is dear.
   They shall pray for him <u>without</u> ceasing
   and bless him <u>all</u> the day.

9. May corn be abundant <u>in</u> the land
   to the peaks <u>of</u> the mountains.
   May its fruit rus<u>tle</u> like Lebanon;
   may people flourish in the cities
      like grass <u>on</u> the earth.

10. May his name be <u>blessed</u> for ever
    and endure <u>like</u> the sun.
    Every tribe <u>shall</u> be blessed in him,
    all nations <u>bless</u> his name.

11. Blessed be the LORD, the <u>God</u> of Israel,
    who a<u>lone</u> works wonders,
    ever blessed God's <u>glorious</u> name.
    Let his glory fill the earth. A<u>men</u>! Amen!

Our City Has No Need of Sun or Moon

Epiphany, Song for the Table

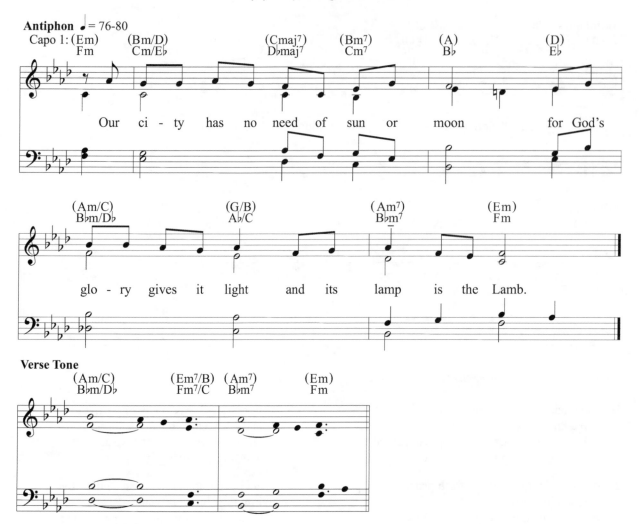

Revelation 21:24-27ac; 22:3b-5

1. The nations will walk <u>by</u> its light,
   and the kings of the earth
      will bring their <u>glo</u>ry into it.

2. Its gates will never be <u>shut</u> by day,
   and there will <u>be</u> no night there.

3. People will bring into <u>it</u> the glory
   and the honor <u>of</u> the nations.

4. Nothing un<u>clean</u> will enter it,
   but only those who are written
      in the Lamb's <u>book</u> of life.

5. The throne of God
      and of the Lamb <u>will</u> be in it,
   and his ser<u>vants</u> will worship him.

6. They will <u>see</u> his face,
   and his name will be <u>on</u> their foreheads.

7. And there will be <u>no</u> more night;
   they need no light of <u>lamp</u> or sun,

8. for the LORD God will <u>be</u> their light,
   and they will reign for <u>ev</u>er and ever.

A-26 ➡ Baptism of the Lord, Song for the Week, *same as A-34*

The Lord Will Bless His People

A-27

Baptism of the Lord, Song for the Word

Psalm 29:1-4, 10

1. O give the LORD, you children of God,
   give the LORD glory and power;
   give the LORD the glory of his name.
   Adore the LORD, resplendent and holy.

2. The LORD's voice resounding on the waters,
   the LORD on the immensity of waters;

   the voice of the LORD, full of power,
   the voice of the LORD, full of splendor.

3. The God of glory thunders.
   In his temple they all cry: "Glory!"
   The LORD sat enthroned over the flood;
   the LORD sits as king for ever.

Performance Notes

The Antiphon is sung twice each time. The Alto canon may give rise to the temptation to sing the Antiphon more than twice, a temptation which should be resisted except perhaps after the final psalm verse!

Clothed in Christ, One in Christ

Baptism of the Lord, Song for the Table
Easter Vigil, Baptismal Acclamation

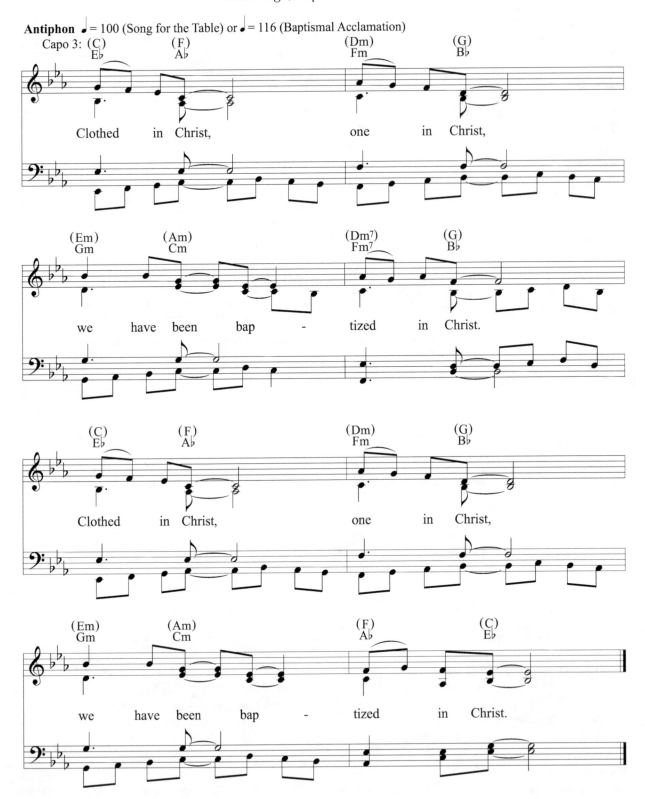

Performance Notes

During the Rite of Baptism, the antiphon may be used as an acclamation immediately after each baptism, or at the clothing with a white garment, or at both moments in the Rite.

Verse Tone

Titus 3:4-7; Ephesians 1:3-12; 1 Timothy 3:16

1. When the goodness and loving kindness of God our Savior appeared,
   he saved us, not because of any works of righteousness that we had done,
   but according to his mercy,
   through the water of rebirth and renewal by the Holy Spirit.

2. This Spirit he poured out on us richly through Jesus Christ our Savior,
   so that, having been justified by his grace,
   we might become heirs
   according to the hope of eternal life.

3. Blessed be the God and Father of our Lord Jesus Christ,
   who has blessed us in Christ with every spiritual blessing in the heavenly places,
   just as he chose us in Christ before the foundation of the world
   to be holy and blameless before him in love.

4. He destined us for adoption as his children through Jesus Christ,
   according to the good pleasure of his will,
   to the praise of his glorious grace
   that he freely bestowed on us in the Beloved.

5. In him we have redemption through his blood,
   the forgiveness of our trespasses,
   according to the riches of his grace
   that he lavished on us.

6. With all wisdom and insight he has made known to us the mystery of his will,
   according to his good pleasure that he set forth in Christ,
   as a plan for the fullness of time,
   to gather up all things in him, things in heaven and things on earth.

7. In Christ we have also obtained an inheritance,
   having been destined according to the purpose of him who accomplishes all things
       according to his counsel and will,
   so that we, who were the first to set our hope on Christ,
   might live for the praise of his glory.

8. He was revealed in flesh, vindicated in spirit,
   seen by angels, proclaimed among Gentiles,
   believed in throughout the world,
   taken up in glory.

Those Who Love Me, I Will Deliver

First Sunday of Lent, Song for the Week

Verse Tone

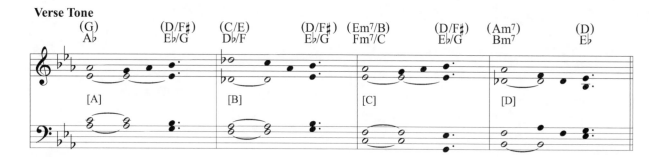

Psalm 91; Isaiah 58:8, 9c-10, 11c-12, 14

1. Those who dwell in the shelter of the Most High
and abide in the shade of the Almighty
say to the LORD: "My refuge, my stronghold,
the God in whom I trust."

2. It is God who will free you from the snare
of the fowler who seeks to destroy you;
God will conceal you with his pinions,
and under his wings you will find refuge.

3. You will not fear the terror of the night
nor the arrow that flies by day,
nor the plague that prowls in the darkness
nor the scourge that lays waste at noon.

4. A thousand may fall at your side,
ten thousand fall at your right,
you, it will never approach;
God's faithfulness is buckler and shield.

5. Your eyes have only to look
to see how the wicked are repaid,
you who have said: "LORD, my refuge!"
and have made the Most High your dwelling.

6. Upon you no evil shall fall,
no plague approach where you dwell.
For you God has commanded the angels
to keep you in all your ways.

7. They shall bear you upon their hands
lest you strike your foot against a stone.
On the lion and the viper you will tread
and trample the young lion and the dragon.

8. You set your love on me so I will save you,
protect you for you know my name.

When you call I shall answer: "I am with you,"
I will save you in distress and give you glory.

9. *[omit A-B]*
With length of days I will content you;
I shall let you see my saving power.

10. Your light shall break forth like the dawn,
and your healing shall spring up quickly;
your vindicator shall go before you,
the glory of the LORD shall be your rearguard.

11. If you remove the yoke from among you,
the pointing of the finger, the speaking of evil,
if you offer your food to the hungry
and satisfy the needs of the afflicted,

12. then your light shall rise in the darkness
and your gloom be like the noonday.
You shall be like a watered garden,
like a spring of water, whose waters never fail.

13. Your ancient ruins shall be rebuilt;
you shall raise up the foundations
of many generations:
you shall be called the repairer of the breach,
the restorer of streets to live in.

14. Then you shall take delight in the LORD,
and I will make you ride
upon the heights of the earth;
I will feed you with the heritage
of your ancestor Jacob,
for the mouth of the LORD has spoken.

We Have Sinned, Lord

First Sunday of Lent, Song for the Word
Ash Wednesday, Song for the Word

Verses Superimposed Tone *Psalm 51:3-6b, 12-14, 17*

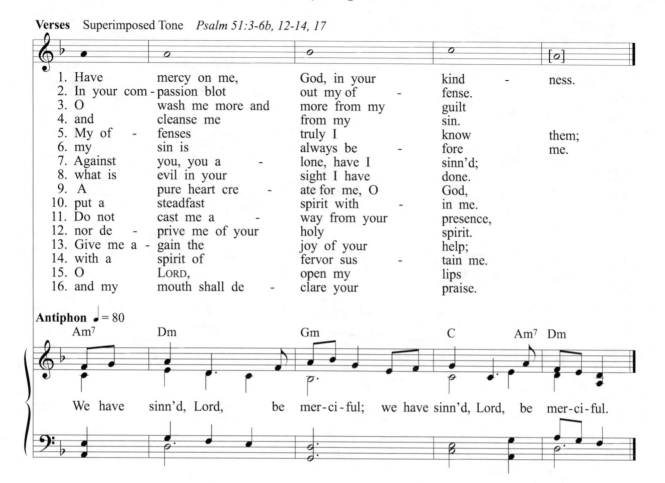

1. Have mercy on me, God, in your kind - ness.
2. In your com - passion blot out my of - fense.
3. O wash me more and more from my guilt
4. and cleanse me from my sin.
5. My of - fenses truly I know them;
6. my sin is always be - fore me.
7. Against you, you a - lone, have I sinn'd;
8. what is evil in your sight I have done.
9. A pure heart cre - ate for me, O God,
10. put a steadfast spirit with - in me.
11. Do not cast me a - way from your presence,
12. nor de - prive me of your holy spirit.
13. Give me a - gain the joy of your help;
14. with a spirit of fervor sus - tain me.
15. O LORD, open my lips
16. and my mouth shall de - clare your praise.

Antiphon ♩ = 80

Am⁷ Dm Gm C Am⁷ Dm

We have sinn'd, Lord, be mer-ci-ful; we have sinn'd, Lord, be mer-ci-ful.

A-31 Not on Bread Alone Are We Nourished

First Sunday of Lent, Song for the Table

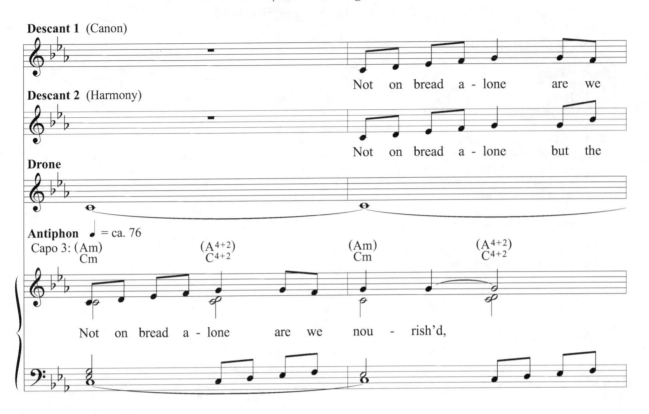

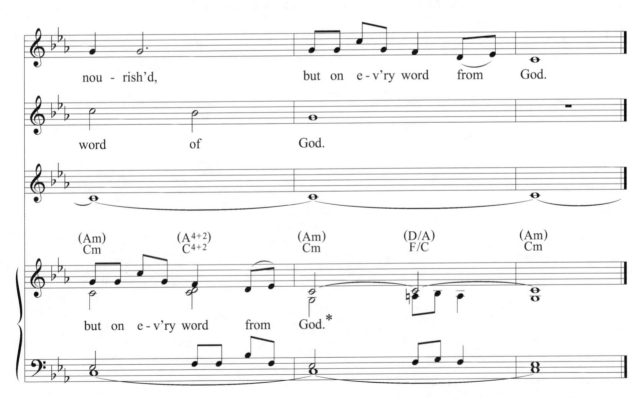

* *The word* God *lasts for four beats only, unless Descant 1 is being sung, when it is prolonged for an additional measure.*

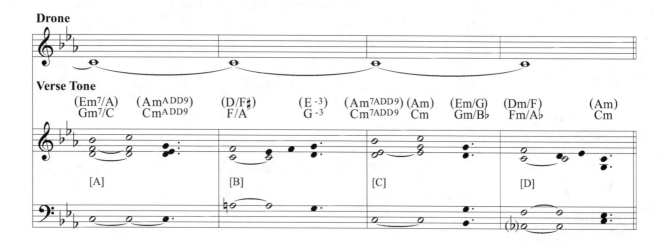

Psalm 19

1. The heavens proclaim the glory of God,
   and the firmament shows forth the work of God's hands.
   Day unto day takes up the story
   and night unto night makes known the message.

2. No speech, no word, no voice is heard
   yet their span extends through all the earth,
   [omit C]
   their words to the utmost bounds of the world.

3. There God has placed a tent for the sun;
   it comes forth like a bridegroom coming from his tent,
   [omit C]
   rejoices like a champion to run its course.

4. At the end of the sky is the rising of the sun;
   to the furthest end of the sky is its course.
   [omit C]
   There is nothing concealed from its burning heat.

5. The law of the Lord is perfect,
   it revives the soul.
   The rule of the Lord is to be trusted,
   it gives wisdom to the simple.

6. The precepts of the Lord are right,
   they gladden the heart.
   The command of the Lord is clear,
   it gives light to the eyes.

7. The fear of the Lord is holy,
   abiding for ever.
   The decrees of the Lord are truth
   and all of them just.

8. They are more to be desired than gold,
   than the purest of gold
   and sweeter are they than honey,
   than honey from the comb.

9. So in them your servant finds instruction;
   great reward is in their keeping.
   But can we discern all our errors?
   From hidden faults acquit us.

10. From presumption restrain your servant
    and let it not rule me.
    Then shall I be blameless,
    clean from grave sin.

11. May the spoken words of my mouth,
    the thoughts of my heart,
    win favor in your sight, O Lord,
    my rescuer, my rock!

Performance Notes
The Antiphon melody is derived from the hymn tune PICARDY.

Seek the Lord! Long for the Lord!

Second Sunday of Lent, Song for the Week
Fourth Sunday in Ordinary Time, Song for the Week
Thirtieth Sunday in Ordinary Time, Song for the Week

Verse Tone with Response

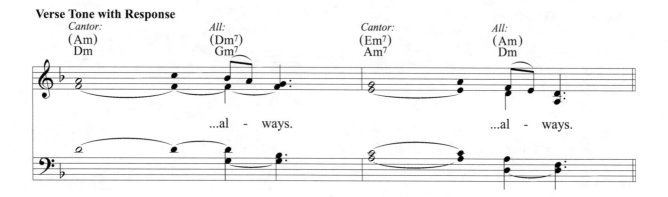

Psalm 105:1-5

1. Give thanks and acclaim God's <u>name</u> *al-ways*,
   make known God's deeds among the peo<u>ples</u> *al-ways*.

2. O sing to the LORD, sing <u>praise</u> *al-ways*;
   tell all his wonderful <u>works</u> *al-ways*!

3. Be proud of God's holy <u>name</u> *al-ways*,
   let the hearts that seek the LORD re<u>joice</u> *al-ways*.

4. Consider the LORD, who is <u>strong</u> *al-ways*;
   constantly seek his <u>face</u> *al-ways*.

5. Remember the wonders of the <u>LORD</u> *al-ways*,
   the miracles and judgements pro<u>nounced</u> *al-ways*.

A-33

Let Your Love Be Upon Us, O Lord

Second Sunday of Lent, Song for the Word

Verse Tone

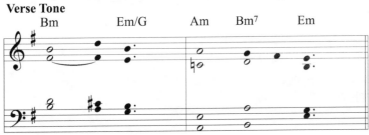

Psalm 33:4-5, 18-21

1. The word of the LORD is faithful
   and all his works done in truth.

2. The LORD loves justice and right
   and fills the earth with love.

3. The LORD looks on those who fear him,
   on those who hope in his love,

4. to rescue their souls from death,
   to keep them alive in famine.

5. Our soul is waiting for the LORD.
   The LORD is our help and our shield.

6. Our hearts find joy in the LORD.
   We trust in God's holy name.

Second Sunday of Lent, Song for the Table
Baptism of the Lord, Song for the Week
The Transfiguration of the Lord (August 6), Song for the Day

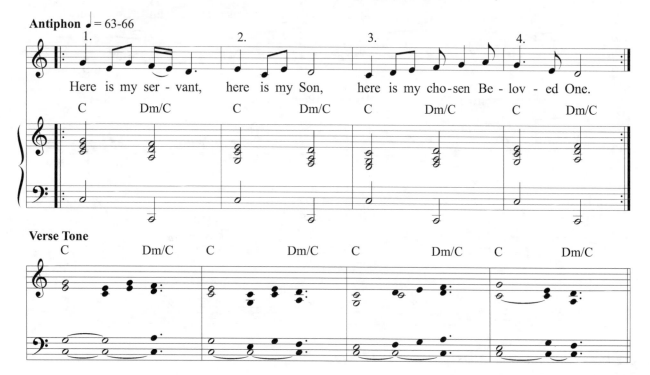

Isaiah 40:1-11

1. Comfort, O comfort my people, <u>says</u> your God.
   Speak tenderly to Jerusalem and <u>cry</u> to her
   that she has served her term, that her penal<u>ty</u> is paid,
   that she has received from the LORD's hand double for
   all <u>her</u> sins.

2. A voice cries out: "In the wilderness prepare the way
   <u>of</u> the LORD,
   make straight in the desert a highway <u>for</u> our God.
   Every valley shall be <u>lift</u>ed up,
   and every mountain and hill be <u>made</u> low;

3. the uneven ground shall become level, and the rough
   pla<u>ces</u> a plain.
   Then the glory of the LORD shall <u>be</u> revealed,
   and all people shall see <u>it</u> together,
   for the mouth of the LORD <u>has</u> spoken."

4. A voice <u>says</u>, "Cry out!"
   And I said, "What <u>shall</u> I cry?"
   All peo<u>ple</u> are grass,
   their constancy is like the flower of <u>the</u> field.

5. The grass withers, the flower fades, when the
   breath of the LORD <u>blows</u> upon it;
   surely the peo<u>ple</u> are grass.
   The grass withers, the <u>flower</u> fades;
   but the word of our God will stand <u>for</u>ever.

6. Get you up to a high mountain, O Zion, herald
   <u>of</u> good tidings,
   lift up your voice with strength, O Jerusalem,
   herald <u>of</u> good tidings,
   lift it up, <u>do</u> not fear;
   say to the cities of Judah, "Here is <u>your</u> God!"

7. See, the LORD God <u>comes</u> with might,
   and his arm <u>rules</u> for him;
   his re<u>ward</u> is with him,
   and his recompense <u>before</u> him.

8. He will feed his flock <u>like</u> a shepherd;
   he will gather the lambs <u>in</u> his arms,
   and carry them <u>in</u> his bosom,
   and gently lead the <u>mother</u> sheep.

Performance Notes
The Antiphon may be sung as a round.

Turn Our Hearts from Stone to Flesh

Third Sunday of Lent, Song for the Week

Ezekiel 36:24-28; Jeremiah 31:33; Ezekiel 37:12-14

1. I will take you from the nations,
   and gather you from all the countries,
   and bring you into your own land.

2. I will sprinkle clean water upon you
   and you shall be clean from all your uncleannesses,
   and from all your idols I will cleanse you.

3. A new heart I will give you,
   and a new spirit I will put within you;
   and I will remove from your body the heart of stone
   and give you a heart of flesh.

4. I will put my spirit within you,
   and make you follow my statutes
   and be careful to observe my ordinances.

5. Then you shall live in the land
   that I gave to your ancestors;
   and you shall be my people,
   and I will be your God.

6. I will put my law within you,
   and I will write it on your hearts;
   and I will be your God,
   and you shall be my people.

7. I am going to open your graves,
   and bring you up from your graves, O my people;
   and I will bring you back
   to the land of Israel.

8. And you shall know that I am the LORD,
   when I open your graves,
   and bring you up from your graves,
   O my people.

9. I will put my spirit within you,
   and you shall live
   and I will place you on your own soil;
   then you shall know that I, the LORD,
   have spoken and will act.

Performance Notes

Percussion or handclaps may be added, as indicated by X's, both during the Antiphon and at the end of the psalm verses to lead back into the Antiphon.
The Antiphon should be repeated every time it is sung.
The entire piece may be transposed down a whole step.

Listen! Listen! Open Your Hearts!

Third Sunday of Lent, Song for the Word
Twenty-third Sunday in Ordinary Time, Song for the Word

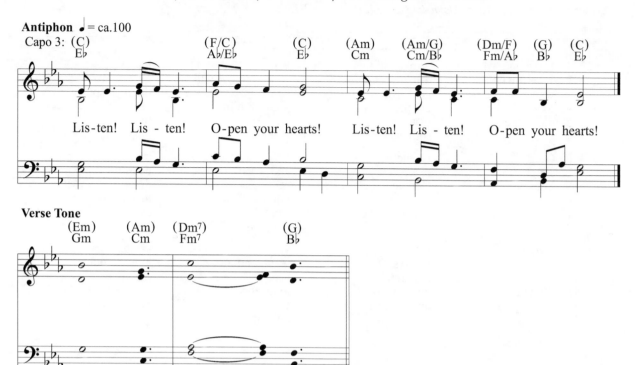

Psalm 95:1-9 [*The Lectionary selections for the day are indicated by an asterisk.*]

1. * Come, ring out our joy to the LORD;
   * hail the rock who saves us.

2. * Let us come before God, giving thanks;
   * with songs let us hail the LORD.

3. A mighty God is the LORD,
   a great king above all gods.

4. In God's hands are the depths of the earth;
   the heights of the mountains as well.

5. The sea belongs to God, who made it
   and the dry land shaped by his hands.

6. * Come in; let us bow and bend low;
   * let us kneel before the God who made us.

7. * This is our God, and we the people
   *   who belong to his pasture,
   * the flock that is led by his hand.

8. * O that today you would listen to God's voice!
   * "Harden not your hearts as at Meribah,
   [repeat the tone]
   * as on that day at Massah in the desert
   * when your ancestors put me to the test;
   *   when they tried me, though they saw my work."

Give Us Living Water

Third Sunday of Lent, Song for the Table

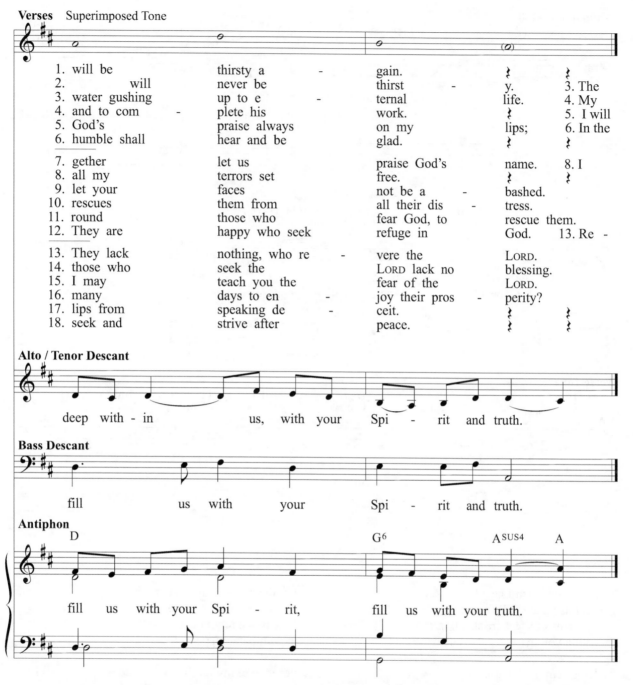

Verses   Superimposed Tone

1. will be	thirsty a -	gain.	
2. will	never be	thirst - y.	3. The
3. water gushing	up to e -	ternal	life. 4. My
4. and to com -	plete his	work.	5. I will
5. God's	praise always	on my	lips; 6. In the
6. humble shall	hear and be	glad.	
7. gether	let us	praise God's	name. 8. I
8. all my	terrors set	free.	
9. let your	faces	not be a -	bashed.
10. rescues	them from	all their dis -	tress.
11. round	those who	fear God, to	rescue them.
12. They are	happy who seek	refuge in	God. 13. Re -
13. They lack	nothing, who re -	vere the	LORD.
14. those who	seek the	LORD lack no	blessing.
15. I may	teach you the	fear of the	LORD.
16. many	days to en -	joy their pros -	perity?
17. lips from	speaking de -	ceit.	
18. seek and	strive after	peace.	

Alto / Tenor Descant

deep with - in   us, with your   Spi - rit and truth.

Bass Descant

fill   us with   your   Spi - rit and truth.

Antiphon

D   G⁶   A^SUS4   A

fill   us with your Spi - rit,   fill   us with your truth.

Rejoice, Rejoice, All You Who Love Jerusalem!

Fourth Sunday of Lent, Song for the Week

Antiphon ♩ = 100

Re - joice, re-joice, all you who love Je - ru - sa - lem! Re -

joice, be glad, for you will be con-soled.

Verse Tone

Psalm 122

1. I rejoiced when I <u>heard</u> them say:
   "Let us go to <u>God's</u> house."
   And now our <u>feet</u> are standing
   within your gates, O <u>Jerusalem</u>.

2. Jerusalem is built <u>as</u> a city
   strongly <u>compact</u>.
   It is there that the <u>tribes</u> go up,
   the tribes <u>of the</u> LORD.

3. For Israel's <u>law</u> it is,
   there to praise <u>the</u> LORD's name.
   There were set the <u>thrones</u> of judgement
   of the house <u>of</u> David.

4. For the peace of Jerusalem pray:
   "Peace be to <u>your</u> homes!
   May peace reign <u>in</u> your walls,
   in your pala<u>ces</u>, peace!"

5. For love of my fam'<u>ly</u> and friends
   I say: "Peace <u>upon</u> you."
   For love of the house <u>of</u> the LORD
   I will ask for <u>your</u> good.

My Shepherd Is the Lord

Fourth Sunday of Lent, Song for the Word
Fourth Sunday of Easter, Song for the Word
Christ the King, Song for the Word

A-39

Psalm 23

1. Fresh and green are <u>the</u> pastures   *there is . . .*
   where you give me <u>re</u>pose.   *my God . . .*
   Near restful waters <u>you</u> lead me   *there is . . .*
   to revive my droop<u>ing</u> spirit.   *my God . . .*

2. You guide me along the <u>right</u> path;   *(simile)*
   you are true to <u>your</u> name.
   If I should walk in the valley <u>of</u> darkness
   no evil would <u>I</u> fear.
   You are there with your crook and <u>your</u> staff;
   with these you give <u>me</u> comfort.

3. You have prepared a banquet <u>for</u> me
   in the sight of <u>my</u> foes.
   My head you have anointed <u>with</u> oil;
   my cup is o<u>ver</u>flowing.

4. Surely goodness and kindness <u>shall</u> follow me
   all the days of <u>my</u> life.
   In the LORD's own house shall <u>I</u> dwell
   for ever <u>and</u> ever.

Psalm text: The Grail (England), © 1963, 1986, 1993, 2000, The Grail, GIA Publications, Inc., agent. All rights reserved. Used with permission.
Music and antiphon text: © 2005, The Collegeville Composers Group. All rights reserved. Published and administered by the Liturgical Press, Collegeville, MN 56321.

Florentino Idosor Phone Number
310-227-5702

A-40

You Are Light in the Lord

Fourth Sunday of Lent, Song for the Table

Verse Tone

Isaiah 58:8-12; 60:1-5, 19-22

1. Your light shall break <u>forth</u> like the <u>dawn</u>,
   and your healing shall spring <u>up</u> quickly;
   your vindicator shall <u>go</u> before you,
   the glory of the LORD shall be <u>your</u> rear guard.

2. Then you shall <u>call</u> and the LORD will <u>answer</u>;
   you shall cry for help, and he will say, Here <u>I</u> am.
   If you remove the yoke <u>from</u> among you,
   the pointing of the finger, the speaking <u>of</u> evil,
   [repeat entire tone]
       if you offer your <u>food</u> to the <u>hungry</u>
       and satisfy the needs of the <u>afflicted</u>,
       then your light shall rise <u>in</u> the darkness
       and your gloom be like <u>the</u> noonday.

3. The LORD will <u>guide</u> you continually,
   and satisfy your needs in parched places,
       and make your <u>bones</u> strong;
   and you shall be like a <u>watered</u> garden,
   like a spring of water, whose waters will ne<u>ver</u> fail.

4. Your ancient <u>ruins</u> shall be re<u>built</u>;
   you shall raise up the foundations
       of many ge<u>nerations</u>;
   you shall be called the repairer <u>of</u> the breach,
   the restorer of streets <u>to</u> live in.

5. Arise, shine; for your <u>light</u> has <u>come</u>,
   the glory of the LORD has risen <u>upon</u> you.
   For darkness shall co<u>ver</u> the earth,
   and thick darkness <u>the</u> peoples.

6. The LORD will <u>rise</u> up<u>on</u> you,
   and his glory will appear o<u>ver</u> you.
   Nations shall come <u>to</u> your light,
   and kings to the brightness of <u>your</u> dawn.

7. Lift up your <u>eyes</u> and look a<u>round</u>;
   they all gather together, <u>they</u> come to you;
   your sons shall come from <u>far</u> away,
   and your daughters shall be carried
       on their nur<u>ses</u>' arms.

8. Then you shall <u>see</u> and be <u>radiant</u>;
   [omit B-C]
       your heart shall thrill and <u>rejoice</u>.

9. The sun shall no longer be your <u>light</u> by <u>day</u>,
   nor for brightness shall the moon
       give light to you <u>by</u> night;
   but the LORD will be your ever<u>lasting</u> light,
   and your God will be <u>your</u> glory.

10. Your sun shall no <u>more</u> go <u>down</u>,
    or your moon withdraw <u>itself</u>;
    for the LORD will be your ever<u>lasting</u> light,
    and your days of mourning shall <u>be</u> ended.

11. Your people shall <u>all</u> be <u>righteous</u>;
    they shall possess the land <u>forever</u>.
    They are the shoot that I planted,
        the work <u>of</u> my hands,
    so that I might <u>be</u> glorified.

12. The least of them shall be<u>come</u> a <u>clan</u>,
    and the smallest one a mighty <u>nation</u>:
    I <u>am</u> the LORD;
    in its time I will accomplish <u>it</u> quickly.

My God, My Strength, Defend My Cause

Fifth Sunday of Lent, Song for the Week

Verse Tone with Response

...my God, my strength, de-fend my cause.

...save me from the hands of the wick-ed.

Psalm 43

1. Defend me, O God, and plead my cause against a <u>god</u>less nation.   *my God, my strength . . .*
   From a deceitful and cunning people rescue <u>me</u>, O God.   *save me from the hands . . .*

2. Since you, O God, are my stronghold, why have <u>you</u> rejected me?   *(simile)*
   Why do I go mourning, oppressed <u>by</u> the foe?

3. O send forth your light and your truth; let these <u>be</u> my guide.
   Let them bring me to your holy mountain, to the place <u>where</u> you dwell.

4. And I will come to your altar, O God, the God <u>of</u> my joy.
   My redeemer, I will thank you on the harp, O <u>God</u>, my God.

5. Why are you cast down, my soul, why <u>groan</u> within me?
   Hope in God; I will praise yet again my savior <u>and</u> my God.

There Is Mercy in the Lord

Fifth Sunday of Lent, Song for the Word

Verse Tone

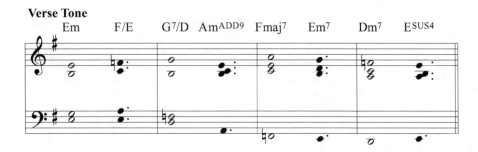

Psalm 130:1-6b, 7b-8

1. Out of the depths I cry to you, O LORD,
   LORD, hear my voice!
   O let your ears be attentive
   to the voice of my pleading.

2. If you, O LORD, should mark our guilt,
   LORD, who would survive?
   But with you is found forgiveness:
   for this we revere you.

3. My soul is waiting for the LORD,
   I count on God's word.
   My soul is longing for the LORD
   more than those who watch for daybreak.

4. Because with the LORD there is mercy
   and fullness of redemption,
   Israel indeed God will redeem
   from all its iniquity.

Performance Notes

The Antiphon may be sung in a two or four-part round as indicated. After the final stanza, the round may continue as long as desired.
The Optional Bass part is only used once the four-part round is firmly established.

I Am the Resurrection
Fifth Sunday of Lent, Song for the Table

John 12:23-26, 31-32, 35-36 (option I)

1. The hour has come for the
    Son of Man to be glorified.
   Very truly, I tell you, unless a grain of wheat
    falls to the ground and dies,
   it remains just a single grain;
   but if it dies, it bears much fruit.

2. Those who love their life lose it,
   and those who hate their life in this world
   will keep it for eternal life.

3. Whoever serves me must follow me,
   and where I am, there will my servant be also.
   Whoever serves me, the Father will honor.

4. Now is the judgement of this world;
   now the ruler of this world will be driven out.
   And I, when I am lifted up from the earth,
   will draw all people to myself.

5. The light is with you for a little longer.
   Walk while you have the light,
   so that the darkness may not overtake you.

6. If you walk in the darkness,
   you do not know where you are going.
   While you have the light, believe in the light,
   so that you may become children of light.

Verse Tone

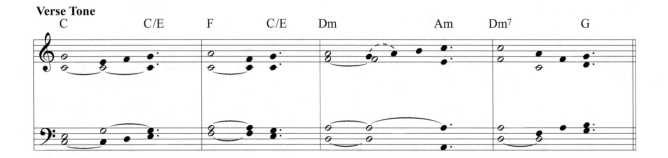

Psalm 34 (option II)

1. I will bless the LORD at all times,
God's praise always on <u>my</u> lips;
in the LORD my soul <u>shall</u> make its boast.
The humble shall hear <u>and</u> be glad.

2. Glorify the LORD with me.
Together let us praise <u>God's</u> name.
I sought the LORD and was heard;
from all my te<u>rrors</u> set free.

3. Look towards God <u>and</u> be radiant;
let your faces not be <u>a</u>bashed.
When the poor cry <u>out</u> the LORD hears them
and rescues them from all <u>their</u> distress.

4. The angel of the LORD <u>is</u> encamped
around those who fear God, <u>to</u> rescue them.
Taste and see that the <u>LORD</u> is good.
They are happy who seek re<u>fuge</u> in God.

5. Revere the LORD, you saints.
They lack nothing, who revere <u>the</u> LORD.
Strong lions suffer <u>want</u> and go hungry
but those who seek the LORD <u>lack</u> no blessing.

6. Come, chil<u>dren</u> and hear me
that I may teach you the fear of <u>the</u> LORD.
Who are those who <u>long</u> for life
and many days, to enjoy <u>their</u> prosperity?

7. Then keep your <u>tongue</u> from evil
and your lips from speaking <u>deceit</u>.
Turn aside from <u>evil</u> and do good;
seek and strive <u>after</u> peace.

8. The eyes of the LORD are <u>toward</u> the just
and his ears toward their <u>appeal</u>.
The face of the LORD <u>re</u>buffs the wicked
to destroy their remembrance <u>from</u> the earth.

9. They call <u>and</u> the LORD hears
and rescues them in all their <u>distress</u>.
The LORD is close to the <u>bro</u>-ken-hearted;
those whose spirit is crushed <u>God</u> will save.

10. Many are the trials <u>of</u> the upright
but the LORD will come <u>to</u> rescue them,
keeping guard over <u>all</u> their bones,
not one of their bones <u>shall</u> be broken.

11. Evil brings death <u>to</u> the wicked;
those who hate the good <u>are</u> doomed.
The LORD ransoms the <u>souls</u> of the faithful.
None who trust in God shall <u>be</u> condemned.

Performance Notes
Words with a double underline are sung over the slurred G–A.

Hosanna, Hosanna, Hosanna in the Highest
Palm Sunday of the Lord's Passion, Opening Song

Final note of tone: sing either G or C

1. The children of Jerusalem
   welcomed Christ the King.
   They carried olive branches
      and loudly praised the Lord.

2. The children of Jerusalem
   welcomed Christ the King.
   They spread their cloaks before him
      and loudly praised the Lord.

3. Hosanna to the Son of David!
   Blessed is he who comes
   in the name of the Lord!

4. The children of Jerusalem
   welcomed Christ the King.
   They proclaimed the resurrection of life.

5. Waving olive branches,
   they loudly praised the Lord:
   Hosanna in the highest.

6. When the people heard that Jesus
   was entering Jerusalem,
   they went to meet him.

7. Waving olive branches,
   they loudly praised the Lord:
   Hosanna in the highest.

My God, My God

Palm Sunday of the Lord's Passion, Song for the Word

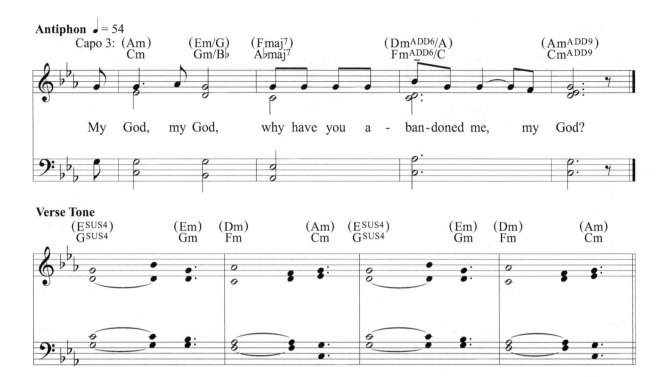

Psalm 22:8-9, 17-18a, 19-20, 23-24

1. All who see me deride me.
   They curl their lips, they toss their heads.
   "He trusted in the LORD, let him save him,
   and release him if this is his friend."

2. Many dogs have surrounded me,
   a band of the wicked beset me.
   They tear holes in my hands and my feet.
   I can count every one of my bones.

3. They divide my clothing among them.
   They cast lots for my robe.
   O LORD, do not leave me alone,
   my strength, make haste to help me.

4. I will tell of your name to my people
   and praise you where they are assembled.
   "You who fear the LORD, give praise;
   all children of Jacob, give glory.
       Revere God, children of Israel."

If I Must Drink This Cup
Palm Sunday of the Lord's Passion, Song for the Table

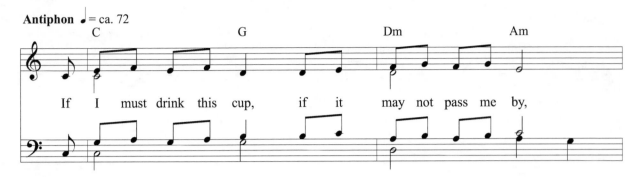

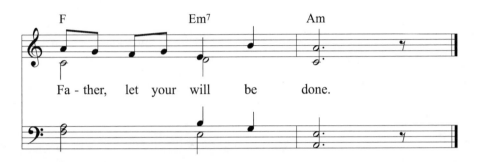

Verse Tone

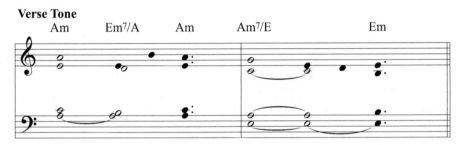

Psalm 116

1. I love the Lord, for the Lord has heard
   the cry of my appeal.

2. The Lord was attentive to me
   in the day when I called.

3. They surrounded me, the snares of death,
   with the anguish of the tomb;

4. they caught me, sorrow and distress.
   I called on the Lord's name.

5. O Lord, my God, deliver me!
   O Lord, my God, deliver me!

6. How gracious is the Lord and just;
   our God has compassion.

7. The Lord protects the simple hearts;
   I was helpless so God saved me.

8. Turn back, my soul, to your rest
   for the Lord has been good.

9. The Lord has kept my soul from death,
   my eyes from tears, my feet from stumbling.

10. I will walk in the presence of the Lord
    in the land of the living.

Our Glory and Pride Is the Cross of Jesus Christ

Holy Thursday, Entrance Song

Exaltation of the Holy Cross (September 14), Song for the Day

Our Cup of Blessing
Holy Thursday, Song for the Word

Psalm 116:12-19

1. How can I repay the LORD
   for his goodness to me?
   The cup of salvation I will raise;
   I will call on the name of the LORD.

2. My vows to the LORD I will fulfill
   before all the people.
   O precious in the eyes of the LORD
   is the death of the faithful.

3. Your servant, LORD, your servant am I;
   you have loosened my bonds.
   A thanksgiving sacrifice I make;
   I will call on the name of the LORD.

4. My vows to the LORD I will fulfill
   before all the people,
   in the courts of the house of the LORD,
   in your midst, O Jerusalem.

A New Commandment I Give to You

Holy Thursday, Song for the Washing of Feet
The Most Sacred Heart of Jesus, Song for the Day

Verses for Holy Thursday *cf. Matthew 20:21, 24; John 13:5, 8, 15, 14, 35, 34; 1 Corinthians 13:13*

Verses for the Sacred Heart *cf. Revelation 21:2-4, 6; John 13:34; 1 Corinthians 13:13*

Antiphon ♩ = 72

Capo 5: (Am) (Dm⁷)   (G)   (Em⁷)   (Am)

Performance Notes

In verse 2 for the Sacred Heart, if you are used to pronouncing "Omega" with the stress on the first and not the second syllable – you should sing "Omega and Alpha."

This Is My Body

Holy Thursday, Song for the Table
The Most Holy Body and Blood of Christ, Song for the Table

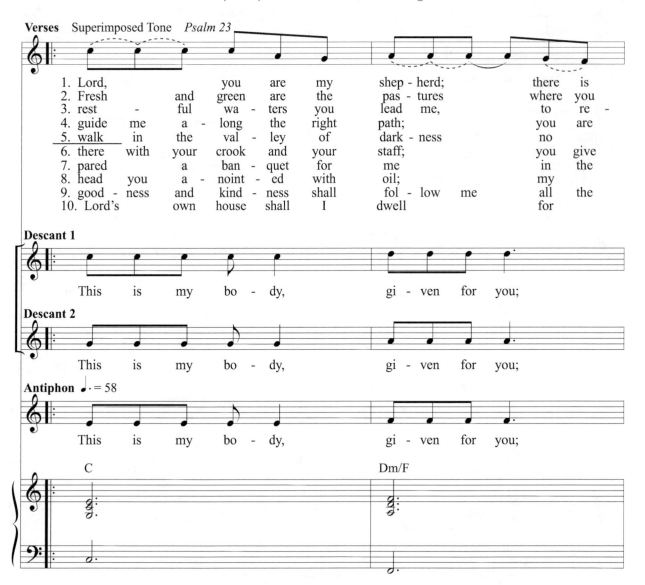

Verses Superimposed Tone *Psalm 23*

1. Lord, you are my shep - herd; there is
2. Fresh and green are the pas - tures where you
3. rest - ful wa - ters you lead me, to re -
4. guide me a - long the right path; you are
5. walk in the val - ley of dark - ness no
6. there with your crook and your staff; you give
7. pared a ban - quet for me in the
8. head you a - noint - ed with oil; my
9. good - ness and kind - ness shall fol - low me all the
10. Lord's own house shall I dwell for

Descant 1

This is my bo - dy, gi - ven for you;

Descant 2

This is my bo - dy, gi - ven for you;

Antiphon ♩. = 58

This is my bo - dy, gi - ven for you;

C   Dm/F

Performance Notes

The first four measures of the Descants and Antiphon are vocalized (perhaps to 'oo') or hummed when a verse is superimposed.

Father, into Your Hands

Good Friday, Song for the Word

Psalm 31:2, 6, 12-13, 15-17, 25

1. In you, O LORD, I take refuge.
    Let me never be put to shame.
   In your justice, set me free.
   Into your hands I commend my spirit.
   It is you who will redeem me, LORD.

2. In the face of all my foes
   I am a reproach,
   an object of scorn to my neighbors
   and of fear to my friends.

3. Those who see me in the street
   run far away from me.
   I am like the dead, forgotten by all,
   like a thing thrown away.

4. But as for me, I trust in you, LORD;
   I say: "You are my God.
   My life is in your hands, deliver me
   from the hands of those who hate me.

5. Let your face shine on your servant.
   Save me in your love."
   Be strong, let your heart take courage,
   all who hope in the LORD.

Send Out Your Spirit

Easter Vigil, Song for the Word: Reading I-a Response

Psalm 104:1-2a, 5-6, 10, 12, 13-14, 24, 35c

1. Bless the LORD, my soul!
   LORD God, how great you are,
   clothed in majesty and glory,
   wrapped in light as in a robe!

2. You founded the earth on its base,
   to stand firm from age to age.
   You wrapped it with the ocean like a cloak:
   the waters stood higher than the mountains.

3. You make springs gush forth in the valleys;
   they flow in between the hills.
   On their banks dwell the birds of heaven;
   from the branches they sing their song.

4. From your dwelling you water the hills;
   earth drinks its fill of your gift.
   You make the grass grow for the cattle
   and the plants to serve our needs.

5. How many are your works, O LORD!
   In wisdom you have made them all.
   The earth is full of your riches.
   Bless the LORD, my soul.

Performance Notes

Percussion or handclaps may be added, as indicated by X's, both during the Antiphon and at the end of the psalm verses to lead back into the Antiphon.

The Antiphon should be repeated every time it is sung.

The entire piece may be transposed down a whole step.

The Earth Is Full of the Goodness of God

Easter Vigil, Song for the Word: Reading I-b Response

My Portion and My Cup
Easter Vigil, Song for the Word: Reading II Response

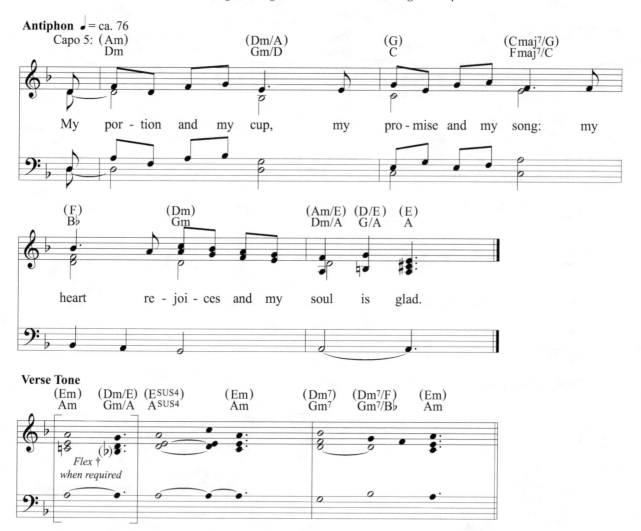

Psalm 16:5, 8-11

1. O LORD, it is you who are my portion <u>and</u> cup,
   it is you yourself who <u>are</u> my prize.

2. I keep you, LORD, ever in <u>my</u> sight;
   since you are at my right hand, I <u>shall</u> stand firm.

3. And so my heart re<u>joi</u>ces, † my soul <u>is</u> glad;
   even my body shall <u>rest</u> in safety.

4. For you will not leave my soul among <u>the</u> dead,
   nor let your beloved <u>know</u> decay.

5. You will show me the path of <u>life</u>, † the fullness of joy in <u>your</u> presence,
   at your right hand happ<u>iness</u> for ever.

Sing to the Lord

Easter Vigil, Song for the Word: Reading III Response

Exodus 15:1-6, 17-18

1. I will sing to the LORD, glo<u>ri</u>ous his triumph!
   Horse and rider he has thrown in<u>to</u> the sea!
   The LORD is my strength, my song, <u>my</u> salvation.
[repeat C]
   This is my God and <u>I</u> extol him,
   my father's God and I <u>give</u> him praise.

2. The LORD is a warrior! The LORD <u>is</u> his name.
   The chariots of Pharaoh he hurled in<u>to</u> the sea,
   the flower of his army is drowned <u>in</u> the sea.
   The deeps hide them; they sank <u>like</u> a stone.

3. Your right hand, LORD, glorious <u>in</u> its power,
   your right hand, LORD, has shat<u>tered</u> the enemy.
[omit C]
   In the greatness of your glory you <u>crushed</u> the foe.

4. You will lead your people and plant them <u>on</u> your mountain,
   the place, O LORD, where you have <u>made</u> your home,
   the sanctuary, LORD, which your <u>hands</u> have made.
   The LORD will reign for <u>ev</u>er and ever.

I Will Praise You, Lord

Easter Vigil, Song for the Word: Reading IV Response

Descant I

I will praise you, Lord.

Descant II

Praise you, Lord, O praise you, Lord.

Antiphon ♩ = 108

Em Am⁷ D Gmaj⁷ Am⁷ Bm⁷ Em

I will praise you, Lord, you have res-cued me; I will praise you, Lord.

Verse Tone

Em Am/C Am Em

Psalm 30:2, 4-6, 11-12a, 13b

1. I will praise you, LORD, you have rescued me
   and have not let my enemies rejoice over me.
   O LORD, you have raised my soul from the dead,
   restored me to life from those who sink into the grave.

2. Sing psalms to the LORD, all you faithful,
   give thanks to his holy name.
   God's anger lasts a moment, God's favor through life.
   At night there are tears, but joy comes with dawn.

3. The LORD listened and had pity.
   The LORD came to my help.
   For me you have changed my mourning into dancing.
   O LORD my God, I will thank you for ever.

Joyfully You Will Draw Water

A-57

Easter Vigil, Song for the Word: Reading V Response
Easter Vigil, Song for the Word: Reading VII-b Response

Performance Notes *The psalm-tone can be superimposed on the Antiphon as shown, or it may be sung separately (but still in rhythm) using a simple chordal accompaniment.*

A-58

Your Word Is Life, Lord

Easter Vigil, Song for the Word: Reading VI Response

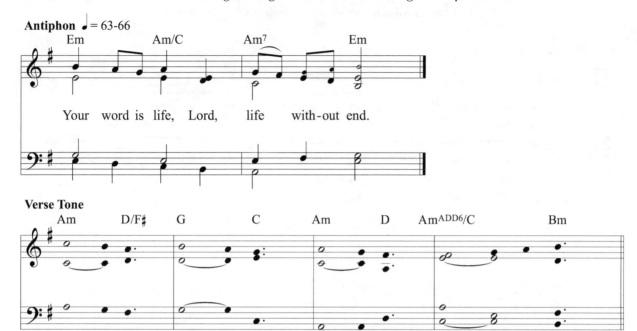

Antiphon ♩ = 63-66

Em   Am/C   Am⁷   Em

Your word is life, Lord, life with-out end.

Verse Tone

Am   D/F♯   G   C   Am   D   Am^{ADD6}/C   Bm

Verses   *Psalm 19:8-11*

1. The law of the LORD is perfect,
   it revives the soul.
   The rule of the LORD is to be trusted,
   it gives wisdom to the simple.

2. The precepts of the LORD are right,
   they gladden the heart.
   The command of the LORD is clear,
   it gives light to the eyes.

3. The fear of the LORD is holy,
   abiding for ever.
   The decrees of the LORD are truth
   and all of them just.

4. They are more to be desired than gold,
   than the purest of gold
   and sweeter are they than honey,
   than honey from the comb.

Like a Deer That Longs for Running Streams

Easter Vigil, Song for the Word: Reading VII-a Response

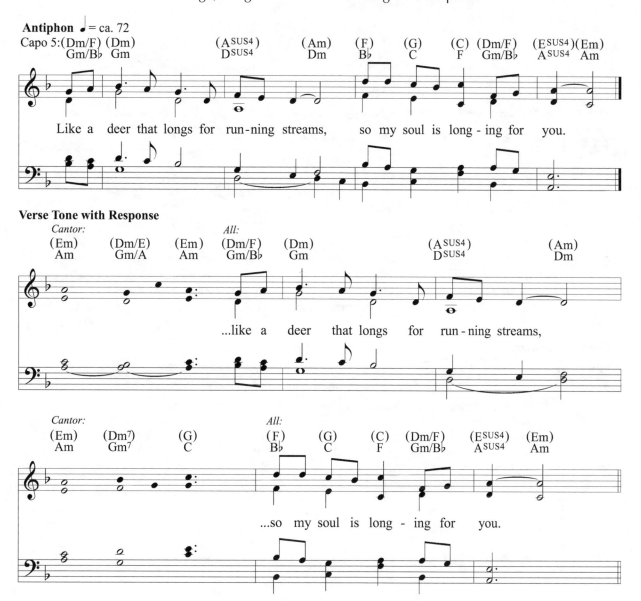

Psalm 42:3, 5; 43:3-4

1. My soul is thirsting for God, the God <u>of</u> my life;   *like a deer . . .*
   when can I enter and see the <u>face</u> of God?   *so my soul . . .*

2. These things will I remember as I pour out my soul:
      how I would lead the rejoicing crowd into the <u>house</u> of God,   *(simile)*
   amid cries of gladness and thanksgiving, the throng <u>wild</u> with joy.

3. O send forth your light and your truth; let these <u>be</u> my guide.
   Let them bring me to your holy mountain, to the place <u>where</u> you dwell.

4. And I will come to your altar, O God, the God <u>of</u> my joy.
   My redeemer, I will thank you on the harp, O <u>God</u>, my God.

A-61

Lord, Cleanse My Heart

Easter Vigil, Song for the Word: Reading VII-c Response

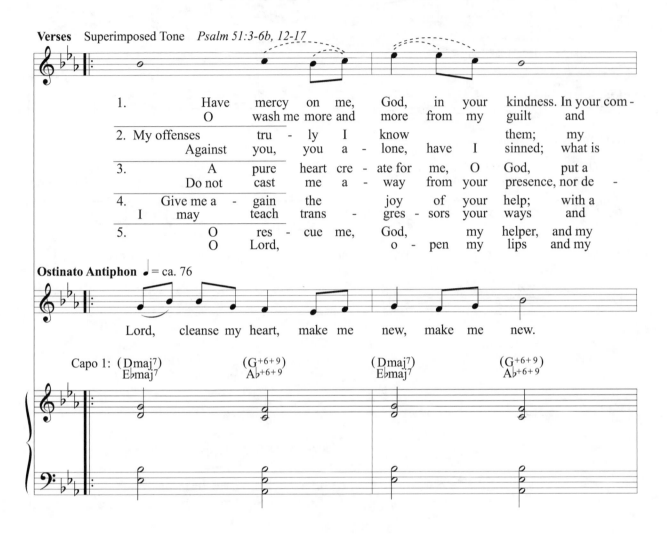

Verses Superimposed Tone *Psalm 51:3-6b, 12-17*

1. Have mercy on me, God, in your kindness. In your com-
   O wash me more and more from my guilt and
2. My offenses tru-ly I know them; my
   Against you, you a-lone, have I sinned; what is
3. A pure heart cre-ate for me, O God, put a
   Do not cast me a-way from your presence, nor de -
4. Give me a-gain the joy of your help; with a
   I may teach trans-gres-sors your ways and
5. O res-cue me, God, my helper, and my
   O Lord, o-pen my lips and my

Ostinato Antiphon ♩ = ca. 76

Lord, cleanse my heart, make me new, make me new.

Capo 1: (Dmaj⁷) (G⁺⁶⁺⁹) (Dmaj⁷) (G⁺⁶⁺⁹)
Ebmaj⁷ Ab⁺⁶⁺⁹ Ebmaj⁷ Ab⁺⁶⁺⁹

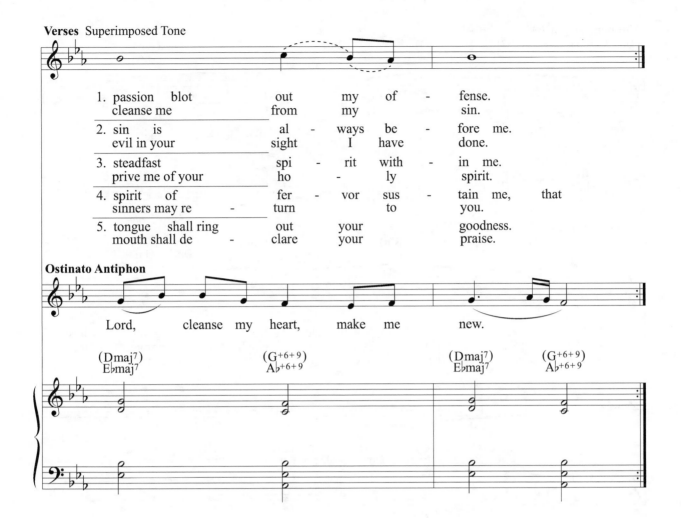

Alleluia, Alleluia, Alleluia!
Easter Vigil, Song for the Word: Epistle Response

Christic the Lord Is Risen Again

A-65

Easter Sunday, Song for the Week

♩ = 84   *Adaptations from Psalm 95*

1. Christ the Lord is ris'n a - gain, al - le - lu - ia, his hand on
2. Christ the Lord is ris'n in - deed, al - le - lu - ia. All pow'r and
3. Cry a - loud to God with joy, al - le - lu - ia; let earth with
4. Peo - ple of the Lord our God, al - le - lu - ia, who made all
5. Faith - ful to the end of time, al - le - lu - ia, is God, whose

1. us to keep us safe, al - le - lu - ia. How his wis - dom is
2. glo - ry be to him, al - le - lu - ia. Praise his name to the
3. glad - ness serve the Lord, al - le - lu - ia; come to God with our
4. things up - on the earth, al - le - lu - ia, sing with praise and thanks -
5. mer - cy co - vers us, al - le - lu - ia, and whose love is e -

1. won - der - ful! al - le - lu - ia, al - le - lu - ia, al - le - lu - ia!
2. end of time, al - le - lu - ia, al - le - lu - ia, al - le - lu - ia!
3. songs of joy, al - le - lu - ia, al - le - lu - ia, al - le - lu - ia!
4. giv - ing, al - le - lu - ia, al - le - lu - ia, al - le - lu - ia!
5. ter - nal, al - le - lu - ia, al - le - lu - ia, al - le - lu - ia!

This Is the Day

Easter Sunday, Song for the Word

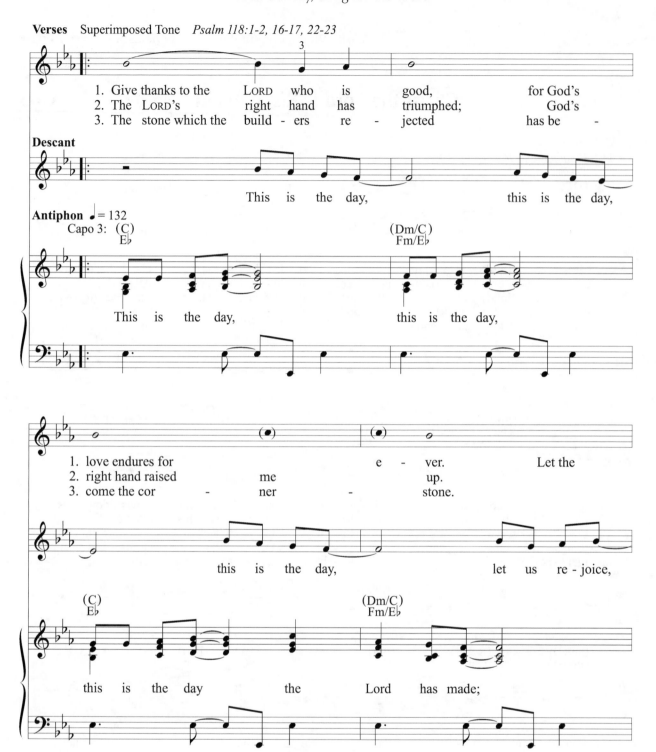

Verses Superimposed Tone *Psalm 118:1-2, 16-17, 22-23*

1. Give thanks to the LORD who is good, for God's
2. The LORD's right hand has triumphed; God's
3. The stone which the build - ers re - jected has be -

Descant

This is the day, this is the day,

Antiphon ♩ = 132

Capo 3: (C) (Dm/C)
Eb Fm/Eb

This is the day, this is the day,

1. love endures for e - ver. Let the
2. right hand raised me up.
3. come the cor - ner - stone.

this is the day, let us re - joice,

(C) (Dm/C)
Eb Fm/Eb

this is the day the Lord has made;

Verses Superimposed Tone

3

1. fam'ly of Is - ra - el say: "God's
2. I shall not die, I shall live
3. This is the work of the LORD, a

Descant

let us re - joice, let us re - joice

Antiphon

(C) (Dm/C)
Eb Fm/Eb

let us re - joice, let us re - joice,

1. love endures for e - ver."
2. and recount God's deeds.
3. marvel in our eyes.

and be glad.

(Am7) (Fmaj7) (G) (C)
Cm7 Abmaj7 Bb Eb

let us re - joice and be glad.

To repeat

A-67

Christ, Our Pasch

Easter Sunday, Song for the Table
Easter Vigil, Song for the Table

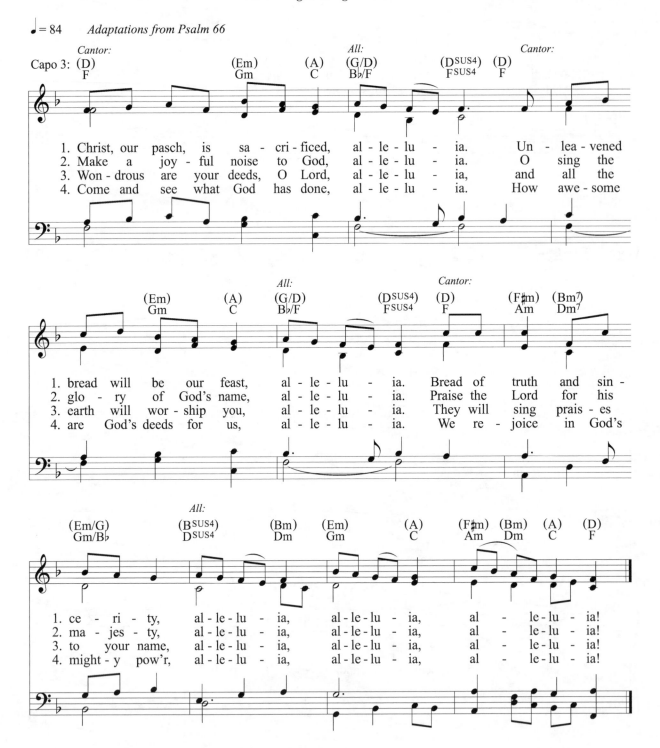

1. Christ, our pasch, is sa - cri - ficed, al - le - lu - ia. Un - lea - vened
2. Make a joy - ful noise to God, al - le - lu - ia. O sing the
3. Won - drous are your deeds, O Lord, al - le - lu - ia, and all the
4. Come and see what God has done, al - le - lu - ia. How awe - some

1. bread will be our feast, al - le - lu - ia. Bread of truth and sin -
2. glo - ry of God's name, al - le - lu - ia. Praise the Lord for his
3. earth will wor - ship you, al - le - lu - ia. They will sing prais - es
4. are God's deeds for us, al - le - lu - ia. We re - joice in God's

1. ce - ri - ty, al - le - lu - ia, al - le - lu - ia, al - le - lu - ia!
2. ma - jes - ty, al - le - lu - ia, al - le - lu - ia, al - le - lu - ia!
3. to your name, al - le - lu - ia, al - le - lu - ia, al - le - lu - ia!
4. might - y pow'r, al - le - lu - ia, al - le - lu - ia, al - le - lu - ia!

Second Sunday of Easter, Song for the Week: Option I

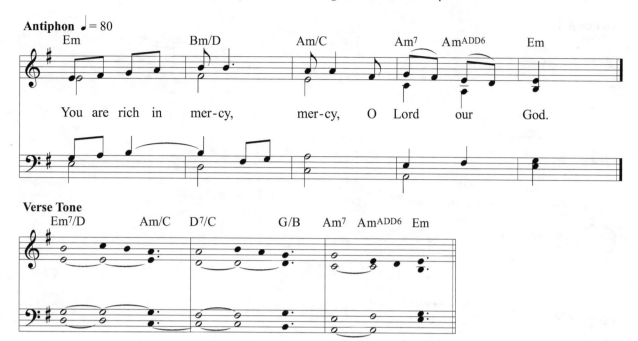

Isaiah 66:10-14

1. Rejoice <u>with</u> Jerusalem,
   and be glad for her, all <u>you</u> who love her;
   rejoice with her in joy, all <u>you</u> who mourn over her—

2. that you may nurse <u>and</u> be satisfied
   from her con<u>sol</u>ing breast;
   that you may drink deeply with delight from her <u>glo</u>rious bosom.

3. For thus <u>says</u> the LORD:
   I will extend prosperity to her <u>like</u> a river,
   and the wealth of the nations like an over<u>flow</u>ing stream;

4. and you shall nurse and be carried <u>on</u> her arm,
   and dandled <u>on</u> her knees.
   As a mother comforts her child, so I will <u>com</u>fort you.

5. You shall be comforted <u>in</u> Jerusalem.
   You shall see, and your heart <u>shall</u> rejoice;
   your bodies shall flourish <u>like</u> the grass.

6. And it <u>shall</u> be known
   that the hand of the LORD is <u>with</u> his servants,
   and his indignation is a<u>gainst</u> his enemies.

Performance Notes

The Antiphon may be sung twice each time. If desired, the repetition could overlap on the final note, with "You are" being sung at the same time as "God."

Like Newborn Children

Second Sunday of Easter, Song for the Week: Option II

Antiphon ♩. = 54

Like new-born child-ren thirst-ing for milk, our spi-rits long to grow in Christ, al-le-lu-ia.

Verse Tone

Isaiah 66:10-14

1. Rejoice with Jerusalem,
   and be glad for her, all you who love her;
   rejoice with her in joy,
   all you who mourn over her—

2. that you may nurse and be satisfied
   from her consoling breast;
   that you may drink deeply
   with delight from her glorious bosom.

3. For thus says the Lord:
   I will extend prosperity to her like a river,
   and the wealth of the nations
   like an overflowing stream;

4. and you shall nurse and be carried on her arm,
   and dandled on her knees.
   As a mother comforts her child,
   so I will comfort you.

5. You shall be comforted in Jerusalem.
   You shall see, and your heart shall rejoice;
   your bodies shall flourish
   like the grass.

6. And it shall be known
   that the hand of the Lord is with his servants,
   and his indignation
   is against his enemies.

Give Thanks to the Lord, Alleluia

Second Sunday of Easter, Song for the Word

Verses Superimposed Tone   *Psalm 118:2-4, 13-15, 22-24*

1. ⸗ Chil-dren of Is-rael and Aa-ron say, "God's love has no
2. Though thrust down and fall-ing, God came to my aid. My sav-ior gives
3. The stone which the build-ers re-ject-ed and scorned is now the
4. ⸗ This day was made, was made by the Lord; let us re-

Antiphon ♩. = 63

Give thanks to the Lord, al-le-lu-ia, for God's love has no

1. end, God's love has no end." All those who fear the Lord,
2. cour-age and strength to my soul. Loud shouts of vic-to-ry
3. key, the cor-ner-stone. This is the work of the
4. joice, re-joice and be glad. Give thanks to the Lord, God's

end, al-le-lu-ia. Al-le-lu-ia, al-le-

1. now let them say: "God's love has no end." Al-le-lu-ia!
2. joy-ful-ly fill the tents of the just. Al-le-lu-ia!
3. Lord our God, great in our eyes. Al-le-lu-ia!
4. love has no end. Al-le-lu-ia! Al-le-lu-ia!

lu-ia, for God's love has no end, al-le-lu-ia!

Touch Me and See

Second Sunday of Easter, Song for the Table: Option I

Psalm 78:1-4, 23-25, 29

1. Give heed, my people, to my <u>teach</u>ing;
   turn your ear to the words of my <u>mouth</u>.
   I will open my mouth <u>in</u> a parable
   and reveal hidden lessons <u>of</u> the past.

2. The things we have heard and under<u>stood</u>,
   the things our ancestors have <u>told</u> us,
   these we will not hide <u>from</u> their children
   but will tell them to the next <u>gen</u>eration:

3. God commanded the clouds a<u>bove</u>
   and opened the gates of <u>heaven</u>;
   rained down manna <u>for</u> their food,
   and gave them <u>bread</u> from heaven.

4. Mere mortals ate the bread of <u>angels</u>.
   The LORD sent them meat in a<u>bun</u>dance;
   so they ate and <u>had</u> their fill;
   for God gave them <u>all</u> they craved.

Put Your Hand Here, Thomas

Second Sunday of Easter, Song for the Table: Option II

Psalm 30

1. *A* I will praise you, LORD, you have rescued me
   D and have not let my enemies rejoice over me.

2. O LORD, I cried to you for help
   and you, my God, have healed me.
   O LORD, you have raised my soul from the dead,
   restored me to life from those who sink into the
   grave.

3. Sing psalms to the LORD, you faithful ones,
   give thanks to his holy name.
   God's anger lasts a moment, God's favor through
   life.
   At night there are tears, but joy comes with dawn.

4. I said to myself in my good fortune:
   "Nothing will ever disturb me."

Your favor had set me on a mountain fastness,
then you hid your face and I was put to confusion.

5. To you, LORD, I cried,
   to my God I made appeal:
   "What profit would my death be,
       my going to the grave?
   Can dust give you praise or proclaim your truth?"

6. The LORD listened and had pity.
   The LORD came to my help.
   For me you have changed my mourning into dancing,
   you removed my sackcloth and clothed me with joy.
   [Repeat C and D]
   So my soul sings psalms to you unceasingly.
   O LORD my God, I will thank you for ever.

A-73

Let All the Earth Cry Out Your Praises/
Let All the Earth Adore and Praise You

Third Sunday of Easter, Song for the Week
Sixth Sunday of Easter, Song for the Word
Second Sunday in Ordinary Time, Song for the Week

The alternate text (italic) is used on the Second Sunday in Ordinary Time.

Verse Tone with Response

...al - le - lu - ia, al - le - lu - ia!
...*sing to your name, O God Most High!*

Psalm 66:1-12, 16-20 [Lectionary selections for the Sixth Sunday of Easter are indicated by an asterisk.]

1. * Cry out with <u>joy</u> to
   * God, <u>all</u> the earth;
      alleluia, alleluia! (or *sing to your name . . .*)

2. * O sing to the glory of his <u>name</u>,
   * rendering <u>glorious</u> praise.
      alleluia, alleluia! (or *sing to your name . . .*)

3. * Say to <u>God</u>: "How tre-
   * <u>mendous</u> your deeds! *(simile)*

4. * Because of the greatness of your <u>strength</u>
   * your enemies <u>cringe</u> before you.

5. * Before you all the earth shall <u>bow</u>,
   * shall sing to you, sing <u>to</u> your name!"

6. * Come and see the works of <u>God</u>,
   * tremendous deeds <u>for</u> the people.

7. * God turned the sea into <u>dry</u> land,
   * they passed through the <u>river</u> dry-shod.

8. * Let our <u>joy</u> then
   * be <u>in</u> the LORD.

9. * The LORD rules for <u>ever</u>,
   * for <u>ever</u> in power.

10. * The LORD's eyes keep watch over <u>nations</u>;
    * let rebels not lift <u>them</u>selves up.

11. O peoples, bless our <u>God</u>, let the
    voice of God's <u>praise</u> resound.

12. Praise God who gave life to our <u>souls</u>
    and kept our <u>feet</u> from stumbling.

13. For you, our God, have <u>tested</u> us,
    you have tried us as sil<u>ver</u> is tried;

14. you led us, God, into the <u>snare</u>;
    you laid a heavy burden <u>on</u> our backs.

15. You let foes ride over our <u>heads</u>;
    we went through fire <u>and</u> through water

16. but then you <u>brought</u> us,
    you brought <u>us</u> relief.

17. * Come and hear, all who fear <u>God</u>,
    * I will tell what God did <u>for</u> my soul;

18. to God I cried a<u>loud</u>,
    with high praise ready <u>on</u> my tongue.

19. If there had been evil in my <u>heart</u>,
    the LORD would <u>not</u> have listened.

20. But truly God has <u>listened</u>;
    has heeded the voice <u>of</u> my prayer.

21. * Blessed be <u>God</u> who has
    * not re<u>jected</u> me.

22. * Blessed be <u>God</u> who has not with-
    * held his <u>love</u> from me.

Performance Notes
Since the psalm verses are fairly short and brisk, it is recommended that the Antiphon only be sung after every two or three verses.

A-74

You Will Show Us the Path of Life
Third Sunday of Easter, Song for the Word

Psalm 16:1-2, 5-11

*1. Preserve me, God, I take re<u>fuge</u> in you.
   I say to you, LORD: "You are my God.
      My happiness lies in <u>you</u> alone."

*2. O LORD, it is you who are my por<u>tion</u> and cup,
   it is you yourself who <u>are</u> my prize.

[3.] The lot marked out for me is <u>my</u> delight,
   welcome indeed the her<u>itage</u> that falls to me!

*4. I will bless you, LORD, you <u>give</u> me counsel,
   and even at night di<u>rect</u> my heart.

*5. I keep you, LORD, ever <u>in</u> my sight;
   since you are at my right hand, I <u>shall</u> stand firm.

6. And so my heart rejoices, my <u>soul</u> is glad;
   even my body shall <u>rest</u> in safety.

*7. For you will not leave my soul <u>among</u> the dead,
   nor let your beloved <u>know</u> decay.

8. You will show me the <u>path</u> of life,
   the fullness of joy in your presence,
      at your right hand happ<u>iness</u> for ever.

Performance Notes
This psalm tone is derived from the old Gregorian chant tonus peregrinus. *The asterisked verses 1, 2, 4, 5 and 7 end with two slurred notes on the final syllable. In verse 3, use the additional cue note in parentheses and no slur.*
[*The Lectionary selection omits verse 3 above, and groups the remainder as 1-2, 4-5, 6-7 and 8.*]

At Your Word Our Hearts Are Burning

Third Sunday of Easter, Song for the Table

Revelation 4:11; 5:9-10, 12b-d, 13b-d; 4:8c

1. You are worthy, our Lord <u>and</u> God,
   to receive glory and h<u>on</u>or and power,
   for you cre<u>at</u>ed all things,
   and by your will <u>they</u> existed
   and <u>were</u> created.

2. You are worthy to take <u>the</u> scroll
   and to <u>op</u>en its seals,
   for you were slaughtered and by <u>your</u> blood
   you ran<u>somed</u> for God
   saints from every tribe and language and
      <u>peo</u>ple and nation;

3. C you have made them to be a kingdom <u>and</u> priests
   D serv<u>ing</u> our God,
   E and they will <u>reign</u> on earth.

4. C Worthy is the Lamb that <u>was</u> slaughtered
   D to receive power and wealth and wis<u>dom</u> and might
   E and honor and glo<u>ry</u> and blessing.

5. C To the one seated on the throne and to <u>the</u> Lamb
   D be blessing and honor and glo<u>ry</u> and might
   E for<u>ev</u>er and ever.

6. C Holy, ho<u>ly</u>, holy,
   D the Lord God <u>the</u> Almighty,
   E who was and is and <u>is</u> to come.

Performance Notes

The Antiphon is the hymn tune STUTTGART. *It would perhaps be preferable to perform this in chant style, unaccompanied, at half-note = ca. 80.*

The Earth Is Full of the Goodness of God

Fourth Sunday of Easter, Song for the Week

Antiphon ♩. = ca. 76

Capo 3:

The earth is full of the good-ness of God, al - le - lu - ia,

al - le - lu - ia; the hea - vens were made by the word of the Lord,

al - le - lu - ia!

Verse Tone with Response

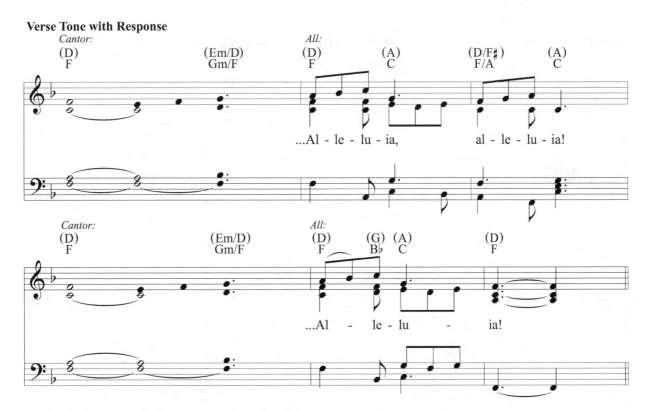

Psalm 33:1-9, 12-13, 20-22

1. Ring out your joy to the LORD, O you just;
   Alleluia, alleluia;
   for praise is fitting for loyal hearts.
   Alleluia!

2. Give thanks to the LORD upon the harp,   *(simile)*
   with a ten-stringed lute play your songs.

3. Sing to the LORD a song that is new,
   play loudly with all your skill.

Antiphon

4. The word of the LORD is faithful
   and all his works done in truth.

5. The LORD loves justice and right
   and fills the earth with love.

Antiphon

6. By God's word the heav'ns were made,
   by the breath of his mouth all the stars.

7. God collects the waves of the ocean;
   and stores up the depths of the sea.

Antiphon

8. Let all the earth fear the LORD,
   all who live in the world stand in awe.

9. For God spoke; it came to be.
   God commanded; it sprang into being.

Antiphon

10. They are happy whose God is the LORD,
    the people who are chosen as his own.

11. From the heavens the LORD looks forth
    and sees all the peoples of the earth.

Antiphon

12. Our soul is waiting for the LORD.
    The LORD is our help and our shield.

13. Our hearts find joy in the LORD.
    We trust in God's holy name.

14. May your love be upon us, O LORD,
    as we place all our hope in you.

Antiphon

A-78

You Are the Shepherd

Fourth Sunday of Easter, Song for the Table

Alto / Tenor Descants

Je - sus the Lamb who was slain.

Bass Descant *(optional)*

Je - sus, slain.

Antiphon

(D) (Em/G) (D)
Eb Fm/Ab Eb

Je - sus, the Lamb who was slain.

Verse Tone

(D) (G) (Em⁷) (A) (D/F♯) (Em⁷) (D/F♯) (G) (G/B) (A)
Eb Ab Fm⁷ Bb Eb/G Fm⁷ Eb/G Ab Ab/C Bb

[A] [B] [C] [D]

Psalm 78:52-55, 70-72; 80:2-4, 18-19

1. God brought forth the people like sheep;
   guided them like a flock in the desert;
   led them safely with nothing to fear,
   while the sea engulfed their foes.

2. So God brought them to that holy land,
   to the mountain that was won by his hand;
   drove out the nations before them,
   and divided the land for their heritage.

3. And God chose David as servant
   and took him away from the sheepfolds.
   From the care of the ewes God called him
      to be shepherd of the people of Jacob,
   of Israel, God's own possession.

4. *[Omit A-B]*
   God tended them wth blameless heart,
   with discerning mind he led them.

5. O shepherd of Israel, hear us,
   you who lead Joseph's flock,
   shine forth from your cherubim throne
   upon Ephraim, Benjamin, Manasseh.

6. O Lord, rouse up your might,
   O Lord, come to our help.
   God of hosts, bring us back;
   let your face shine on us and we shall be saved.

7. May your hand be on the one you have chosen,
   the one you have given your strength.
   And we shall never forsake you again;
   give us life that we may call upon your name.

Sing to God a New Song

Fifth Sunday of Easter, Song for the Week
The Immaculate Conception of the Blessed Virgin Mary (December 8), Song for the Word

Psalm 98 [*The Lectionary selections for the Immaculate Conception are indicated by an asterisk.*]

1. * Sing a new song to the LORD who
    *   has worked wonders; *Sing to God . . .*
    * whose right hand and holy arm have
    *   brought salvation. *Sing alleluia!*

2. * The LORD has made known salvation;
    *   has shown justice to the nations; *(simile)*
    * has remembered truth and love
    *   for the house of Israel.

3. * All the ends of the earth have seen
    *   the salvation of our God.
    * Shout to the LORD, all the earth,
    *   ring out your joy.

4. Sing psalms to the LORD with the harp,
    with the sound of music.
    With trumpets and the sound of the horn
    acclaim the King, the LORD.

5. Let the sea and all within it thunder;
    the world, and all its peoples.
    Let the rivers clap their hands
    and the hills ring out their joy

6. at the presence of the LORD who comes,
    who comes to rule the earth.
    God will rule the world with justice
    and the peoples with fairness.

Let Your Love Be Upon Us, O Lord

Fifth Sunday of Easter, Song for the Word

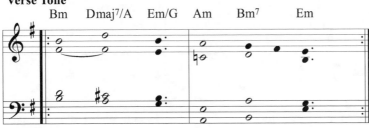

Psalm 33:1-2, 4-5, 18-19

1. Ring out your joy to the LORD, O you just;
   for praise is fitting for loyal hearts.
   Give thanks to the LORD upon the harp,
   with a ten-stringed lute play your songs.

2. The word of the LORD is faithful
   and all his works done in truth.
   The LORD loves justice and right
   and fills the earth with love.

3. The LORD looks on those who fear him,
   on those who hope in his love,
   to rescue their souls from death,
   to keep them alive in famine.

I Am the Way: Follow Me

Fifth Sunday of Easter, Song for the Table: Option I

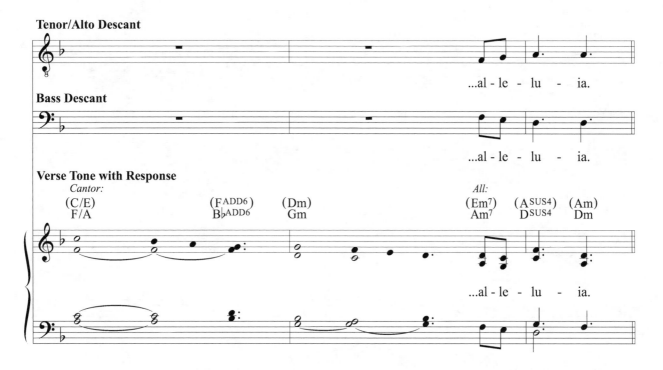

Cf. John 15:5; 10:11; 14:27; Revelation 19:5; 12:10; Romans 6:8; Psalm 71:8, 23a; 2 Corinthians 5:15; Revelation 5:12; Colossians 2:12; John 17:20-21

1. I am the vine and you are the branches,
   <u>says</u> the Lord;
   those who abide in me, and I in them, <u>bear</u> much
   fruit, *alleluia.*

2. The Good Shepherd is risen, who laid down his
   life <u>for</u> his sheep,
   the one is risen who died <u>for</u> his flock, *alleluia.*

3. Peace I leave with you, my peace I give to you,
   <u>says</u> the Lord.
   Not as the world gives <u>do</u> I give to you, *alleluia.*

4. Praise our God, all <u>you</u> his servants,
   and all who fear him, <u>small</u> and great, *alleluia.*

5. Now have come the salvation <u>and</u> the power
   and the kingdom of our God
   and the authority of <u>his</u> Anointed, *alleluia.*

6. If we have <u>died</u> with Christ,
   we believe that we will also <u>live</u> with him, *alleluia.*

7. Our lips are filled with your praise <u>and</u> your glory;
   when we sing to you our lips <u>shall</u> rejoice, *alleluia.*

8. Christ has risen and <u>shines</u> upon us;
   he has redeemed us <u>with</u> his blood, *alleluia.*

9. Christ died for all, so that those who live might
   live no longer <u>for</u> themselves,
   but for him who died <u>and</u> was raised for them,
   alleluia.

10. Worthy is the Lamb <u>that</u> was slain
    to receive power and wealth and wisdom and
    might and honor and <u>glory</u> and blessing,
    alleluia.

11. The one who died on the cross has risen <u>from</u>
    the dead,
    and has rescued our <u>lives</u> from death, *alleluia.*

12. When we were buried with Christ in baptism,
    we were <u>also</u> raised with him
    through faith in the power of God, who raised
    him <u>from</u> the dead, *alleluia.*

13. I pray for them, Father, that they may be one
    in us, <u>says</u> the Lord,
    so that the world may believe that <u>you</u> have
    sent me, *alleluia.*

You Are the Vine

Fifth Sunday of Easter, Song for the Table: Option II

Antiphon ♩. = 63

You are the vine, we are the branch-es: Liv-ing in you, may we bear much fruit.

Verse Tone

Psalm 80:2ac, 3bc, 9-16, 20

1. O shepherd of Is<u>ra</u>el, hear us,
   shine forth from your che<u>ru</u>bim throne.
   O L<small>ORD</small>, rouse <u>up</u> your might,
   O L<small>ORD</small>, come <u>to</u> our help.

2. You brought a vine <u>out</u> of Egypt;
   to plant it you drove <u>out</u> the nations.
   Before it you <u>cleared</u> the ground;
   it took root and spread <u>through</u> the land.

3. The mountains were covered <u>with</u> its shadow,
   the cedars of God <u>with</u> its boughs.
   It stretched out its branches <u>to</u> the sea,
   to the Great River it stretched <u>out</u> its shoots.

4. Then why have you broken <u>down</u> its walls?
   It is plucked by all <u>who</u> pass by.
   It is ravaged by the boar <u>of</u> the forest,
   devoured by the beasts <u>of</u> the field.

5. God of hosts, turn again, <u>we</u> implore,
   look down from hea<u>ven</u> and see.
   Visit this vine <u>and</u> protect it,
   the vine your right <u>hand</u> has planted.

6. God of hosts, <u>bring</u> us back;
   let your face shine on us and we <u>shall</u> be saved.
   God of hosts, <u>bring</u> us back;
   let your face shine on us and we <u>shall</u> be saved.

A-83 ➞ Sixth Sunday of Easter, Song for the Week, *same as A-89*

A-84 ➞ Sixth Sunday of Easter, Song for the Word, *same as A-73*

Live on in My Love

Sixth Sunday of Easter, Song for the Table

Verses *John 15:9-16*

1. As the Fa - ther loved me, so I have loved you:
2. If you keep my com - mands, you will live in my love,
3. May my joy be in you, may your joy be com - plete:
4. 𝄾 𝄾 Love one an - o - ther as I have loved you:
5. 𝄾 𝄾 No great - er love than to lay down your life:
6. 𝄾 𝄾 You are my friends if you keep to my word:
7. 𝄾 𝄾 No long - er slaves, but I call you friends:
8. Not you who chose me, but I who chose you:
9. Go forth and bear fruit, and your fruit must en - dure:

Alto Descant

(Text as above)

(Verses) *All:* live on in my love. **Antiphon** Live on in my love, live on in my love.

Alto Descant
Live on in my love. Live on in my love, live on in my love.

Tenor Descant
Live on in my love. Live on in my love, live on in my love.

Bass Descant
Live on in my love, live on in my love.

Why Stare into the Sky?
The Ascension of the Lord, Song for the Day/Week

Verses Superimposed tone

Antiphon *(can be sung in unison or as a 3-part round)*

Why stare in-to the sky?
Christ as - cend - ed and will come a - gain,
al - le - lu - ia, al - le - lu - ia!

♩ = 88-92

Psalm 68:2-6, 19-22, 33-36

1. Let God arise, let the foes be scattered.
   Let those who hate God take to flight.

2. As smoke is blown away so will they be blown away;
   like wax that melts before the fire,
   so the wicked shall perish at the presence of God.

3. But the just shall rejoice at the presence of God,
   they shall exult and dance for joy.
   O sing to the LORD, make music to God's name;
   make a highway for the One who rides upon the clouds.

4. Rejoice in the LORD, exult before God.
   Father of the orphan, defender of the widow,
   such is God in the holy place.

5. You have gone up on high; you have taken captives,
   receiving people in tribute, O God,
   even those who rebel, into your dwelling, O LORD.
   May the LORD be blessed day after day.

6. God our savior bears our burdens;
   this God of ours is a God who saves.
   The LORD our God holds the keys of death.
   And God will smite the heads of foes,
   the crowns of those who persist in their sins.

7. Kingdoms of the earth, sing to God,
      praise the LORD
   who rides on the heavens, the ancient
      heavens.
   God's mighty voice thunders and roars.

8. Come, acknowledge the power of God,
   whose glory is on Israel;
   whose might is in the skies.

9. God is to be feared in the holy place.
   This is the LORD, Israel's God,
   who gives strength and power to the people.

God Goes Up with Shouts of Joy

The Ascension of the Lord, Song for the Word

Psalm 47 [*The Lectionary selections for the day are indicated by an asterisk.*]

1. * All peoples, <u>clap</u> your hands,
   * cry to God with <u>shouts</u> of joy! *alleluia!*
   * For the LORD, the Most High, <u>we</u> must fear,
   * great king over <u>all</u> the earth. *alleluia!*

2. God subdues <u>peoples</u> under us
   and nations <u>under</u> our feet. *(simile)*
   Our inheritance, our glory <u>is</u> from God,
   given to Jacob <u>out</u> of love.

3. * God goes up with <u>shouts</u> of joy;
   * the LORD goes up with <u>trumpet</u> blast.
   * Sing praise for <u>God</u>, sing praise,
   * sing praise to our <u>king</u>, sing praise.

4. * God is king of <u>all</u> the earth,
   * sing praise with <u>all</u> your skill.
   * God is king <u>over</u> the nations;
   * God reigns <u>enthroned</u> in holiness.

5. The leaders of the people <u>are</u> assembled
   with the people of Abraham's God.
   The rulers of the earth be<u>long</u> to God,
   to God who reigns <u>over</u> all.

I Will See You Again

The Ascension of the Lord, Song for the Table

Verse Tone

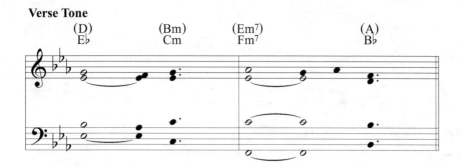

cf. John 14:18; 16:22; Revelation 1:17-18; John 14:26; 16:7; 16:13; 15:26-27; Acts 1:8

1. I will not leave <u>you</u> orphans;
   I will come back to you and your hearts <u>will</u> rejoice.

2. I am the beginning and the end of <u>all</u> things;
   I have met death, but I <u>am</u> alive.

3. The Holy Spirit whom the Father <u>will</u> send
   will teach you, and remind you of all <u>I</u> have said.

4. It is best for me <u>to</u> leave you,
   because if I do not go the Spirit <u>will</u> not come to you.

5. When the Spirit of truth comes <u>to</u> you,
   you will be led to the full<u>ness</u> of truth.

6. When the Advocate comes whom I will send you from the Father,
   the Spirit of truth who comes from <u>my</u> Father,
   he will testify on <u>my</u> behalf.

7. You also are <u>to</u> testify
   because you have been with me from <u>the</u> beginning.

8. When the Holy Spirit comes <u>to</u> you,
   you will be my witnesses to <u>all</u> the world.

Shout to the Ends of the Earth

Seventh Sunday of Easter, Song for the Week
Sixth Sunday of Easter, Song for the Week

Verse Tone with Response

...al - le - lu - ia!

...al - le - lu - ia!

Verses for the Seventh Sunday of Easter   *Psalm 66:1-12, 16-20*

1. Cry out with joy to God, all the <u>earth</u>.   *alleluia!*
   O sing to the glory of his name, rendering <u>glo</u>rious praise.   *alleluia!*

2. Say to God: "How tremendous your <u>deeds</u>!   *(simile)*
   Because of the greatness of your strength your enemies <u>cringe</u> before you.

3. Before you all the earth shall <u>bow</u>,
   shall sing to you, sing <u>to</u> your name!"

4. Come and see the works of <u>God</u>,
   tremendous deeds <u>for</u> the people.

5. God turned the sea into <u>dry</u> land,
   they passed through the ri<u>ver</u> dry-shod.

Verse Tone with Response

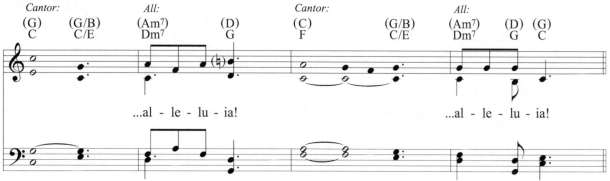

6. Let our joy then be in the LORD,
   who rules for ever in power.

7. The LORD's eyes keep watch over nations;
   let rebels not lift themselves up.

8. O peoples, bless our God,
   let the voice of God's praise resound.

9. Praise God who gave life to our souls
   and kept our feet from stumbling.

10. For you, our God, have tested us,
    you have tried us as silver is tried;

11. you led us, God, into the snare;
    you laid a heavy burden on our backs.

12. You let foes ride over our heads;
    we went through fire and through water

13. but then you brought us,
    you brought us relief.

14. Come and hear, all who fear God,
    I will tell what God did for my soul;

15. to God I cried aloud,
    with high praise ready on my tongue.

16. If there had been evil in my heart,
    the LORD would not have listened.

17. But truly God has listened;
    has heeded the voice of my prayer.

18. Blessed be God
    who has not rejected me.

19. Blessed be God
    who has not withheld his love from me.

Verses for the Sixth Sunday of Easter   *Psalm 98*

1. Sing a new song to the LORD   *alleluia!*
   who has worked wonders   *alleluia!*
   whose right hand and holy arm   *alleluia!*
   have brought salvation.   *alleluia!*

2. The LORD has made known salvation;   *(simile)*
   has shown justice to the nations;
   has remembered truth and love
   for the house of Israel.

3. All the ends of the earth have seen
   the salvation of our God.
   Shout to the LORD, all the earth,
   ring out your joy.

4. Sing psalms to the LORD with the harp,
   with the sound of music.
   With trumpets and the sound of the horn
   acclaim the King, the LORD.

5. Let the sea and all within it, thunder,
   the world, and all its peoples.
   Let the rivers clap their hands
   and the hills ring out their joy.

6. Ring out your joy at the presence of
      the LORD, who comes,
   who comes to rule the earth.
   God will rule the world with justice
   and the peoples with fairness.

Performance Notes
The Verse Tone is repeated for each stanza on the Sixth Sunday of Easter.

Seventh Sunday of Easter, Song for the Word

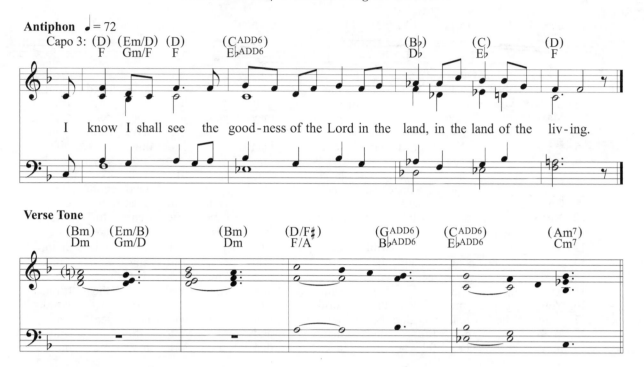

Psalm 27:1, 3-5, 7-14   *[The Lectionary selections for the day are indicated by an asterisk.]*

1. * The LORD is my light and my help;
   * whom shall I fear?
   * The LORD is the stronghold of my life;
   * before whom shall I shrink?

2. Though an army encamp against me
   my heart would not fear.
   Though war break out against me
   even then would I trust.

3. * There is one thing I ask of the LORD, for this I long,
   * to live in the house of the LORD, all the days of my life,
   * to savor the sweetness of the LORD,
   * to behold his temple.

4. For God makes me safe in his tent
   in the day of evil.
   God hides me in the shelter of his tent,
   on a rock I am secure.

5. * O LORD, hear my voice when I call;
   * have mercy and answer.
   * Of you my heart has spoken:
   * "Seek God's face."

6. It is your face, O LORD, that I seek;
   hide not your face.
   Dismiss not your servant in anger;
   you have been my help.

7. Do not abandon or forsake me,
   O God my help!
   Though father and mother forsake me,
   the LORD will receive me.

8. Instruct me, LORD, in your way;
   on an even path lead me.
   When they lie in ambush, protect me
       from my enemies' greed.
   False witnesses rise against me,
       breathing out fury.

9. I am sure I shall see the LORD's goodness
   in the land of the living.
   In the LORD, hold firm and take heart.
   Hope in the LORD!

Live on in My Love

Seventh Sunday of Easter, Song for the Table

Verses *John 15:9-16; 17:11b-12, 14, 17-18, 21, 23*

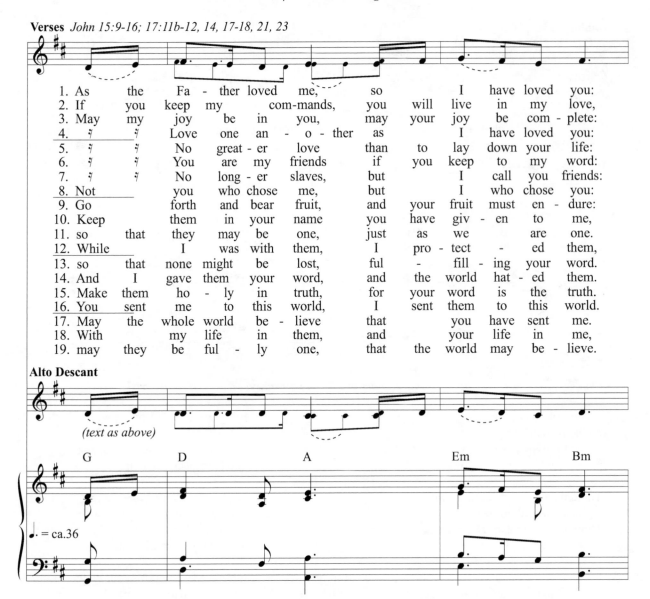

1. As the Fa - ther loved me, so I have loved you:
2. If you keep my com-mands, you will live in my love,
3. May my joy be in you, may your joy be com - plete:
4. 〉 〉 Love one an - o - ther as I have loved you:
5. 〉 〉 No great - er love than to lay down your life:
6. 〉 〉 You are my friends if you keep to my word:
7. 〉 〉 No long - er slaves, but I call you friends:
8. Not you who chose me, but I who chose you:
9. Go forth and bear fruit, and your fruit must en - dure:
10. Keep them in your name you have giv - en to me,
11. so that they may be one, just as we are one.
12. While I was with them, I pro - tect - ed them,
13. so that none might be lost, ful - fill - ing your word.
14. And I gave them your word, and the world hat - ed them.
15. Make them ho - ly in truth, for your word is the truth.
16. You sent me to this world, I sent them to this world.
17. May the whole world be - lieve that you have sent me.
18. With my life in them, and your life in me,
19. may they be ful - ly one, that the world may be - lieve.

Alto Descant

(text as above)

G D A Em Bm

♩. = ca.36

A-92

The Love of God

Pentecost Sunday, Song for the Week
The Most Holy Trinity, Song for the Table

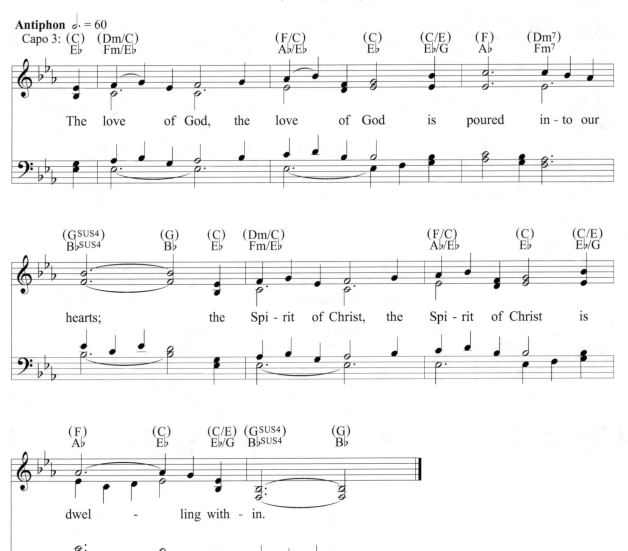

The love of God, the love of God is poured in-to our

hearts; the Spi-rit of Christ, the Spi-rit of Christ is

dwel - ling with - in.

Verse Tone

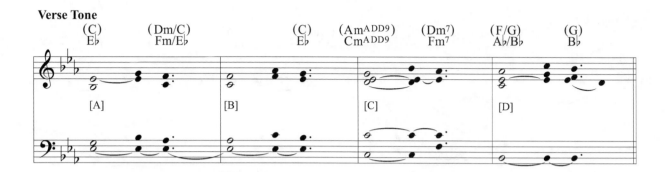

[A] [B] [C] [D]

Verses for Pentecost Sunday *Psalm 103*

1. My soul, give thanks to the LORD,
   all my being, bless God's holy name.
   My soul, give thanks to the LORD
   and never forget all God's blessings.

2. It is God who forgives all your guilt,
   who heals every one of your ills,
   who redeems your life from the grave,
   who crowns you with love and compassion,
   [repeat C-D]
   who fills your life with good things,
   renewing your youth like an eagle's.

3. The LORD does deeds of justice,
   gives judgement for all who are oppressed.
   The LORD's ways were made known to Moses;
   the LORD's deeds to Israel's children.

4. The LORD is compassion and love,
   slow to anger and rich in mercy.
   The LORD will not always chide,
   will not be angry for ever.
   [repeat C-D]
   God does not treat us according to our sins
   nor repay us according to our faults.

5. For as the heavens are high above the earth,
   so strong is God's love for the God-fearing;
   as far as the east is from the west,
   so far does God remove our sins.

6. As parents have compassion on their children,
   the LORD has pity on those who are God-fearing
   for God knows of what we are made,
   and remembers that we are dust.

7. As for us, our days are like grass;
   we flower like the flower of the field;
   the wind blows and we are gone
   and our place never sees us again.

8. But the love of the LORD is everlasting
   upon those who fear the LORD.
   God's justice reaches out to children's children
   when they keep his covenant in truth,
   [repeat D]
   when they keep his will in their mind.

9. The LORD has set his throne in heaven
   and his kingdom rules over all.
   Give thanks to the LORD, all you angels,
   mighty in power, fulfilling God's word,
   [repeat D]
   who heed the voice of that word.

10. Give thanks to the LORD, all you hosts,
    you servants who do God's will.
    Give thanks to the LORD, all God's works,
    in every place where God rules.
    [repeat D]
    My soul, give thanks to the LORD!

Verse Tone

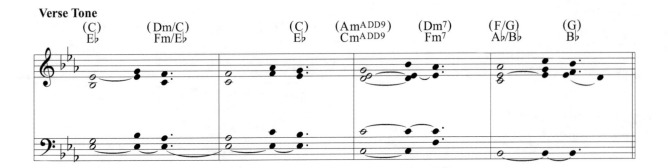

Verses for Trinity Sunday   *Ephesians 1:3-14*

1. Blessed be the God and Father of our Lord Je<u>sus</u> Christ,
   who has blessed us in Christ with every spiritual blessing in the heaven<u>ly</u> places,
   just as he chose us in Christ before the foundation of <u>the</u> world
   to be holy and blameless before him <u>in</u> love.

2. He destined us for adoption as his children through Je<u>sus</u> Christ,
   according to the good pleasure of <u>his</u> will,
   to the praise of his glo<u>rious</u> grace
   that he freely bestowed on us in the <u>Be</u>loved.

3. In him we have redemption through <u>his</u> blood,
   the forgiveness of <u>our</u> trespasses,
   according to the riches of <u>his</u> grace
   that he lavished <u>on</u> us.

4. With all wisdom and insight he has made known to us the mystery of <u>his</u> will,
   according to his good pleasure that he set forth <u>in</u> Christ,
   as a plan for the fullness <u>of</u> time,
   to gather up all things in him, things in heaven and things <u>on</u> earth.

5. In Christ we have also obtained an <u>in</u>heritance,
   having been destined according to the purpose of him who accomplishes all things
      according to his counsel <u>and</u> will,
   so that we, who were the first to set our hope <u>on</u> Christ,
   might live for the praise of <u>his</u> glory.

6. In him you also, when you had heard the word of truth, the gospel of your salvation,
      and had believed <u>in</u> him,
   were marked with the seal of the promised Ho<u>ly</u> Spirit;
   this is the pledge of our inheritance toward redemption as God's <u>own</u> people,
   to the praise of <u>his</u> glory.

Alleluia, Send Out Your Spirit

Pentecost Sunday, Song for the Word

Psalm 104:1ab, 24ac, 29b-31, 34

1. Bless the LORD, <u>my</u> soul!
   LORD God, how <u>great</u> you are!
   How many are your works, <u>O</u> LORD!
   The earth is full of <u>your</u> riches.

2. You take back your spirit, <u>they</u> die,
   returning to the dust from <u>which</u> they came.
   You send forth your spirit, they are <u>created</u>;
   and you renew the face of <u>the</u> earth.

3. May the glory of the LORD last <u>for</u> ever!
   May the LORD rejoice <u>in</u> creation!
   May my thoughts be pleasing <u>to</u> God.
   I find my joy in <u>the</u> LORD.

Performance Notes
Percussion or handclaps may be added, as indicated by X's, both during the Antiphon and at the end of the psalm verses to lead back into the Antiphon.
The Antiphon should be repeated every time it is sung.
The entire piece may be transposed down a whole step.

A-94

Come to Me and Drink
Pentecost Sunday, Song for the Table

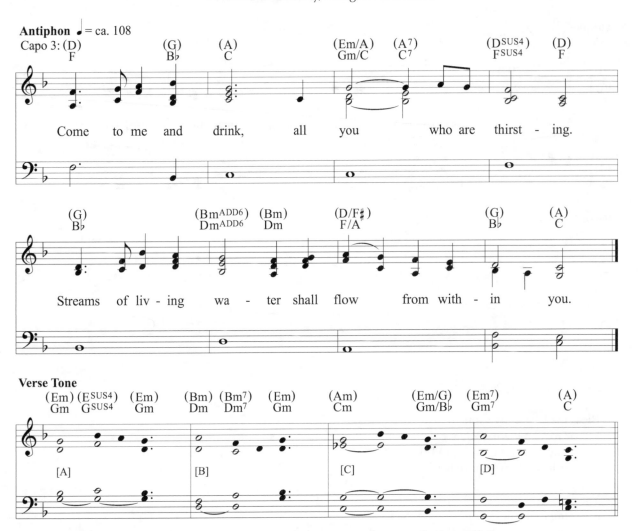

Psalm 63:2-9; 42:2-3, 8-9

1. O God, you are my God, for <u>you</u> I long;
   for you my <u>soul</u> is thirsting.
   My body <u>pines</u> for you
   like a dry, weary land with<u>out</u> water.

2. So I gaze on you <u>in</u> the sanctuary
   to see your strength <u>and</u> your glory.
   For your love is bet<u>ter</u> than life,
   my lips will <u>speak</u> your praise.

3. So I will bless you <u>all</u> my life,
   in your name I will lift <u>up</u> my hands.
   My soul shall be filled as <u>with</u> a banquet,
   my mouth shall praise <u>you</u> with joy.

4. On my bed <u>I</u> remember you.
   On you I muse <u>through</u> the night

for you have <u>been</u> my help;
in the shadow of your wings <u>I</u> rejoice.

5. My soul <u>clings</u> to you;
   [omit B-C]
   your right hand <u>holds</u> me fast.

6. Like the deer that yearns for <u>running</u> streams,
   so my soul is yearning for <u>you</u>, my God.
   My soul is thirsting for God, the God <u>of</u> my life;
   when can I enter and see the <u>face</u> of God?

7. Deep is calling on deep, in the <u>roar</u> of waters;
   your torrents and all your waves swept <u>over</u> me.
   By day the LORD will send forth <u>loving</u> kindness;
   by night I will sing to the LORD,
   praise the God <u>of</u> my life.

Here I Am

A-96

Second Sunday in Ordinary Time, Song for the Word

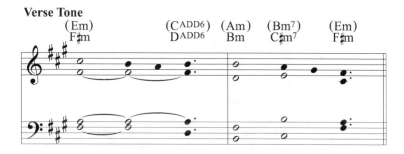

Psalm 40:2, 4ab, 7-11

1. I waited, I waited <u>for</u> the LORD
   who stooped down to me, and <u>heard</u> my cry.

2. God put a new song <u>into</u> my mouth,
   praise <u>of</u> our God.

3. You do not ask for sac<u>ri</u>fice and offerings,
   but an <u>open</u> ear.

4. You do not ask for holo<u>caust</u> and victim.
   Instead, <u>here</u> am I.

5. In the scroll of the book <u>it</u> stands written
   that I should <u>do</u> your will.

6. My God, I delight <u>in</u> your law
   in the depth <u>of</u> my heart.

7. Your justice I <u>have</u> proclaimed
   in the <u>great</u> assembly.

8. My lips I <u>have</u> not sealed;
   you know <u>it</u>, O LORD.

9. I have not hidden your justice <u>in</u> my heart
   but declared your <u>faithful</u> help.

10. I have not hidden your love <u>and</u> your truth
    from the <u>great</u> assembly.

Performance Notes
The Antiphon may be sung twice each time if desired.
The descants are intended for equal voices.

Behold the Lamb of God!

Second Sunday in Ordinary Time, Song for the Table

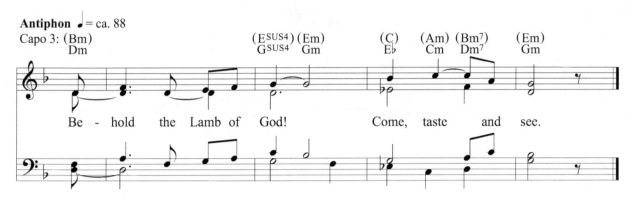

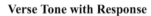

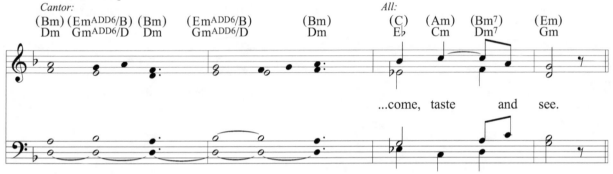

Psalm 34:2-15

1. I will bless the LORD <u>at</u> all times,
   God's praise always <u>on</u> my lips;   *come, taste . . .*

2. In the LORD my soul shall <u>make</u> its boast;
   the humble shall hear <u>and</u> be glad.   *(simile)*

3. Glorify the <u>LORD</u> with me.
   Together let us <u>praise</u> God's name.

4. I sought the LORD <u>and</u> was heard;
   from all my ter<u>rors</u> set free.

5. Look towards God <u>and</u> be radiant;
   let your faces not <u>be</u> abashed.

6. When the poor cry out <u>the</u> LORD hears them
   and rescues them from all <u>their</u> distress.

7. The angel of the LORD <u>is</u> encamped
   around those who fear <u>God</u>, to rescue them.

8. Taste and see that the <u>LORD</u> is good.
   They are happy who seek re<u>fuge</u> in God.

9. Revere the LORD, <u>you</u> his saints.
   They lack nothing, who re<u>vere</u> the LORD.

10. Strong lions suffer want <u>and</u> go hungry
    but those who seek the LORD <u>lack</u> no blessing.

11. Come, child<u>ren</u>, and hear me
    that I may teach you the fear <u>of</u> the LORD.

12. Who are those who <u>long</u> for life
    and many days to enjoy <u>their</u> prosperity?

13. Keep your <u>tongue</u> from evil
    and your lips from speak<u>ing</u> deceit.

14. Turn aside from evil <u>and</u> do good;
    seek and strive <u>after</u> peace.

The Message Goes Forth

Third Sunday in Ordinary Time, Song for the Week

Psalm 19:2-11

1. The heavens proclaim the glory of God,
   and the firmament shows forth the work of God's hands.
   Day unto day takes up the story
   and night unto night makes known the message.

2. No speech, no word, no voice is heard
   yet their span extends through all the earth,
   their words to the utmost bounds of the world.

3. There God has placed a tent for the sun;
   it comes forth like a bridegroom coming from his tent,
   rejoices like a champion to run its course.

4. At the end of the sky is the rising of the sun;
   to the furthest end of the sky is its course.
   There is nothing concealed from its burning heat.

5. The law of the LORD is perfect,
   it revives the soul.

The rule of the LORD is to be trusted,
   it gives wisdom to the simple.

6. The precepts of the LORD are right,
   they gladden the heart.
   The command of the LORD is clear,
   it gives light to the eyes.

7. The fear of the LORD is holy,
   abiding for ever.
   The decrees of the LORD are truth
   and all of them just.

8. They are more to be desired than gold,
   than the purest of gold
   and sweeter are they than honey,
   than honey from the comb.

The Lord Is My Light

Third Sunday in Ordinary Time, Song for the Word
Tenth Sunday in Ordinary Time, Song for the Week

Psalm 27:1, 3-5, 7-14   [The Lectionary selections for the Third Sunday in Ordinary Time are indicated by an asterisk.]

1. * The LORD is my light and my help;
   * whom shall I fear?
   * The LORD is the stronghold of my life;
   * before whom shall I shrink?

2. Though an army encamp against me
   my heart would not fear.
   Though war break out against me
   even then would I trust.

3. * There is one thing I ask of the LORD, for this I long,
   * to live in the house of the LORD all the days of my life,
   * to savor the sweetness of the LORD,
   * to behold his temple.

4. For God makes me safe in his tent
   in the day of evil.
   God hides me in the shelter of his tent,
   on a rock I am secure.

5. O LORD, hear my voice when I call;
   have mercy and answer.
   Of you my heart has spoken:
   "Seek God's face."

6. It is your face, O LORD, that I seek;
   hide not your face.
   Dismiss not your servant in anger;
   you have been my help.

7. Do not abandon or forsake me,
   O God my help!
   Though father and mother forsake me,
   the LORD will receive me.

8. Instruct me, LORD, in your way;
   on an even path lead me.
   When they lie in ambush, protect me
      from my enemies' greed.
   False witnesses rise against me,
      breathing out fury.

9. * I am sure I shall see the LORD's goodness
   * in the land of the living.
   * In the LORD, hold firm and take heart.
   * Hope in the LORD!

Light of the World

Third Sunday in Ordinary Time, Song for the Table

we are the light of the world, we are the light of the world.

we are the light of the world, we are the light of the world.

Ah . . . Ah . . .

Verse Tone *Isaiah 9:2-6; Psalm 27:1, 3, 13-14*
Cantor:

1. The peo - ple in dark - ness have seen a great light.
2. You have filled them with glad - ness and joy in a - bun - dance.
3. For the yoke of their bur - den, the rod of op - pres - sion,
4. For the boots of the bat - tle, the cloaks rolled in blood,
5. For a child has been born for us, a son has been giv'n.
6. He is Won - der - ful Coun - sel - lor, Might - y God,
7. The Lord is my light, the Lord is my help.
8. Though an ar - my be - siege me, my heart shall not fear.
9. I know I shall see the good - ness of God.

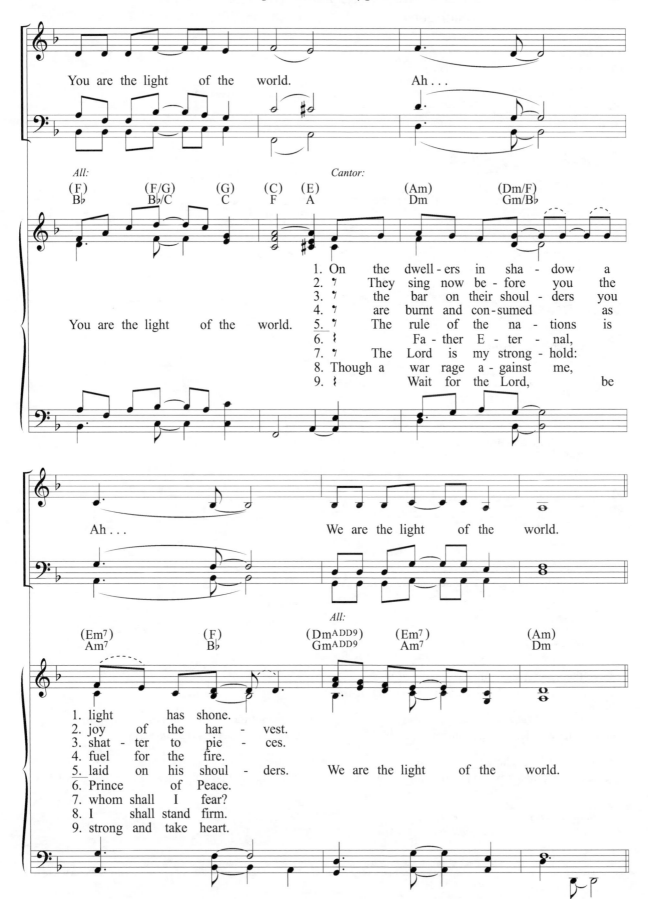

Seek the Lord! Long for the Lord!
Fourth Sunday in Ordinary Time, Song for the Week

Psalm 105:1-5

1. Give thanks and acclaim God's <u>name</u> *al-ways*,
   make known God's deeds among the peo<u>ples</u> *al-ways*.

2. O sing to the Lord, sing <u>praise</u> *al-ways*;
   tell all his wonderful <u>works</u> *al-ways*!

3. Be proud of God's holy <u>name</u> *al-ways*,
   let the hearts that seek the Lord re<u>joice</u> *al-ways*.

4. Consider the Lord, who is <u>strong</u> *al-ways*;
   constantly seek his <u>face</u> *al-ways*.

5. Remember the wonders of the Lord *al-ways*,
   the miracles and judgements pro<u>nounced</u> *al-ways*.

Performance Notes
Descants for the antiphon are available at A-32.

Blest Are the Poor in Spirit

Fourth Sunday in Ordinary Time, Song for the Word

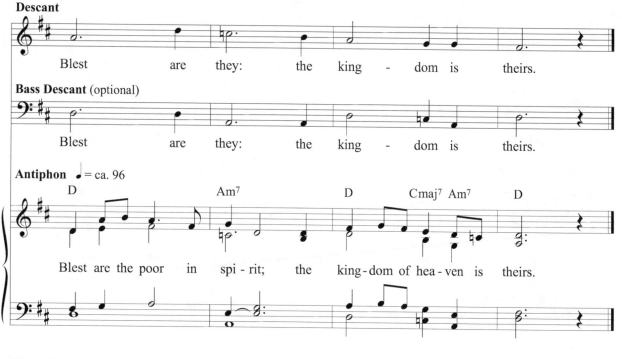

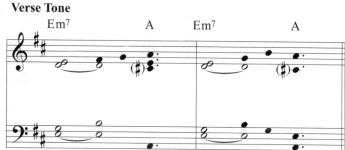

Psalm 146:2-10b [*The Lectionary selections for the day are indicated by an asterisk.*]

1. I will praise the LORD <u>all</u> my days,
   make music to my God <u>while</u> I live.

2. Put no trust <u>in</u> the powerful,
   mere mortals in whom there <u>is</u> no help.

3. Take their breath, they <u>return</u> to clay
   and their plans that day <u>come</u> to nothing.

4. They are happy who are helped by <u>Jacob's</u> God,
   whose hope is in the <u>LORD</u> their God,

5. the LORD who alone made <u>heav'n</u> and earth,
   the seas and all <u>they</u> contain.

6. * It is the LORD who keeps <u>faith</u> for ever,
   * who is just to those who <u>are</u> oppressed.

7. * It is God who gives bread <u>to</u> the hungry,
   * the LORD, who sets <u>pris'ners</u> free,

8. * the LORD who gives sight <u>to</u> the blind,
   * who raises up those who <u>are</u> bowed down,

9. * the LORD, who <u>protects</u> the stranger
   * and upholds the <u>widow</u> and orphan.

10. * It is the LORD who <u>loves</u> the just
    * but thwarts the path <u>of</u> the wicked.

11. * The LORD will <u>reign</u> for ever,
    * Zion's God from <u>age</u> to age.

A-103

Blest Are the Poor in Spirit

Fourth Sunday in Ordinary Time, Song for the Table

Cf. Psalm 1:1-3; Matthew 5:4-10; Psalm 15:2-5

1. Happy indeed <u>are</u> those
   who follow not the counsel <u>of</u> the wicked:
      the kingdom of heaven is theirs.

2. They do not linger in the way <u>of</u> sinners
   nor sit in the comp<u>any</u> of scorners;
      (simile)

3. Their delight is the law of <u>the</u> Lord
   and they ponder God's law <u>day</u> and night;

4. They are like a tree that <u>is</u> planted
   beside the <u>flowing</u> waters;

5. They yield their fruit in <u>due</u> season
   and their leaves shall <u>never</u> fade;
[repeat B]
   and all that they <u>do</u> shall prosper.

Descant

...the king - dom is theirs.

Bass Descant (optional)

...the king - dom is theirs.

Verse Tone with Response

Cantor:
Bm   Bm/A Em⁷   A G/A D   Cmaj⁷ Am⁷   D

All:

...the king - dom of hea - ven is theirs.

6. Blessed are those who mourn,
   for they will be comforted:

7. Blessed are the meek
   for they will inherit the earth:

8. Blessed are those who hunger and thirst for
     righteousness,
   for they will be filled:

9. Blessed are the merciful,
   for they will receive mercy:

10. Blessed are the pure in heart,
    for they will see God:

11. Blessed are the peacemakers,
    for they will be called children of God:

12. Blessed are those who are persecuted
    for righteousness' sake:

13. Those who walk without fault,
    those who act with justice:

14. Those who speak the truth from their hearts,
    and do not slander with their tongue:

15. Those who do no wrong to their kindred,
    who cast no slur on their neighbors:

16. Those who hold the godless in disdain,
    and honor those who fear the LORD:

17. Those who keep their word, come what may,
    who take no interest on a loan:

18. Those who accept no bribes against the innocent,
    they will stand firm for ever:

A-105

Those Who Fear the Lord

Fifth Sunday in Ordinary Time, Song for the Word

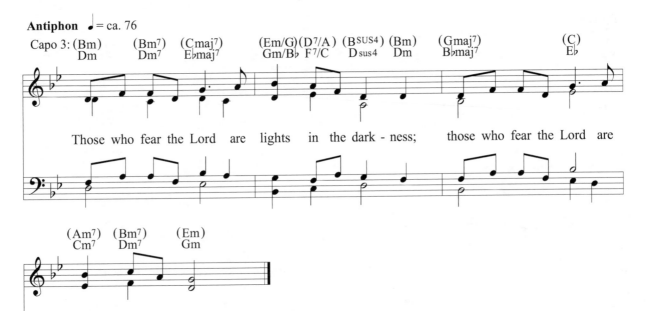

Antiphon ♩ = ca. 76

Those who fear the Lord are lights in the dark-ness; those who fear the Lord are light for the world.

Verse Tone with Response

Cantor: *All:* *Cantor:* *All:*

...lights in the dark - ness. ...light for the world.

Psalm 112:4-8a, 9

1. They are lights in the darkness for <u>the</u> upright;
   lights in the darkness.
   they are generous, merciful <u>and</u> just.
   light for the world.

2. Good people take pity <u>and</u> lend,
   (simile)
   they conduct their affairs <u>with</u> honor.

3. The just will ne<u>ver</u> waver,
   they will be remembered <u>for</u> ever.

4. They have no fear of e<u>vil</u> news;
   with firm hearts they trust in <u>the</u> LORD.

5. With steadfast hearts they will <u>not</u> fear;
   openhanded, they give to <u>the</u> poor.

6. Their justice stands firm <u>for</u> ever.
   Their heads will be raised <u>in</u> glory.

Light of the World

Fifth Sunday in Ordinary Time, Song for the Table

Alto Descant

Light, light, You are the light of the

Tenor / Bass Descants

Antiphon ♩ = 92-96

Capo 5: (C) (G) (Em⁷) (Am) (F) (F/G) (G)
F C Am⁷ Dm B♭ B♭/C C

Light of the world, light of the world, You are the light of the

world. Dark - ness in - to light,

(C) (E) (Am) (Dm/F) (Em⁷) (Am)
F A Dm Gm/B♭ Am⁷ Dm

world. From the dark-ness to light lead us, O Lord, so that

we are the light of the world, we are the light of the world.

(Dm^{ADD9}) (Em⁷) (Am) (G) (C) (Em⁷) (Am)
Gm^{ADD9} Am⁷ Dm C F Am⁷ Dm

we are the light of the world, we are the light of the world.

Ah . . . Ah . . .

Verse Tone *Isaiah 58:7-11; Matthew 5:13a, 14; Psalm 27:1, 3, 13-14*
Cantor:

(C) (G) (Em⁷) (Am)
F C Am⁷ Dm

1.	Share	your	bread	with	the	hun -	gry,		shel - ter	the	home-	less,
2.	Then	your	light	shall	break	forth		and	shine like	the	dawn.
3.	⁊	When - e -	ver	you	call,		God	sure - ly	will	an -	swer;
4.	Do	a -	way	with	op - pres -	sion,		the	speak - ing	of	e -	vil.
5.	⁊	Like	light	in	the	dark -	ness	your	glo - ry	will	shine;
6.	God	will	guide	you	for	e -	ver,		re - fresh - ing	your	soul,
7.	You	are	salt	of	the	earth		and	light	of	the	world,
8.	⁊	The	Lord	is	my	light,		the	Lord	is	my	help.
9.	Though	an	ar -	my	be - siege	me,		my	heart shall	not	fear.
10.	⁊	I	know	I	shall	see		the	good - ness	of	God.

Lead Me, Guide Me

Sixth Sunday in Ordinary Time, Song for the Week

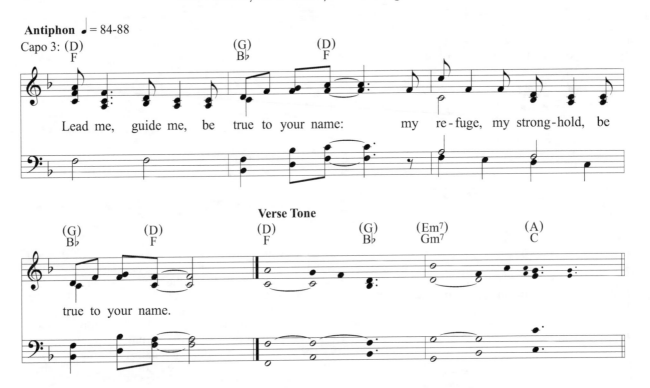

Psalm 31:2-6, 10, 15-17, 25

1. In you, O LORD, I take refuge.
   Let me never be put to shame.

2. In your justice, set me free,
   *hear me and speedily rescue me.

3. Be a rock of refuge for me,
   *a mighty stronghold to save me,

4. for you are my rock, my stronghold.
   *For your name's sake lead me and guide me.

5. Release me from the snares they have hidden
   for you are my refuge, LORD.

6. Into your hands I commend my spirit.
   It is you who will redeem me, LORD.

7. Have mercy on me, O LORD,
   for I am in distress.

8. Tears have wasted my eyes,
   my throat and my heart.

9. As for me, I trust in you, LORD.
   I say: "You are my God.

10. My life is in your hands, deliver me
    *from the hands of those who hate me.

11. Let your face shine on your servant.
    Save me in your love."

12. Be strong, let your heart take courage,
    all who hope in the LORD.

Performance Notes

Use the small cue-size notes (second measure of the verse tone) on the verse lines marked with an asterisk.

Happy Are They Who Follow

A-108

Sixth Sunday in Ordinary Time, Song for the Word

Psalm 119:1-2, 4-5, 17-18, 33-34

1. They are happy whose <u>life</u> is blameless,
   who fol<u>low</u> God's law!
   They are happy who <u>do</u> God's will,
   seeking God with <u>all</u> their hearts.

2. You have laid <u>down</u> your precepts
   to be o<u>beyed</u> with care.
   May my foot<u>steps</u> be firm
   to o<u>bey</u> your statutes.

3. Bless your servant and <u>I</u> shall live
   and o<u>bey</u> your word.
   Open my eyes that <u>I</u> may see
   the wonders <u>of</u> your law.

4. Teach me the demands <u>of</u> your statutes
   and I will keep them <u>to</u> the end.
   Train me to ob<u>serve</u> your law,
   to keep it <u>with</u> my heart.

Heaven and Earth Will Fade Away

Sixth Sunday in Ordinary Time, Song for the Table

Psalm 119:7-16, 27-28, 35-38, 49-50, 57, 72, 89-91, 103, 105-112

1. I will thank you with an <u>up</u>right heart
   as I learn <u>your</u> decrees.
   I will o<u>bey</u> your statutes;
   do <u>not</u> forsake me.

2. How shall the young <u>re</u>main sinless?
   By obey<u>ing</u> your word.
   I have sought you with <u>all</u> my heart;
   let me not stray from <u>your</u> commands.

3. I treasure your promise <u>in</u> my heart
   lest I <u>sin</u> against you.
   Blessed are <u>you</u>, O LORD;
   teach <u>me</u> your statutes.

4. With my tongue I <u>have</u> recounted
   the decrees <u>of</u> your lips.
   I rejoiced to <u>do</u> your will
   as though all ric<u>hes</u> were mine.

5. I will ponder <u>all</u> your precepts
   and consi<u>der</u> your paths.
   I take delight <u>in</u> your statutes;
   I will not for<u>get</u> your word.

6. Make me grasp the way <u>of</u> your precepts
   and I will muse <u>on</u> your wonders.
   My soul pines a<u>way</u> with grief;
   by your word <u>raise</u> me up.

Verse Tone

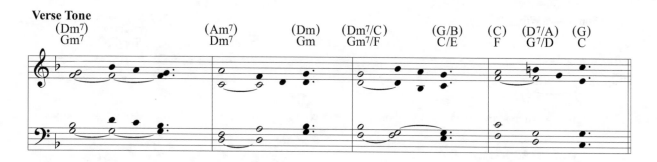

7. Guide me in the path of <u>your</u> commands;
   for there is <u>my</u> delight.
   Bend my heart <u>to</u> your will
   and not to <u>love</u> of gain.

8. Keep my eyes from <u>what</u> is false;
   by your word, <u>give</u> me life.
   Keep the promise <u>you</u> have made
   to the ser<u>vant</u> who fears you.

9. Remember your word <u>to</u> your servant
   by which you <u>gave</u> me hope.
   This is my com<u>fort</u> in sorrow:
   that your promise <u>gives</u> me life.

10. My part, I have re<u>solved</u>, O LORD,
    is to o<u>bey</u> your word.
    The law from your <u>mouth</u> means more to me
    than sil<u>ver</u> and gold.

11. Your word, O <u>LORD</u>, for ever
    stands firm <u>in</u> the heavens:
    your truth lasts from <u>age</u> to age,
    like the earth <u>you</u> created.

12. By your decree it endures <u>to</u> this day;
    for <u>all</u> things serve you.
    Your promise is sweeter <u>to</u> my taste
    than honey <u>in</u> the mouth.

13. Your word is a lamp <u>for</u> my steps
    and a light <u>for</u> my path.
    I have sworn and have made <u>up</u> my mind
    to obey <u>your</u> decrees.

14. LORD, I am deep<u>ly</u> afflicted;
    by your word <u>give</u> me life.
    Accept, LORD, the homage <u>of</u> my lips
    and teach me <u>your</u> decrees.

15. Though I carry my life <u>in</u> my hands,
    I remem<u>ber</u> your law.
    Though the wicked try <u>to</u> ensnare me,
    I do not stray <u>from</u> your precepts.

16. Your will is my her<u>itage</u> for ever,
    the joy <u>of</u> my heart.
    I set myself to carry <u>out</u> your statutes
    in full<u>ness</u>, for ever.

Your Mercy Is My Hope

Seventh Sunday in Ordinary Time, Song for the Week

A-110

Antiphon ♩ = ca. 76

Your mer-cy is my hope, your pro-mise is my song: my
heart re-joi-ces in your pow'r to save.

Verse Tone   *Psalm 13*

— Flex measure for verses 2 and 4

1. How long, O LORD, will you   for - get me?
   this sorrow in my heart day   and night?
3. { Look at me, answer me, LORD   my God!
     lest my enemy say: "I have   pre - vailed;"
   I trust in your merci   -   ful love.
5. Let me sing to you, LORD, for your goodness   to   me,

2. How long must I bear grief in my soul,

4. As for   me,

1. How long will you   hide   your   face?
2. How long shall my ene -   my   pre -   vail?
3. Give light to my eyes lest I fall a - sleep in   death, }
   lest my foes rejoice to   see   my   fall. }
4. Let my heart rejoice in your   sav - ing   help.
5. sing psalms to your name, O   LORD, Most   High.

Merciful and Tender

Seventh Sunday in Ordinary Time, Song for the Word
The Most Sacred Heart of Jesus, Song for the Word

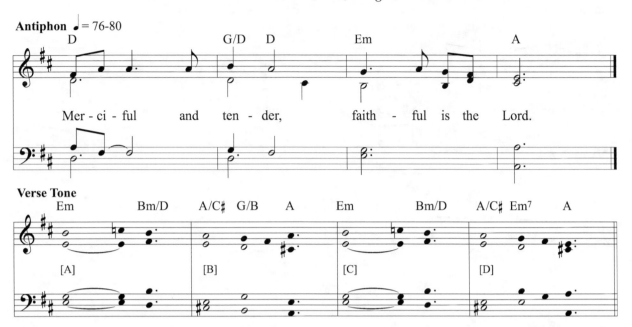

Antiphon ♩ = 76-80

Mer - ci - ful and ten - der, faith - ful is the Lord.

Verse Tone

[A] [B] [C] [D]

Psalm 103 [*The Lectionary selections for the Seventh Sunday in Ordinary Time are indicated by an asterisk and those for the Sacred Heart are indicated by a bullet.*]

1. *• My soul, give thanks to the Lord,
   *• all my being, bless God's holy name.
   *• My soul, give thanks to the Lord
   *• and never forget all God's blessings.

2. *• It is God who forgives all your guilt,
   *• who heals every one of your ills,
   *• who redeems your life from the grave,
   *• who crowns you with love and compassion,
   [repeat C-D]
   who fills your life with good things,
   renewing your youth like an eagle's.

3. • The Lord does deeds of justice,
   • gives judgement for all who are oppressed.
   The Lord's ways were made known to Moses;
   the Lord's deeds to Israel's children.

4. *• The Lord is compassion and love,
   *• slow to anger and rich in mercy.
   The Lord will not always chide,
   will not be angry forever.
   [repeat C-D]
   *• God does not treat us according to our sins
   *• nor repay us according to our faults.

5. For as the heavens are high above the earth
   so strong is God's love for the God-fearing;
   * as far as the east is from the west
   * so far does he remove our sins.

6. * As parents have compassion on their children,
   * the Lord has pity on those who are God-fearing
   for he knows of what we are made,
   and remembers that we are dust.

7. As for us, our days are like grass;
   we flower like the flower of the field;
   the wind blows and we are gone
   and our place never sees us again.

8. A But the love of the Lord is everlasting
   B upon those who fear the Lord.
   A God's justice reaches out to children's children
   B when they keep his covenant in truth,
   D when they keep his will in their mind.

9. A The Lord has set his throne in heaven
   B and his kingdom rules over all.
   A Give thanks to the Lord, all you angels,
   B mighty in power, fulfilling God's word,
   D who heed the voice of that word.

10. A Give thanks to the Lord, all you hosts,
    B you servants who do God's will.
    A Give thanks to the Lord, all his works,
    B in every place where God rules.
    D My soul, give thanks to the Lord!

Love the Lord Your God
Seventh Sunday in Ordinary Time, Song for the Table

Antiphon ♩ = 76

Love the Lord your God, your neigh-bor as your-self: do this and you shall live.

Verse Tone with Response

Cantor:

All:

...Do this and you shall live.

Psalm 119:1-8

1. They are happy whose <u>life</u> is blameless,
   who fo<u>llow</u> God's law!   *Do this . . .*

2. They are happy who <u>do</u> God's will,
   seeking God with <u>all</u> their hearts.   *Do this . . .*

3. They never do <u>any</u>thing evil
   but walk <u>in</u> God's ways.   *(simile)*

4. You have laid <u>down</u> your precepts
   to be o<u>beyed</u> with care.

5. May my foot<u>steps</u> be firm
   to o<u>bey</u> your statutes.

6. Then I shall not be <u>put</u> to shame
   as I heed <u>your</u> commands.

7. I will thank you with an <u>up</u>right heart
   as I learn <u>your</u> decrees.

8. I will o<u>bey</u> your statutes;
   do <u>not</u> forsake me.

Performance Notes
Descants for the antiphon and verses are available at A-185.

In God Alone Is My Soul at Rest

Eighth Sunday in Ordinary Time, Song for the Word

Psalm 62:2-3, 6-9c

1. In God alone is my soul <u>at</u> rest;
   in God alone
   from God <u>comes</u> my help.

2. God alone is my rock, <u>my</u> stronghold,
   in God alone
   my fortress; <u>I</u> stand firm.

3. In God alone be at rest, <u>my</u> soul;
   in God alone
   from God <u>comes</u> my hope.

4. God alone is my rock, <u>my</u> stronghold,
   in God alone
   my fortress; <u>I</u> stand firm.

5. In God is my safety <u>and</u> glory,
   in God alone
   the rock <u>of</u> my strength.

6. Take refuge in God, all <u>you</u> people;
   in God alone
   trusting always, pour out your hearts <u>to</u> the LORD.

God Feeds Us, God Saves Us

Eighth Sunday in Ordinary Time, Song for the Table

Verse Tone

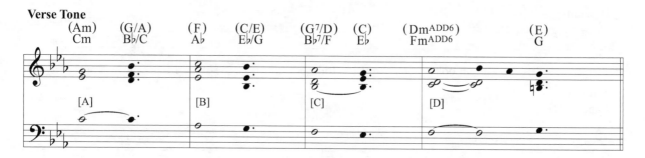

Psalm 33

1. Ring out your joy to the LORD, O you just;
[Omit B-C]
   for praise is fitting for loyal hearts.

2. Give thanks to the LORD upon the harp,
   with a ten-stringed lute play your songs.
   Sing to the LORD a song that is new,
   play loudly, with all your skill.

3. For the word of the LORD is faithful
   and all his works done in truth.
   The LORD loves justice and right
   and fills the earth with his love.

4. By God's word the heavens were made,
   by the breath of his mouth all the stars.
   God collects the waves of the ocean,
   and stores up the depths of the sea.

5. Let all the earth fear the LORD,
   all who live in the world stand in awe.
   For God spoke; it came to be.
   God commanded; it sprang into being.

6. The LORD foils the designs of the nations,
   and defeats the plans of the peoples.
   The counsel of the LORD stands forever,
   the plans of God's heart from age to age.

7. They are happy, whose God is the LORD,
   the people who are chosen as his own.
   From the heavens the LORD looks forth
   and sees all the peoples of the earth.

8. From the heavenly dwelling God gazes
   on all the dwellers on the earth;
   God who shapes the hearts of them all
   and considers all their deeds.

9. A king is not saved by his army,
   nor a warrior preserved by his strength.
   A vain hope for safety is the horse;
   despite its power it cannot save.

10. The LORD looks on those who revere him,
    on those who hope in his love,
    to rescue their souls from death,
    to keep them alive in famine.

11. Our soul is waiting for the LORD.
    The LORD is our help and our shield.
    Our hearts find joy in the LORD.
    We trust in God's holy name.

12. May your love be upon us, O LORD,
[Omit B-C]
    as we place all our hope in you.

Look on My Toil

Ninth Sunday in Ordinary Time, Song for the Week

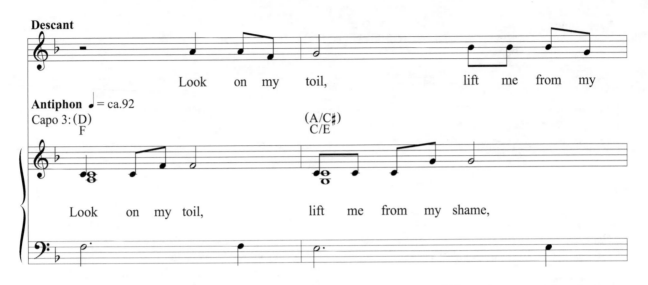

Verse Tone

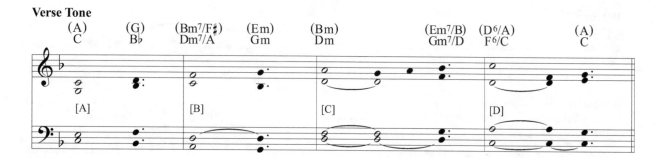

Psalm 25:2-21

1. My God, I trust in you, let me not be disap<u>po</u>inted;
   do not let my enemies <u>tri</u>umph.
   Those who hope in you shall not be <u>dis</u>appointed,
   but only those who wantonly <u>break</u> faith.

2. L<small>ORD</small>, make me know your <u>ways</u>.
   L<small>ORD</small>, teach me your <u>paths</u>.
   Make me walk in your <u>truth</u>, and teach me,
   for you are God <u>my</u> savior.

3. In you I hope all the day <u>long</u>
   because of your goodness, O L<small>ORD</small>.
   Remember your <u>mercy</u>, L<small>ORD</small>,
   and the love you have shown from <u>of</u> old.
   [repeat C-D]
   Do not remember the sins <u>of</u> my youth.
   In your love <u>remem</u>ber me.

4. The L<small>ORD</small> is good and <u>upright</u>,
   showing the path to those who <u>stray</u>,
   guiding the humble <u>in</u> the right path,
   and teaching the way to <u>the</u> poor.

5. God's ways are steadfastness and <u>truth</u>
   for those faithful to the covenant de<u>crees</u>.
   L<small>ORD</small>, for the sake <u>of</u> your name
   forgive my guilt, for it <u>is</u> great.

6. Those who revere the L<small>ORD</small>
   will be shown the path they should <u>choose</u>.
   Their souls will <u>live</u> in happiness
   and their children will possess <u>the</u> land.
   [repeat C-D]
   The L<small>ORD</small>'s friendship is <u>for</u> the God-fearing;
   and the covenant is revealed <u>to</u> them.

7. My eyes are always on the L<small>ORD</small>,
   who will rescue my feet from the <u>snare</u>.
   Turn to me <u>and</u> have mercy
   for I am lonely <u>and</u> poor.

8. Relieve the anguish of my <u>heart</u>
   and set me free from my di<u>stress</u>.
   See my affliction <u>and</u> my toil
   and take all my sins <u>away</u>.

9. See how many are my <u>foes</u>,
   how violent their hatred for <u>me</u>.
   Preserve my <u>life</u> and rescue me.
   Do not disappoint me, you are <u>my</u> refuge.
   [repeat C-D]
   May innocence and upright<u>ness</u> protect me,
   for my hope is in you, <u>O</u> L<small>ORD</small>.

A-117

Save Me, O Lord
Ninth Sunday in Ordinary Time, Song for the Word

Descant

Save me, you are my rock. Lead me, O Lord; let me see you.

Antiphon ♩ = 72-76

Em   Bm   Em   Bm   Em   Em/G   Em/B Bm

Save me, O Lord; you are my rock. Lead me, O Lord; let me see you.

Descant

...you are my rock.

Verse Tone with Response   *Psalm 31:2-4, 17, 25*

Cantor:

Em   Em/D   Am/C   *All:* Em   Bm

1. In you, O LORD, I take refuge.   Let me never be put to shame;   you are my rock.
2. Be a rock of refuge for me,   a mighty strong - hold to save me;
3. Let your face shine on your servant.   Save me in your love;

Cantor:

Em   Em/D   Am/C

1. In your justice set me free,   hear me and speed - i - ly rescue me;
2. for you are my rock, my stronghold.   For your name's sake, lead me and guide me;
3. Be strong, let your heart take courage,   all who hope in the LORD;

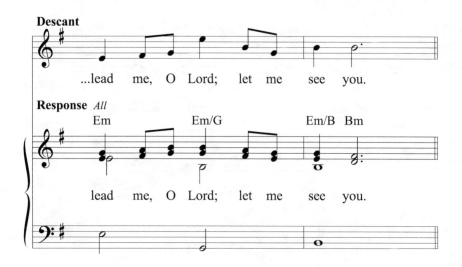

Descant

...lead me, O Lord; let me see you.

Response *All*

Em   Em/G   Em/B   Bm

lead me, O Lord; let me see you.

Keep These Words in Your Heart and Soul

Ninth Sunday in Ordinary Time, Song for the Table

Psalm 17:1-9, 15

1. LORD, hear a <u>cause</u> that is <u>just</u>,
   pay heed to <u>my</u> cry.
   Turn your <u>ear</u> to my <u>prayer</u>,
   no deceit <u>is</u> on my lips.

2. From you may my <u>judgement</u> come <u>forth</u>.
   Your eyes discern <u>the</u> truth.
   You search my heart, you <u>visit</u> me by <u>night</u>.
   You test me and you find <u>in</u> me no wrong.

3. My words are not <u>sinful</u> like human <u>words</u>.
   I kept from violence because of <u>your</u> word,
   I kept my feet <u>firmly</u> in your <u>paths</u>;
   there was no falter<u>ing</u> in my steps.

4. I am here and I call, you will <u>hear</u> me, O <u>God</u>.
   Turn your ear to me; hear <u>my</u> words.
   Display your great love, you whose <u>right</u> hand <u>saves</u>
   your friends from those who <u>rebel</u> against them.

5. Guard me as the <u>apple</u> of your <u>eye</u>.
   Hide me in the shadow of <u>your</u> wings
   from the violent at<u>tack</u> of the <u>wicked</u>.
   My foes encircle me <u>with</u> <u>deadly</u> intent.

6. As for <u>me</u>, in my <u>justice</u>,
   I shall see <u>your</u> face
   and be <u>filled</u>, when I a<u>wake</u>,
   with <u>the</u> <u>sight of</u> your glory.

Performance Notes

In verses 5 and 6, line 4, the double underlined text is sung on a single note.

A-119 → Tenth Sunday in Ordinary Time, Song for the Week, *same as A-99*

I Will Show God's Salvation

Tenth Sunday in Ordinary Time, Song for the Word

Psalm 50:1, 8, 12-15

1. The God of gods, the LORD, has spoken
   and <u>sum</u>moned the <u>earth</u>,
   from the rising of the <u>sun</u> to its <u>set</u>ting.
   "I find no fault <u>with</u> your sacrifices,
   your offerings are al<u>ways</u> before me.

2. Were I hungry, I <u>would</u> not <u>tell</u> you,
   for I own the <u>world</u> and all it <u>holds</u>.
   Do you think I eat the <u>flesh</u> of bulls,
   or drink the <u>blood</u> of goats?

3. Offer to <u>God</u> your <u>sacri</u>fice;
   to the Most High <u>pay</u> your <u>vows</u>.
   Call on me in the day <u>of</u> distress.
   I will free you and <u>you</u> shall honor me."

Love Is My Desire

Tenth Sunday in Ordinary Time, Song for the Table

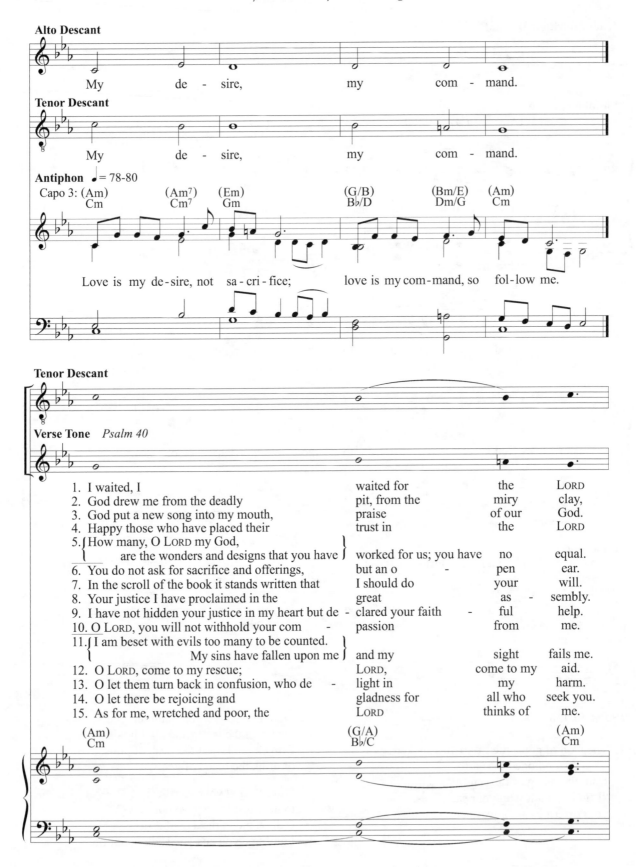

Tenor Descant

Verse Tone

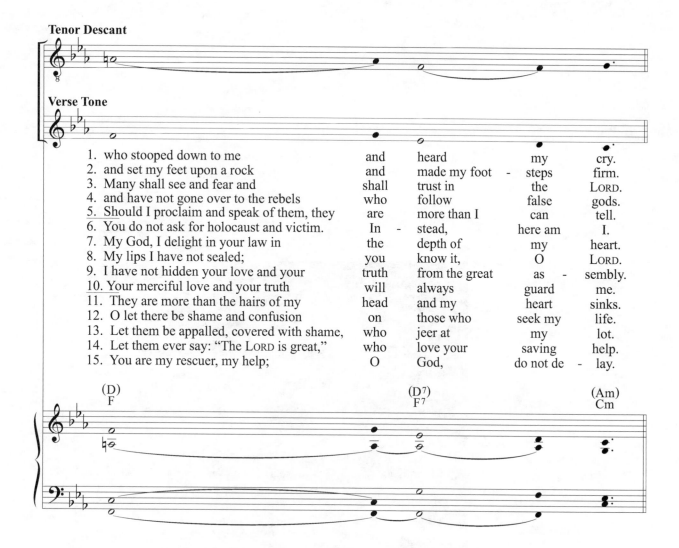

1. who stooped down to me	and	heard	my	cry.
2. and set my feet upon a rock	and	made my foot -	steps	firm.
3. Many shall see and fear and	shall	trust in	the	LORD.
4. and have not gone over to the rebels	who	follow	false	gods.
5. Should I proclaim and speak of them, they	are	more than I	can	tell.
6. You do not ask for holocaust and victim.	In -	stead,	here am	I.
7. My God, I delight in your law in	the	depth of	my	heart.
8. My lips I have not sealed;	you	know it,	O	LORD.
9. I have not hidden your love and your	truth	from the great	as -	sembly.
10. Your merciful love and your truth	will	always	guard	me.
11. They are more than the hairs of my	head	and my	heart	sinks.
12. O let there be shame and confusion	on	those who	seek my	life.
13. Let them be appalled, covered with shame,	who	jeer at	my	lot.
14. Let them ever say: "The LORD is great,"	who	love your	saving	help.
15. You are my rescuer, my help;	O	God,	do not de -	lay.

(D)
F

(D7)
F7

(Am)
Cm

One Thing I Seek

Eleventh Sunday in Ordinary Time, Song for the Week

Antiphon ♩ = 72

One thing I seek: to dwell in your house all the days of my life.

Verse Tone

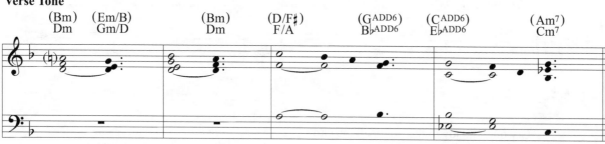

Psalm 27:1, 3-5, 7-14

1. The LORD is my light and my help;
   whom shall I fear?
   The LORD is the stronghold of my life;
   before whom shall I shrink?

2. Though an army encamp against me
   my heart would not fear.
   Though war break out against me
   even then would I trust.

3. There is one thing I ask of the LORD, for this I long,
   to live in the house of the LORD all the days of my life,
   to savor the sweetness of the LORD,
   to behold his temple.

4. For God makes me safe in his tent
   in the day of evil.
   God hides me in the shelter of his tent,
   on a rock I am secure.

5. O LORD, hear my voice when I call;
   have mercy and answer.
   Of you my heart has spoken:
   "Seek God's face."

6. It is your face, O LORD, that I seek;
   hide not your face.
   Dismiss not your servant in anger;
   you have been my help.

7. Do not abandon or forsake me,
   O God my help!
   Though father and mother forsake me,
   the LORD will receive me.

8. Instruct me, LORD, in your way;
   on an even path lead me.
   When they lie in ambush, protect me
       from my enemies' greed.
   False witnesses rise against me,
       breathing out fury.

9. I am sure I shall see the LORD's goodness
   in the land of the living.
   In the LORD, hold firm and take heart.
   Hope in the LORD!

People of God, Flock of the Lord

Eleventh Sunday in Ordinary Time, Song for the Word

Verses Superimposed Tone *Psalm 100*

4. In -

Antiphon ♩ = ca. 46

Capo 4: (Am) (Dm) (G) (C) (F) (Dm/F) (E)
C♯m F♯m B E A F♯m/A G♯

Peo - ple of God, flock of the Lord, al - le - lu - ia, sing to the Lord.
Al - le - lu - ia, al - le - lu - ia, al - le - lu - ia, al - le - lu - ia.

*1. Cry out with joy to the LORD, all the earth. Serve the LORD with gladness.
*2. Know the the LORD is God, our Maker, to whom we belong.
3. Enter the gates with thanksgiving, God's courts with songs of praise.
*4. deed how good is the LORD, whose merciful love is eternal, whose

(Am) (Dm) (G) (C)
C♯m F♯m B E

Peo - ple of God, flock of the Lord,
Al - le - lu - ia, al - le - lu - ia,

1. Come before God singing for joy.
2. We are God's people, sheep of the flock.
3. Give thanks to God and bless his name.
4. faithfulness lasts for - ever.

(F) (Dm/F) (E) (Am)
A F♯m/A G♯ C♯m

al - le - lu - ia, sing to the Lord.
al - le - lu - ia, al - le - lu - ia.

The Lectionary selections for the day are indicated by an asterisk.

Descant 1 (Soprano)

Descant 2 (Alto)

Descant 3 (Bass)

Performance Notes

The text in italics could be used for an additional final refrain instead of the main text.

You Shall Be a Royal Priesthood

Eleventh Sunday in Ordinary Time, Song for the Table

Antiphon ♩ = ca. 76

You shall be a roy - al priest - hood, ho - ly na - tion that I keep. Go, pro - claim the com - ing king - dom; tend my lost and scat - tered sheep.

Verse Tone

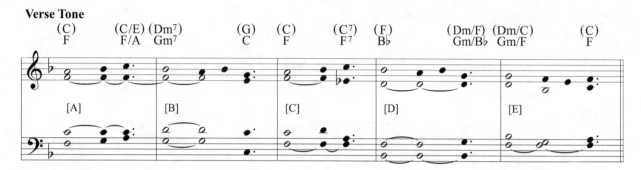

Revelation 4:11; 5:9-10, 12b-d, 13b-d; 4:8c; Romans 5:6, 8-12

1. You are worthy, our Lord <u>and</u> God,
   to receive glory and h<u>on</u>or and power,
   for you cre<u>at</u>ed all things,
   and by your will <u>they</u> existed
   and <u>were</u> created.

2. You are worthy to take <u>the</u> scroll
   and to <u>op</u>en its seals,
   for you were slaughtered and by <u>your</u> blood
   you ran<u>som</u>ed for God
   saints from every tribe and language and
      peo<u>ple</u> and nation;

3. *C* you have made them to be a kingdom
      <u>and</u> priests
   D serv<u>ing</u> our God,
   E and they will <u>reign</u> on earth.

4. *C* Worthy is the Lamb that <u>was</u> slaughtered
   D to receive power and wealth and
      wis<u>dom</u> and might
   E and honor and glo<u>ry</u> and blessing.

5. *C* To the one seated on the throne and
      to <u>the</u> Lamb
   D be blessing and honor and glo<u>ry</u> and might
   E fore<u>ver</u> and ever.

6. *C* Holy, ho<u>ly</u>, holy,
   D the Lord God <u>the</u> Almighty,
   E who was and is and <u>is</u> to come.

7. *C* While we were <u>still</u> weak,
   D at <u>the</u> right time,
   E Christ died for <u>the</u> ungodly.

8. God proves his love <u>for</u> us
   in that while we still were sinners Christ <u>died</u> for us.
   Much more sure<u>ly</u> then,
   now that we have been justified <u>by</u> his blood,
   will we be saved through him from the <u>wrath</u> of God.

9. *A* For if while we <u>were</u> enemies,
   B we were reconciled to God through the death
      <u>of</u> his Son,
   C much more surely, having <u>been</u> reconciled,
   E will we be saved <u>by</u> his life.

10. We even boast in God through our Lord Je<u>sus</u> Christ,
    through whom we have now received reconci<u>li</u>ation.
    Just as sin came into the world <u>through</u> one man,
    and death <u>came</u> through sin,
    so death spread to all because <u>all</u> have sinned.

Performance Notes

The Antiphon is the hymn tune STUTTGART. *It would perhaps be preferable to perform this in chant style, unaccompanied, at half-note = ca. 80.*

Save Us, Lord

Twelfth Sunday in Ordinary Time, Song for the Week

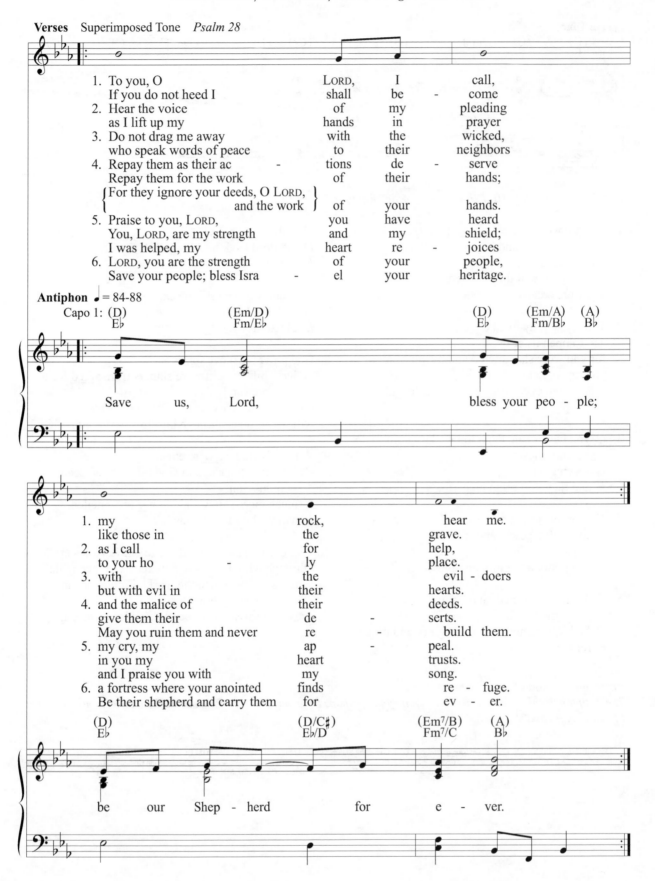

Verses Superimposed Tone   *Psalm 28*

1. To you, O LORD, I call,
   If you do not heed I shall be - come
2. Hear the voice of my pleading
   as I lift up my hands in prayer
3. Do not drag me away with the wicked,
   who speak words of peace to their neighbors
4. Repay them as their ac - tions de - serve
   Repay them for the work of their hands;
   { For they ignore your deeds, O LORD,
   and the work } of your hands.
5. Praise to you, LORD, you have heard
   You, LORD, are my strength and my shield;
   I was helped, my heart re - joices
6. LORD, you are the strength of your people,
   Save your people; bless Isra - el your heritage.

Antiphon ♩ = 84-88

Capo 1: (D)   (Em/D)   (D)   (Em/A) (A)
        E♭   Fm/E♭   E♭   Fm/B♭   B♭

Save   us,   Lord,   bless your peo - ple;

1. my rock, hear me.
   like those in the grave.
2. as I call for help,
   to your ho - ly place.
3. with the evil - doers
   but with evil in their hearts.
4. and the malice of their deeds.
   give them their de - serts.
   May you ruin them and never re - build them.
5. my cry, my ap - peal.
   in you my heart trusts.
   and I praise you with my song.
6. a fortress where your anointed finds re - fuge.
   Be their shepherd and carry them for ev - er.

(D)   (D/C♯)   (Em⁷/B) (A)
E♭   E♭/D   Fm⁷/C   B♭

be   our   Shep - herd   for   e - ver.

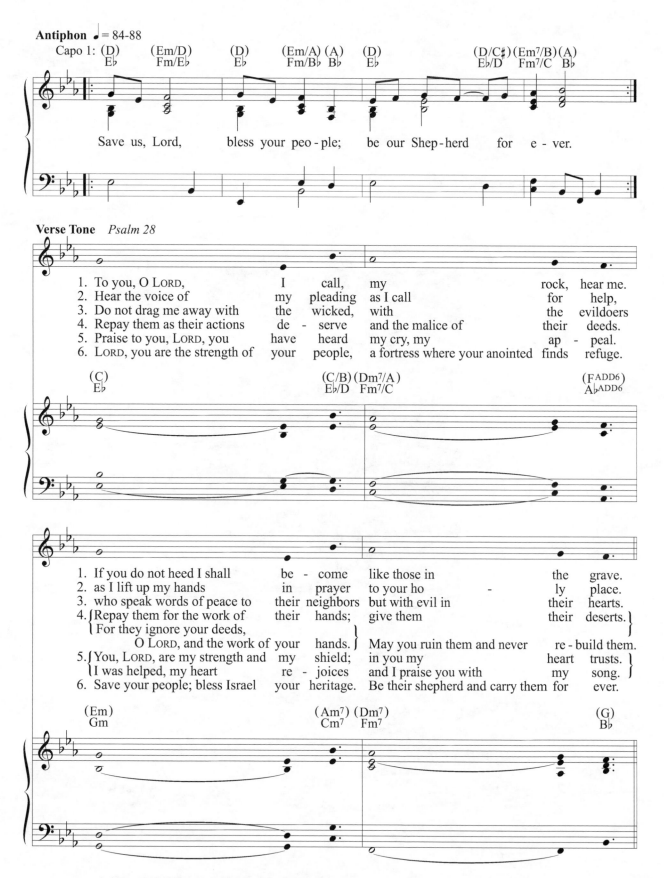

In Your Abundant Love

Twelfth Sunday in Ordinary Time, Song for the Word

Psalm 69:8-10, 14, 17, 33-35

1. It is for you that I suffer taunts, *answer me . . .*
   that shame covers my face. *answer me . . .*

2. I have become a stranger to my family, *(simile)*
   an alien to my brothers and sisters.

3. I burn with zeal for your house
   and taunts against you fall on me.

4. This is my prayer to you,
   my prayer for your favor.

5. In your great love, answer me, O God,

6. LORD, answer, for your love is kind;
   in your compassion turn towards me.

7. The poor when they see it will be glad
   and God-seeking hearts will revive;

8. the LORD listens to the needy
   and does not spurn captives in their chains.

9. Let the heavens and the earth give God praise,
   the sea and all its living creatures.

with your help that never fails.

You Open Your Hand

Twelfth Sunday in Ordinary Time, Song for the Table
Eighteenth Sunday in Ordinary Time, Song for the Word

Verses Superimposed Tone *Psalm 145:1-2, 8-11, 13c-18*

1. I will give you glory, O God, my king, I will
   I will bless you day after day and
*2. You are kind and full of com - passion,
* How good you are, LORD, to all,
3. All your creatures shall thank you, O LORD,
   They shall speak of the glory of your reign
4. You are faithful in all your words
   You sup - port all those who are falling and
*5. The eyes of all creatures look to you and you
* You open wide your hand,
*6. You are just in all your ways
* You are close to all who call you,

Alto descant *(hum)*

Antiphon ♩. = ca. 52

Capo 3: (A) (D/A) (A) (G/B) (D)
C F/C C B♭/F F

You o - pen your hand, you o - pen your hand, you

1. bless your name for e - ver.
   praise your name for e - ver.
2. slow to anger, a - bounding in love.
   com - passionate to all your creatures.
3. and your friends shall re - peat their blessing.
   and de - clare your might, O God.
4. and loving in all your deeds.
   raise up all who are bowed down.
5. give them their food in due sea - son.
   grant the de - sires of all who live.
6. and loving in all your deeds.
   who call on you from their hearts.

(G) (D) (G/B) (A)
B♭ F B♭/D C

o - pen your hand to fill our need.

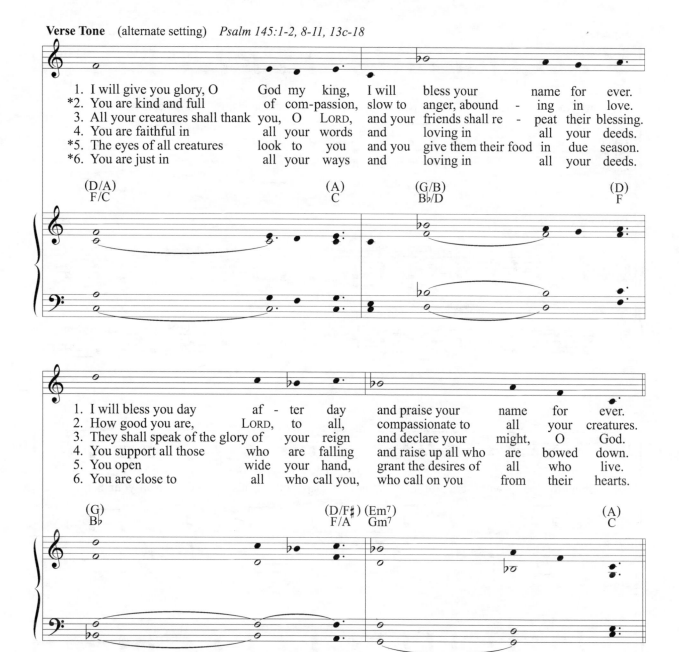

Verse Tone (alternate setting)   *Psalm 145:1-2, 8-11, 13c-18*

1. I will give you glory, O God my king, I will bless your name for ever.
*2. You are kind and full of com-passion, slow to anger, abound - ing in love.
3. All your creatures shall thank you, O LORD, and your friends shall re - peat their blessing.
4. You are faithful in all your words and loving in all your deeds.
*5. The eyes of all creatures look to you and you give them their food in due season.
*6. You are just in all your ways and loving in all your deeds.

(D/A)   (A)   (G/B)   (D)
F/C   C   Bb/D   F

1. I will bless you day af - ter day, and praise your name for ever.
2. How good you are, LORD, to all, compassionate to all your creatures.
3. They shall speak of the glory of your reign and declare your might, O God.
4. You support all those who are falling and raise up all who are bowed down.
5. You open wide your hand, grant the desires of all who live.
6. You are close to all who call you, who call on you from their hearts.

(G)   (D/F#) (Em⁷)   (A)
Bb   F/A Gm⁷   C

Performance Notes
Stanzas 2, 5, and 6 are the Lectionary verses for the Eighteenth Sunday in Ordinary Time.
The psalm verses are pointed separately for use by either the Superimposed Tone or the alternate Verse Tone.

All You Nations

Thirteenth Sunday in Ordinary Time, Song for the Week

Soprano / Melody

Alto

All you na - tions, all you peo - ples, clap your hands, O clap your hands.

Tenor

Bass

Antiphon ♩ = 138-144

G   D   C   G

Shout to God with cries of glad - ness: clap your hands, O clap your hands.

G   D   C   G

Alto Descant

Hum to 'Nn...' (lips open)

Bass Descant

Hum to 'Nn...' (lips open)

Verse Tone   *Psalm 47*

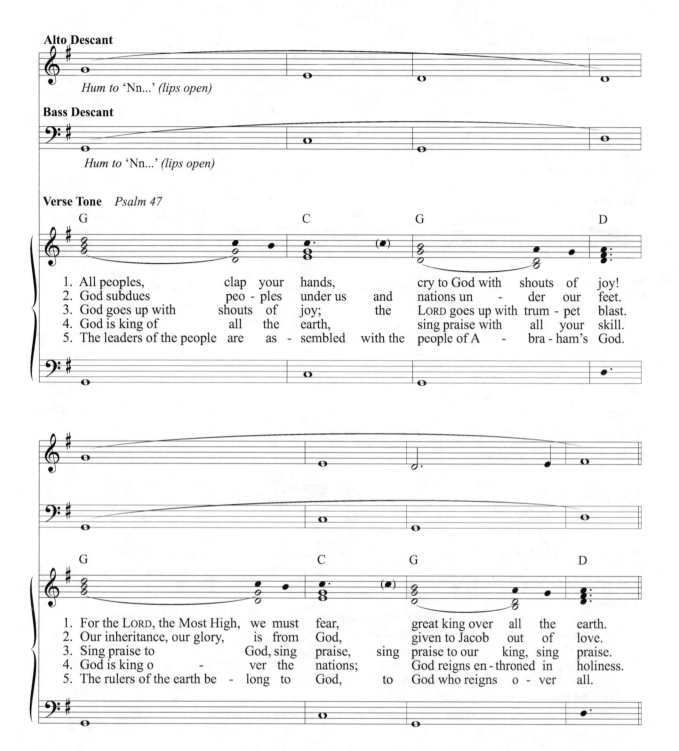

1. All peoples,   clap   your   hands,   cry to God with   shouts   of   joy!
2. God subdues   peo - ples   under us   and   nations un - der   our   feet.
3. God goes up with   shouts   of   joy;   the   LORD goes up with trum - pet   blast.
4. God is king of   all   the   earth,   sing praise with   all   your   skill.
5. The leaders of the people   are   as - sembled   with the   people of A - bra - ham's God.

1. For the LORD, the Most High,   we must   fear,   great king over   all   the   earth.
2. Our inheritance, our glory,   is from   God,   given to Jacob   out   of   love.
3. Sing praise to   God, sing   praise,   sing   praise to our   king, sing   praise.
4. God is king o -   ver the   nations;   God reigns en - throned in   holiness.
5. The rulers of the earth be - long to   God,   to   God who reigns o - ver   all.

Performance Notes
The verses should be sung in approximately the same tempo as the Antiphon.
Light percussion instruments may easily be added to the Antiphon.

I Will Sing For Ever of Your Love

Thirteenth Sunday in Ordinary Time, Song for the Word

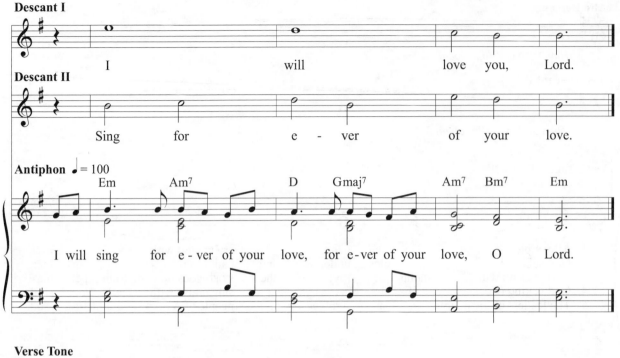

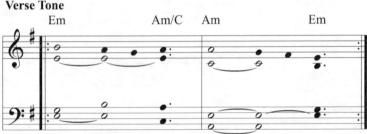

Psalm 89:2-3, 16-19

1. I will sing for ever of your <u>love</u>, O Lord;
   through all ages my mouth will pro<u>claim</u> your truth.
   Of this I am sure, that your love <u>lasts</u> for ever,
   that your truth is firmly established <u>as</u> the heavens.

2. Happy the people who acclaim <u>such</u> a God,
   who walk, O Lord, in the light <u>of</u> your face,
   who find their joy every day <u>in</u> your name,
   who make your justice the source <u>of</u> their bliss.

3. For you, O Lord, and the glory <u>of</u> their strength;
   by your favor it is that our might <u>is</u> exalted;
   for our ruler is in the keeping <u>of</u> the Lord;
   our king is in the keeping of the Holy <u>One</u> of Israel.

Within Your Temple

Fourteenth Sunday in Ordinary Time, Song for the Week
Anniversary of the Dedication of a Church, Song for the Day

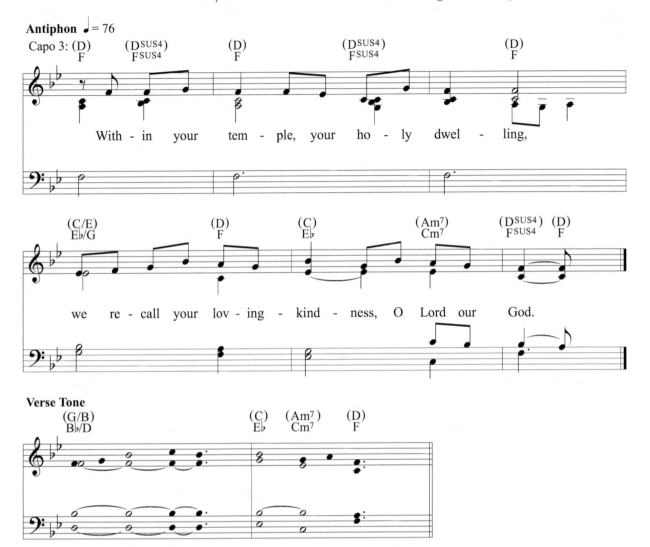

Psalm 48

1. The LORD | is great and worthy to be praised in the city of <u>our</u> God,
   whose holy mountain rises in beauty, the joy of <u>all</u> the earth.

2. Mount Zi- | on, true pole of the earth, the Great <u>King's</u> city!
   God, in the midst of its citadels, is known to <u>be</u> its stronghold.

3. For the | kings assembled together, together they <u>advanced</u>.
   They saw; at once they were astounded; dismayed, they <u>fled</u> in fear.

4. A trem- | bling seized them there, like the pangs <u>of</u> birth.
   By the east wind you have destroyed the <u>ships</u> of Tarshish.

5. As we | have heard, so we have seen in the city of <u>our</u> God,
   in the city of the LORD of hosts, which God up<u>holds</u> for ever.

Verse Tone

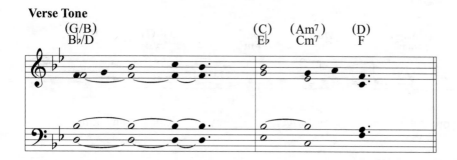

6. God, we | ponder your love within <u>your</u> temple.
   Your praise, O God, like your name reaches the ends <u>of</u> the earth.

7. With just- | ice your right hand is filled. Mount Zion re<u>joi</u>ces;
   the people of Judah rejoice at the sight <u>of</u> your judgements.

8. Walk through | Zion, walk all around it; count the number of <u>its</u> towers.
   Review all its ramparts, exa<u>mine</u> its castles,

9. that you | may tell the next generation that such is <u>our</u> God,
   our God for ever and ever will <u>al</u>ways lead us.

I Will Praise Your Name For Ever

Fourteenth Sunday in Ordinary Time, Song for the Word

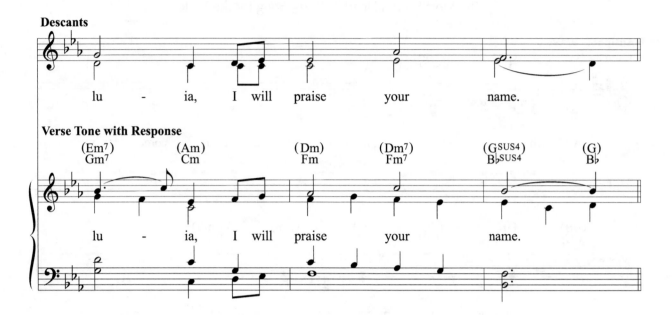

Descants

lu - ia, I will praise your name.

Verse Tone with Response

(Em⁷) (Am) (Dm) (Dm⁷) (Gˢᵁˢ⁴) (G)
Gm⁷ Cm Fm Fm⁷ B♭ˢᵁˢ⁴ B♭

lu - ia, I will praise your name.

Psalm 145:1-2, 8-11, 13c-14

1. I will give you glory, O God my king,
   I will bless your name for ever. *Alleluia . . .*

2. I will bless you day after day
   and praise your name for ever. *(simile)*

3. You are kind and full of compassion,
   slow to anger, abounding in love.

4. How good you are, Lord, to all,
   compassionate to all your creatures.

5. All your creatures shall thank you, O Lord,
   and your friends shall repeat their blessing.

6. They shall speak of the glory of your reign
   and declare your might, O God.

7. You are faithful in all your words
   and loving in all your deeds.

8. You support all those who are falling
   and raise up all who are bowed down.

A-133

All Who Labor, Come to Me

Fourteenth Sunday in Ordinary Time, Song for the Table
The Most Sacred Heart of Jesus, Song for the Table

All who la-bor, come to me; tired and wea-ry, come to me.
I am gen-tle, I am hum-ble; I will give you rest.

Psalm 33:1, 12-13, 18-22

1. *[Omit A-B]*
   Ring out your joy to the LORD, O you just,
   for praise is fitting for loyal hearts.

2. They are happy whose God is the LORD,
   the people who are chosen as his own.
   From the heavens the LORD looks forth
   and sees all the peoples of the earth.

3. The LORD looks on those who fear him,
   on those who hope in his love,

   to rescue their souls from death,
   to keep them alive in famine.

4. Our soul is waiting for the LORD.
   The LORD is our help and our shield.
   Our hearts find joy in the LORD.
   We trust in God's holy name.

5. *[Omit A-B]*
   May your love be upon us, O LORD,
   as we place all our hope in you.

Performance Notes   *The Antiphon may be sung SATB.*

To Gaze on Your Glory

Fifteenth Sunday in Ordinary Time, Song for the Week

Verses Superimposed Tone *Psalm 17*

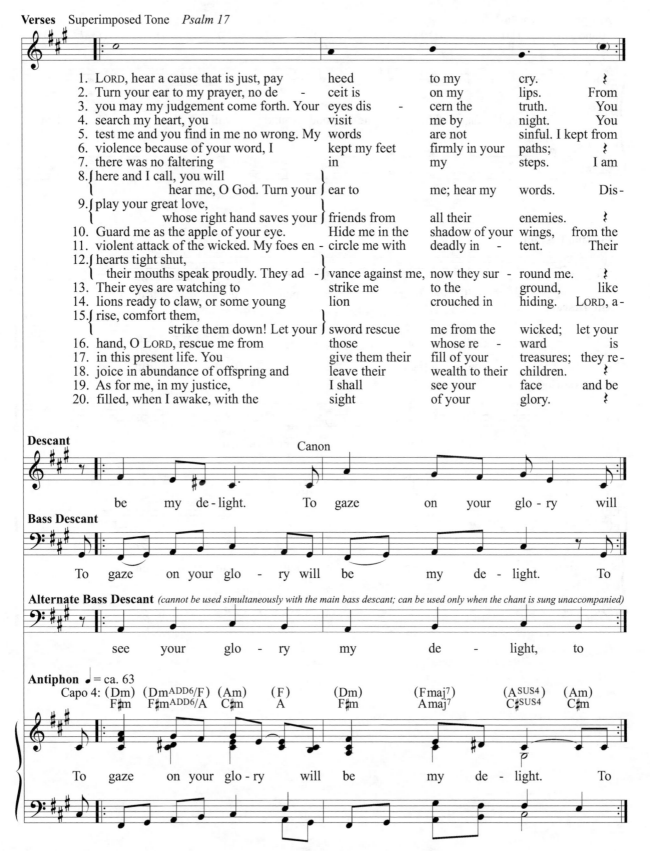

1. LORD, hear a cause that is just, pay heed to my cry.
2. Turn your ear to my prayer, no de- ceit is on my lips. From
3. you may my judgement come forth. Your eyes dis- cern the truth. You
4. search my heart, you visit me by night. You
5. test me and you find in me no wrong. My words are not sinful. I kept from
6. violence because of your word, I kept my feet firmly in your paths;
7. there was no faltering in my steps. I am
8. here and I call, you will hear me, O God. Turn your ear to me; hear my words. Dis-
9. play your great love, whose right hand saves your friends from all their enemies.
10. Guard me as the apple of your eye. Hide me in the shadow of your wings, from the
11. violent attack of the wicked. My foes en- circle me with deadly in - tent. Their
12. hearts tight shut, their mouths speak proudly. They ad- vance against me, now they sur - round me.
13. Their eyes are watching to strike me to the ground, like
14. lions ready to claw, or some young lion crouched in hiding. LORD, a-
15. rise, comfort them, strike them down! Let your sword rescue me from the wicked; let your
16. hand, O LORD, rescue me from those whose re - ward is
17. in this present life. You give them their fill of your treasures; they re-
18. joice in abundance of offspring and leave their wealth to their children.
19. As for me, in my justice, I shall see your face and be
20. filled, when I awake, with the sight of your glory.

Descant Canon

be my de - light. To gaze on your glo - ry will

Bass Descant

To gaze on your glo - ry will be my de - light. To

Alternate Bass Descant *(cannot be used simultaneously with the main bass descant; can be used only when the chant is sung unaccompanied)*

see your glo - ry my de - light, to

Antiphon ♩ = ca. 63

Capo 4: (Dm) (Dm^ADD6/F) (Am) (F) (Dm) (Fmaj^7) (A^SUS4) (Am)
F#m F#m^ADD6/A C#m A F#m Amaj^7 C#SUS4 C#m

To gaze on your glo - ry will be my de - light. To

A-135

The Seed That Falls on Good Ground

Fifteenth Sunday in Ordinary Time, Song for the Word

Verse Tone

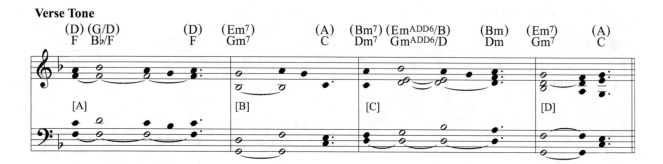

Psalm 65:10-14

1. You | care for the earth, <u>give</u> it water;
   you fill <u>it</u> with riches.
   Your | river in hea<u>ven</u> brims over
   to provide <u>its</u> grain.

2. And | thus you provide <u>for</u> the earth;
   you <u>drench</u> its furrows;
   you | level it, soften <u>it</u> with showers;
   you bless <u>its</u> growth.

3. You | crown the year <u>with</u> your goodness.
   [Omit B]
   A- | bundance flows <u>in</u> your steps;
   in the pastures of the wilderness <u>it</u> flows.

4. The | hills are gir<u>ded</u> with joy,
   the meadows co<u>vered</u> with flocks,
   the | valleys are <u>decked</u> with wheat.
   They shout for joy, yes, <u>they</u> sing.

A-136

As Seed for the Sowing

Fifteenth Sunday in Ordinary Time, Song for the Table

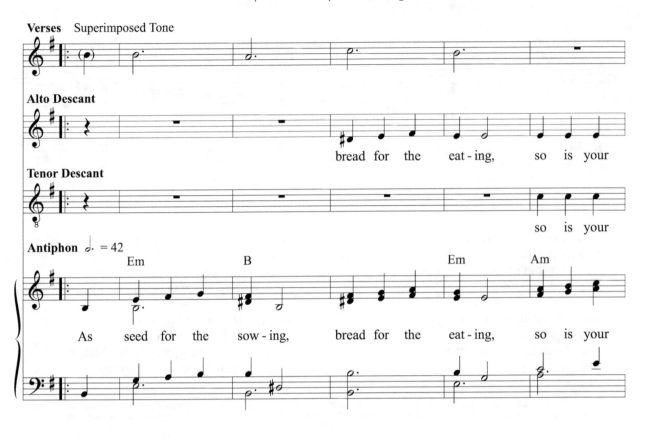

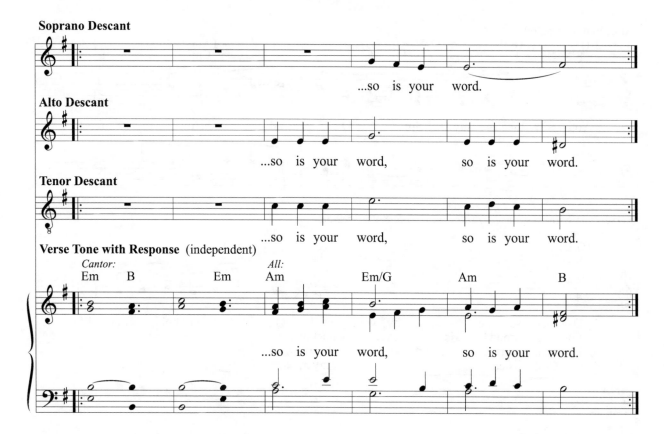

Soprano Descant

...so is your word.

Alto Descant

...so is your word, so is your word.

Tenor Descant

...so is your word, so is your word.

Verse Tone with Response (independent)

Cantor: Em B Em Am All: Em/G Am B

...so is your word, so is your word.

Wisdom 16:20; Psalm 78:23-25, 27, 29; 23:5-6; 145:15-16

1. You gave your <u>peo</u>ple <u>food</u> from <u>an</u>gels,   *so is your word, so is your word.*
   supplied them from <u>heav'n</u> with bread <u>rea</u>dy to <u>eat</u>,   *so is your word, so is your word.*
   providing every <u>plea</u>sure and <u>suit</u>ed to every <u>taste</u>.   *so is your word, so is your word.*

2. God commanded the clouds a<u>bove</u> and <u>o</u>pened the gates of <u>heav</u>en;   *(simile)*
   rained down manna for their <u>food</u>, and <u>gave</u> them bread from <u>heav</u>en.

3. Mere mortals ate the bread of <u>an</u>gels. The Lord <u>sent</u> them meat in a<u>bun</u>dance;
   God rained food on them like <u>dust</u>, winged <u>fowl</u> like the sands of the <u>sea</u>.
   So they ate and had their <u>fill</u>, for God <u>gave</u> them all they <u>craved</u>.

4. You have prepared a banquet for <u>me</u> in the <u>sight</u> of my <u>foes</u>.
   My head you have anointed with <u>oil</u>; my <u>cup</u> is over<u>flow</u>ing.

5. Surely goodness and kindness shall <u>fol</u>low me all the <u>days</u> of my <u>life</u>.
   In the Lord's own house shall I <u>dwell</u> for <u>ev</u>er and <u>ev</u>er.

6. The eyes of all creatures look to <u>you</u> and you <u>give</u> them their food in due <u>sea</u>son.
   You open wide your <u>hand</u>, grant the de<u>sires</u> of all who <u>live</u>.

Performance Notes

The Verse Tone may be superimposed as shown on the previous page (with the text sung metrically or free), while the others parts vocalize to "oo" or hum over the first half, responding with "so is your word, so is your word"; or the Verse Tone may be sung separately (using the same tone, as shown on this page).

You Alone Are My Help

Sixteenth Sunday in Ordinary Time, Song for the Week

Antiphon ♩. = ca. 60

You a-lone are my help: O Lord, up-hold my life.

Verse Tone with Response *Psalm 54:3, 4b-5, 8-9a; 55:2-3a*

Cantor:

1. O God save me by your name; O Lord, up-hold my life.
2. For the proud have ris - en a - gainst me,
3. I will sacrifice to you with will - ing heart
4. O God, listen to my prayer,

Cantor:

1. by your power, up - hold my cause. O Lord, up-hold my life.
2. ruthless foes seek my life.
3. and praise your name, O Lord, for it is good;
4. do not hide from my pleading,

Cantor:

1. Listen to the words of my mouth. O Lord, up-hold my life.
2. They have no re - gard for God.
3. for you have rescued me from all my dis - tress.
4. attend to me and re - ply.

You Are Good and Forgiving

Sixteenth Sunday in Ordinary Time, Song for the Word

Psalm 86:5-6, 9-10, 15-16

1. O LORD, you are good and <u>for</u>giving,
   full of love to <u>all</u> who call.
   Give heed, O LORD, to <u>my</u> prayer
   and attend to <u>the</u> sound of my voice.

2. All the nations shall come to <u>a</u>dore you
   and glorify your <u>name</u>, O LORD,

   for you are great and do mar<u>vel</u>ous deeds,
   you who a<u>lone</u> are God.

3. You, God of mercy and com<u>pas</u>sion,
   slow to <u>an</u>ger, O LORD,
   abounding in love <u>and</u> truth,
   turn and <u>take</u> pity on me.

As Seed for the Sowing

Sixteenth Sunday in Ordinary Time, Song for the Table: Option I

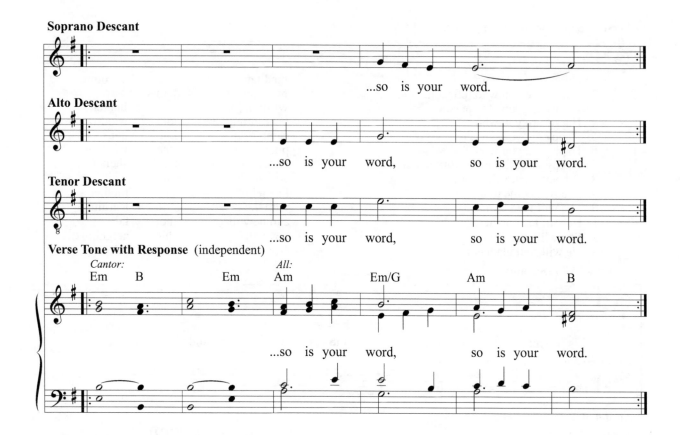

Soprano Descant

...so is your word.

Alto Descant

...so is your word, so is your word.

Tenor Descant

...so is your word, so is your word.

Verse Tone with Response (independent)

Cantor: Em   B   Em   *All:* Am   Em/G   Am   B

...so is your word, so is your word.

cf. Psalm 111:2-5, 7-9b, 6a, 9c; 138:4-6, 8bc

1. Great are your works, O LORD,
   to be pondered by all who love them.
      so is your word, so is your word.
   Majestic and glorious your work,
   your justice stands firm for ever.
      so is your word, so is your word.

2. You make us remember these wonders.
   You, LORD, are compassion and love. *(simile)*
   You give food to those who fear you,
   keep your covenant ever in mind.

3. Your works are justice and truth,
   your precepts are all of them sure.
   They stand firm for ever and ever;
   they are made in uprightness and truth.

4. You have sent deliverance to your people
   and established your covenant for ever.
   You show mighty works to your people.
   Holy is your name, to be feared.

5. All the rulers of the earth shall thank you
   when they hear the words of your mouth.
   They shall sing of the LORD's ways:
   "How great is your glory, O LORD!"

6. LORD, you are high yet look on the lowly
   and the haughty you know from afar.
   Your love, O LORD is eternal,
   discard not the work of your hands.

Performance Notes

The Verse Tone may be superimposed as shown on the previous page (with the text sung metrically or free), while the others parts vocalize to "oo" or hum over the first half, responding with "so is your word, so is your word"; or the Verse Tone may be sung separately (using the same tone, as shown on this page).

Listen: I Stand at the Door and Knock

Sixteenth Sunday in Ordinary Time, Song for the Table: Option II

Verses Superimposed Tone *Sirach 14:20-26; 15:1-6*

1. Happy are you who meditate on wisdom,
2. Happy are you who reflect in your heart on wis - dom's ways,
3. Happy are you who pursue wisdom like a hunter,
4. Happy are you who peer through wis - dom's windows,
5. Happy are you who camp near wis - dom's house,
6. Happy are you who pitch your tent near wisdom,
7. Happy you who place your children under wis - dom's shelter,
8. Whoever fears the Lord will act in this way;
9. She will come to meet him like a lov - ing mother,
10. She will feed him with the bread of learning,
11. He will lean on her and he will not fall,
12. She will exalt him a - bove all his neighbors,
13. He will find gladness and a crown of re - joicing,

Soprano / Alto Descants

Lis - ten: I stand at the door and knock.

Bass Descant

Antiphon ♩ = ca. 78

Capo 3: (D)
F

(G)
B♭

(D)
F

Lis - ten: I stand at the door and knock.

O - pen, and we shall feast.

(A)
C

O - pen, and we shall feast.

Verses   Superimposed Tone

1. happy are you who — reason with — in - tel - li - gence.
2. happy are you who — ponder — her — se - crets.
3. happy are you who lie in — wait on — her — paths.
4. happy are you who — listen at — her — doors.
5. you who fasten your — tent peg to — her — walls.
6. who so occupy an — excel - lent — lodg-ing place.
7. happy are you who lodge — under wis - dom's — boughs.
8. whoever holds to the law — will ob - tain — wis - dom.
9. like a young bride — wisdom — will — wel-come him.
10. she will give him the water of — wisdom — to — drink.
11. he will rely on her and — not be put — to — shame.
12. she will open his mouth in the — midst of the — as - sem - bly.
13. he will inherit an — everlast - ing — name.

Soprano / Alto Descants

Lis - ten: I stand at the door and knock.

Bass Descant

Antiphon

(D) (D7) (G) (D)
F   F7   Bb   F

Lis - ten: I stand at the door and knock.

O - pen, and we shall feast.

(D/A) (Em/A) (D)
F/C   Gm/C   (F)

O - pen and we shall feast.

Performance Notes

When the Antiphon is sung alone, sing all the text; when the verse is superimposed, vocalize to "oo" in measures 1–2 and 5–6 while the cantor sings the verse text.

I Loved Wisdom More Than Health or Beauty

Seventeenth Sunday in Ordinary Time, Song for the Week
Thirty-second Sunday in Ordinary Time, Song for the Week: Option II

Antiphon (optional 4-part round)

1. I loved wis-dom more than health or beau-ty,
2. and I chose her e-ven o-ver light;
3. for her ra - diance ne - ver cea - ses,
4. and I chose her e-ven o-ver light.

Capo 3: (Am) (D) (Am)
Cm F Cm

♩ = ca.72

Verse Tone

(Am) (D/A) (Am) (Am/C) (D) (Am) (Em⁷/B) (Am/C) (D) (Em⁷) (Am)
Cm F/C Cm Cm/E♭ F Cm Gm⁷/D Cm/E♭ F Gm⁷ Cm

[A] [B] [C] [D]

Wisdom 9:9-11, 13-14, 17

1. With you is wisdom, she who <u>knows</u> your <u>works</u>
   and was present when you <u>made</u> the <u>world</u>;
   she understands what is <u>pleasing</u> in your <u>sight</u>
   and what is right according to <u>your</u> commandments.

2. Send her forth from the <u>holy heavens</u>,
   from the throne of your <u>glory send</u> her,
   that she may <u>labor</u> at my <u>side</u>,
   that I may learn what is <u>pleasing</u> to you.

3. For she knows and under<u>stands</u> all <u>things</u>,
   she will guide me <u>wisely</u> in my <u>actions</u>

[omit C]
   and guard me <u>with</u> her glory.

4. For who can learn the <u>counsel</u> of <u>God</u>?
   Who can discern what the LORD <u>wills</u>?
   For the reasoning of <u>mortals</u> is <u>worthless</u>,
   and our designs are <u>likely</u> to fail.

5. Who has <u>learned</u> your <u>counsel</u>,
   unless you have <u>given wisdom</u>
[omit C]
   and sent your holy spirit <u>from</u> on high?

With All My Heart I Cry

A-142

Seventeenth Sunday in Ordinary Time, Song for the Word

Psalm 119:57, 72, 76-77, 127-130

1. My part, I have resolved, O LORD,   *how I love . . .*
   is to obey your <u>word</u>.   *how I love . . .*

2. The law from your mouth means <u>more</u> to me *(simile)*
   than silver and <u>gold</u>.

3. Let your love be ready to con<u>sole</u> me
   by your promise to your <u>servant</u>.

4. Let your love come and I shall <u>live</u>
   for your law is my de<u>light</u>.

5. That is why I love your com<u>mands</u>
   more than finest <u>gold</u>,

6. why I rule my life by your <u>precepts</u>,
   and hate <u>false</u> ways.

7. Your will is wonderful in<u>deed</u>;
   therefore I o<u>bey</u> it.

8. The unfolding of your word gives <u>light</u>
   and teaches the <u>simple</u>.

Performance Notes

The verses may be sung in pairs, the Antiphon only occurring after the even-numbered verses.

A-143

Ask and Receive

Seventeenth Sunday in Ordinary Time, Song for the Table

Psalm 73:1-2, 25-26, 28; 33:12-15, 18-21

1. How good is God to Israel,
   to those who are pure of heart.
   Yet my feet came close to stumbling,
   my steps had almost slipped.

2. What else have I in heaven but you?
   Apart from you I want nothing on earth.
   My body and my heart faint for joy;
   God is my possession for ever.

3. To be near God is my happiness.
   I have made the LORD God my refuge.
   I will tell of all your works
   at the gates of the city of Zion.

4. They are happy, whose God is the LORD,
   the people who are chosen as his own.

From the heavens the LORD looks forth
and sees all the peoples of the earth.

5. From the heavenly dwelling God gazes
   on all the dwellers on the earth;
   God who shapes the hearts of them all
   and considers all their deeds.

6. The LORD looks on those who fear him,
   on those who hope in his love,
   to rescue their souls from death,
   to keep them alive in famine.

7. Our soul is waiting for the LORD.
   The LORD is our help and our shield.
   Our hearts find joy in the LORD.
   We trust in God's holy name.

God, Come to My Aid

Eighteenth Sunday in Ordinary Time, Song for the Week

A-144

Psalm 70

1. O God, make haste to <u>my</u> rescue,   *O Lord, make haste . . .*
   Lord, come to <u>my</u> aid.   *O Lord, do not . . .*

2. Let there be shame and <u>con</u>fusion,   *(simile)*
   on those who seek <u>my</u> life.

3. O let them turn back in <u>con</u>fusion,
   who delight in <u>my</u> harm.

4. Let them retreat, covered <u>with</u> shame,
   who jeer at <u>my</u> lot.

5. Let there be rejoicing <u>and</u> gladness
   for all <u>who</u> seek you.

6. Let them say for ever: "God <u>is</u> great,"
   who love your sav<u>ing</u> help.

7. As for me, wretched <u>and</u> poor,
   come to me, <u>O</u> God.

8. You are my rescuer, <u>my</u> help,
   O Lord, do not <u>de</u>lay.

A-146

Come, Come to the Banquet

Eighteenth Sunday in Ordinary Time, Song for the Table: Option I

Verse Tone

Psalm 78:13-16, 23-29, 35, 52-53

1. God divided the sea and <u>led</u> them through
   and made the waters stand up <u>like</u> a wall;
   leading them by day <u>with</u> a cloud,
   by night, with a light <u>of</u> fire.

2. God split the rocks <u>in</u> the desert;
   gave them plentiful drink as <u>from</u> the deep;
   made streams flow out <u>from</u> the rock,
   and made waters run down <u>like</u> rivers.

3. God commanded the <u>clouds</u> above
   and opened the <u>gates</u> of heaven;
   rained down manna <u>for</u> their food,
   and gave them bread <u>from</u> heaven.

4. Mere mortals ate the <u>bread</u> of angels.
   The Lord sent them meat <u>in</u> abundance;

   made the east wind <u>blow</u> from heaven
   and roused the south wind <u>with</u> might.

5. God rained food on <u>them</u> like dust,
   winged fowl like the sands <u>of</u> the sea;
   let it fall in the midst <u>of</u> their camp
   and all around <u>their</u> tents.

6. So they ate and <u>had</u> their fill;
   for God gave them <u>all</u> they craved.
   They remembered that God <u>was</u> their rock,
   God, the Most High, their <u>redeemer</u>.

7. God brought forth the <u>people</u> like sheep;
   guided them like a flock <u>in</u> the desert;
   led them safely with <u>nothing</u> to fear,
   while the sea engulfed <u>their</u> foes.

Come to Me and You Shall Never Hunger

Eighteenth Sunday in Ordinary Time, Song for the Table: Option II

Verse Tone with Response

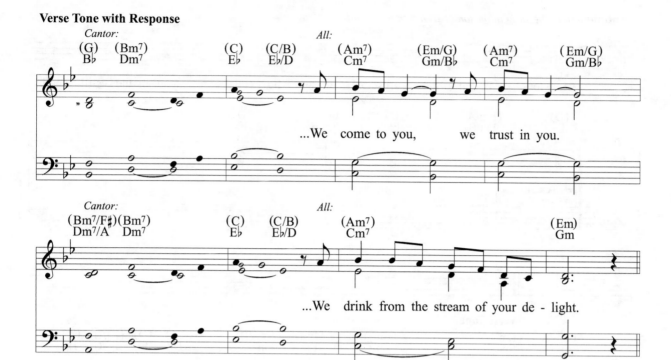

Psalm 36:6-11; Wisdom 16:20-21

1. *Your love, LORD, reaches to the <u>heav</u>ens, your truth <u>to</u> the skies. *We come to you . . .*
   *Your justice is like God's mountain, your <u>judge</u>ments <u>like</u> the deep. *We drink . . .*

2. To mortals and <u>beasts</u> you <u>give</u> protection. *(simile)*
   *O LORD, how <u>precious is</u> your love.

3. *My God, the <u>chil</u>dren <u>of</u> the earth
   *find refuge in the <u>shel</u>ter <u>of</u> your wings.

4. *They feast on the <u>rich</u>es <u>of</u> your house;
   *they drink from the <u>stream</u> of <u>your</u> delight.

5. *In <u>you</u> is the <u>source</u> of life
   *and in your <u>light</u> <u>we</u> see light.

6. Keep on <u>loving</u> <u>those</u> who know you,
   *doing <u>justice</u> for <u>up</u>right hearts.

7. You gave your <u>people</u> <u>food</u> of angels,
   you supplied them from heaven with bread ready to eat,
       *providing every <u>pleasure</u> and suited to <u>every</u> taste.

8. Your sustenance manifested your <u>sweetness</u> to<u>ward</u> your children;
   and the bread, ministering to the desire of the one who took it,
       was <u>changed</u> to suit <u>every</u>one's liking.

Performance Notes
*Lines in the psalm verses marked with an asterisk take the single cue-size note at the end of the line;
the remainder take the two full-size notes.*

Listen, Listen to the Words of Jesus

Nineteenth Sunday in Ordinary Time, Song for the Week

Antiphon *(can be sung in unison or as a 4-voice round)*

Lis-ten, lis-ten to the words of Je-sus, who calls to you in the still, small voice.

Psalm 74:12-13, 16-17, 22-23; 12:7-8; 24:1-4b, 5-6

1. God is our king <u>from</u> time past,
   the giver of help through <u>all</u> the land.
   It was you who divided the sea <u>by</u> your might,
   who shattered the heads of the monsters <u>in</u> the sea.

2. Yours is the day and yours <u>is</u> the night.
   It was you who appointed the light <u>and</u> the sun;
   it was you who fixed the bounds <u>of</u> the earth;
   you who made both sum<u>mer</u> and winter.

3. Arise, O God, and de<u>fend</u> your cause!
   Remember how the senseless revile you
     <u>all</u> the day.
   Do not forget the clamor <u>of</u> your foes,
   the daily increasing uproar <u>of</u> your foes.

4. The words of the LORD are words <u>without</u> alloy,
   [Omit B-C]
     silver from the furnace, seven <u>times</u> refined.

5. The LORD's is the earth <u>and</u> its fullness,
   the world and <u>all</u> its peoples.
   It is God who set it <u>on</u> the seas;
   who made it firm <u>on</u> the waters.

6. Who shall climb the mountain <u>of</u> the LORD?
   Who shall stand in God's <u>holy</u> place?
   Those with clean hands <u>and</u> pure heart,
   who desire not <u>worthless</u> things.

7. They shall receive blessings <u>from</u> the LORD
   and reward from the <u>God</u> who saves them.
   These are the <u>ones</u> who seek,
   seek the face of the <u>God</u> of Jacob.

Show Us, Lord, Your Kindness

A-149

Nineteenth Sunday in Ordinary Time, Song for the Word

Verses Superimposed Tone *Psalm 85:9-14*

1. I will hear what the LORD has to say,
   peace for his people and his friends
2. Salvation is near for the God-fearing,
3. Mercy and faithfulness have met;
   Faithfulness shall spring from the earth
4. The LORD will make us prosper
   Justice shall march in the forefront,

Antiphon ♩ = 66

D   F♯m   Bm

Show us, Lord, your kind - ness,

1. a voice that speaks of peace,
   and those who turn to God in their hearts.
2. and his glory will dwell in our land.
3. justice and peace have em - braced.
   and justice look down from heaven.
4. and our earth shall yield its fruit.
   and peace shall fol - low the way.

Em⁷   A^SUS4   A

grant us your sal - va - tion.

Performance Notes

The psalm tone may be superimposed on an ostinato Antiphon as shown; or tone and Antiphon may be used separately, in which case the Antiphon should be sung twice after each verse.

Don't Be Afraid

Nineteenth Sunday in Ordinary Time, Song for the Table

Verses Superimposed Tone   *Psalm 31:2-4, 15-17, 25; 103:1-4, 8, 10-14, 17-18*

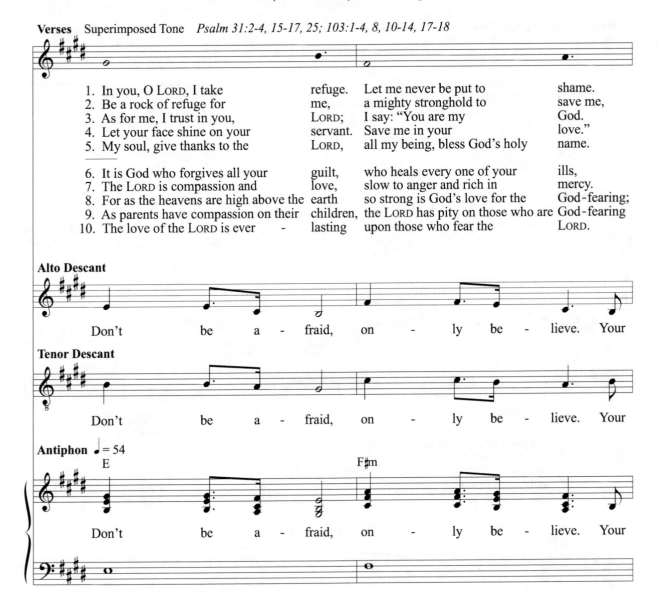

1. In you, O Lord, I take refuge. Let me never be put to shame.
2. Be a rock of refuge for me, a mighty stronghold to save me,
3. As for me, I trust in you, Lord; I say: "You are my God.
4. Let your face shine on your servant. Save me in your love."
5. My soul, give thanks to the Lord, all my being, bless God's holy name.

6. It is God who forgives all your guilt, who heals every one of your ills,
7. The Lord is compassion and love, slow to anger and rich in mercy.
8. For as the heavens are high above the earth so strong is God's love for the God-fearing;
9. As parents have compassion on their children, the Lord has pity on those who are God-fearing
10. The love of the Lord is ever - lasting upon those who fear the Lord.

Alto Descant

Don't be a - fraid, on - ly be - lieve. Your

Tenor Descant

Don't be a - fraid, on - ly be - lieve. Your

Antiphon ♩ = 54

E   F♯m

Don't be a - fraid, on - ly be - lieve. Your

Verses Superimposed Tone

1. In your justice, set me free, hear me and speedily rescue me.
2. for you are my rock, my stronghold. For your name's sake, lead me and guide me.
3. My life is in your hands, de - liver me from the hands of those who hate me.
4. Be strong, let your heart take courage, all who hope in the LORD.
5. My soul, give thanks to the LORD and never forget all God's blessings.

6. who redeems your life from the grave, who crowns you with love and com-passion.
7. God does not treat us according to our sins nor repay us according to our faults.
8. as far as the east is from the west so far does he remove our sins.
9. for he knows of what we are made, and remembers that we are dust.
10. God's justice reaches out to children's children when they keep his covenant in truth.

Alto Descant

faith will save you: on - ly be - lieve.

Tenor Descant

faith will save you: on - ly be - lieve.

Antiphon

E   F♯m/E   E   E/B B   E

faith will save you: on - ly be - lieve.

Performance Notes

As the cantor sings the verses, the other voices may vocalize to 'oo' under the superimposed tone instead of singing the words.

Those Who Do Justice

Twentieth Sunday in Ordinary Time, Song for the Week

Psalm 15:2-5b; 112:1bc, 4-5, 7, 9ab; 119:1-3

1. Those who walk without <u>fault</u>,
   those who act with <u>justice</u>   *shall dwell . . .*
   those who speak the truth from their <u>hearts</u>,
   who do not slander with their <u>tongue</u>   *shall dwell . . .*

2. those who do no wrong to their <u>kindred</u>,
   those who cast no slur on their <u>neighbors</u>   *(simile)*
   those who hold the godless in dis<u>dain</u>,
   but honor those who fear the L<small>ORD</small>;

3. those who keep their word, come what <u>may</u>,
   those who take no interest on a <u>loan</u>
   those who accept no <u>bribes</u>
   against the <u>innocent</u>.

4. Those who fear the L<small>ORD</small>,
   who take delight in all God's com<u>mands</u>,

who are lights in the darkness
   for the <u>upright</u>,
   who are generous, merciful and <u>just</u>.

5. Good people who take pity and <u>lend</u>,
   who conduct their affairs with <u>honor</u>;
   those who have no fear of evil <u>news</u>,
   who with firm hearts trust in the L<small>ORD</small>.

6. The openhanded who give to the <u>poor</u>,
   whose justice stands firm for <u>ever</u>,
   whose life is <u>blameless</u>,
   who follow God's <u>law</u>.

7. Those who do God's <u>will</u>,
   seeking God with all their <u>hearts</u>,
   who never do anything <u>evil</u>
   but walk in God's <u>ways</u>.

Performance Notes
The bass line of the keyboard accompaniment can be used as a bass descant if desired

God, Let All the Peoples Praise You

Twentieth Sunday in Ordinary Time, Song for the Word

Descant

Let all peo - ples praise you, O God.

Antiphon ♩ = 88

God, let all the peo-ples praise you, all the na-tions of the earth.

Verse Tone

Psalm 67:2-3, 5-6, 8ab

1. O God, be gracious <u>and</u> bless us
   and let your face shed its light up<u>on</u> us.
   So will your ways be known <u>up</u>on earth
   and all nations learn your <u>sav</u>ing help.

2. Let the nations be glad and ex<u>ult</u>
   for you rule the world <u>with</u> justice.

With fairness you <u>rule</u> the peoples,
you guide the <u>nations</u> on earth.

3. Let the peoples praise you, <u>O</u> God;
   let all the <u>peoples</u> praise you.
   May God still <u>give</u> us blessing
   till the ends of the earth <u>stand</u> in awe.

The Mercy of God Is for All

Twentieth Sunday in Ordinary Time, Song for the Table

Soprano Descant

The mer-cy of God is for all, the mer-cy of God is for all, the

Alto Descant

The mer-cy of God is for all, the mer-cy of God is for all, the

Antiphon ♩ = 63

Capo 5: (Am) (DmADD6/A) (AmADD9) (Am) (Dm) (Am) (ESUS4) (E)
Dm GmADD6/D DmADD9 Dm Gm Dm ASUS4 A

The mer-cy of God is for all, the mer-cy of God is for all, the

mer-cy of God, mer-cy of God, the mer-cy of God is for all.

mer-cy of God, mer-cy of God, the mer-cy of God is for all.

(Am) (Cmaj7) (DmADD6) (Am/E) (Em7) (Am)
Dm Fmaj7 GmADD6 Dm/A Am7 Dm

mer-cy of God, mer-cy of God, the mer-cy of God is for all.

Verse Tone with Response *Psalm 130:1-6b, 7b-8; 103:1-4, 8, 10-14, 17-18*

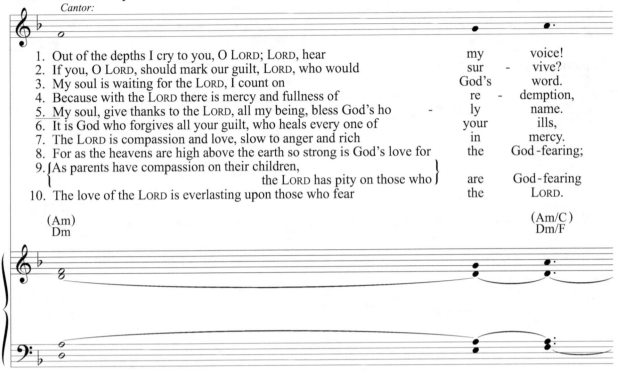

Cantor:

1. Out of the depths I cry to you, O LORD; LORD, hear my voice!
2. If you, O LORD, should mark our guilt, LORD, who would sur - vive?
3. My soul is waiting for the LORD, I count on God's word.
4. Because with the LORD there is mercy and fullness of re - demption,
5. My soul, give thanks to the LORD, all my being, bless God's ho - ly name.
6. It is God who forgives all your guilt, who heals every one of your ills,
7. The LORD is compassion and love, slow to anger and rich in mercy.
8. For as the heavens are high above the earth so strong is God's love for the God-fearing;
9. {As parents have compassion on their children, the LORD has pity on those who} are God-fearing
10. The love of the LORD is everlasting upon those who fear the LORD.

(Am)
Dm

(Am/C)
Dm/F

Soprano Descant

...the mer - cy of God is for all.

Alto Descant

...the mer - cy of God is for all.

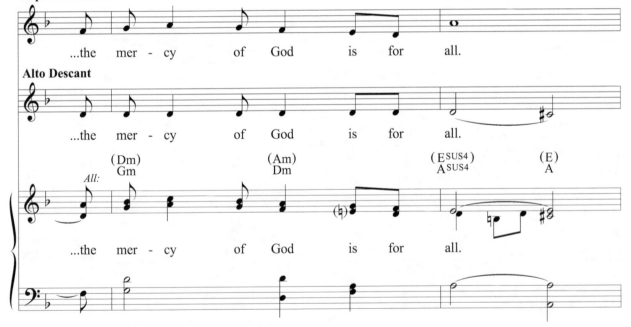

(Dm)
Gm

(Am)
Dm

(E SUS4)
A SUS4

(E)
A

All:

...the mer - cy of God is for all.

Verse Tone with Response

Cantor:

1. O let your ears be attentive to the voice | of | my | pleading;
2. But with you is found forgiveness: for this | we | re - vere you.
3. My soul is longing for the LORD more than those who | watch | for | daybreak.
4. Israel indeed God will redeem from all | its | in - iquity.
5. My soul, give thanks to the LORD and never forget | all | God's | blessings.
6. who redeems your life from the grave, who crowns you with love | and | com - passion.
7. God does not treat us according to our sins nor repay us according | to | our | faults.
8. As far as the east is from the west so far does he re - | move | our | sins.
9. for he knows of what we are made, and remembers that | we | are | dust.
10. { God's justice reaches out to children's children / when they keep his covenant in truth, when they keep his will } in their mind.

Soprano Descant

Alto Descant

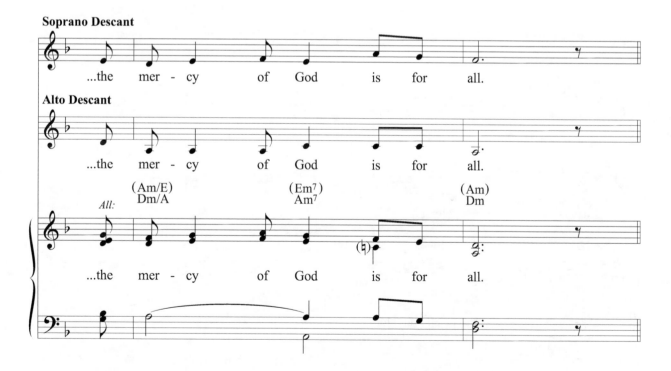

...the mer - cy of God is for all.

...the mer - cy of God is for all.

All:

...the mer - cy of God is for all.

A-154

Turn to Me, Answer Me

Twenty-first Sunday in Ordinary Time, Song for the Week
Twenty-second Sunday in Ordinary Time, Song for the Week

Verses Superimposed Tone *Psalm 86*

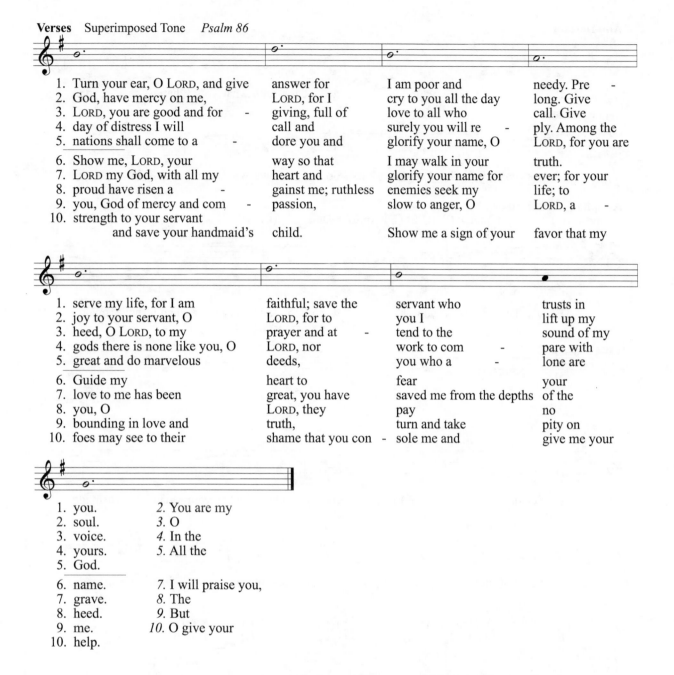

1. Turn your ear, O LORD, and give / answer for / I am poor and / needy. Pre -
2. God, have mercy on me, / LORD, for I / cry to you all the day / long. Give
3. LORD, you are good and for - / giving, full of / love to all who / call. Give
4. day of distress I will / call and / surely you will re - / ply. Among the
5. nations shall come to a - / dore you and / glorify your name, O / LORD, for you are

6. Show me, LORD, your / way so that / I may walk in your / truth.
7. LORD my God, with all my / heart and / glorify your name for / ever; for your
8. proud have risen a - / gainst me; ruthless / enemies seek my / life; to
9. you, God of mercy and com - / passion, / slow to anger, O / LORD, a -
10. strength to your servant
   and save your handmaid's / child.   Show me a sign of your / favor that my

1. serve my life, for I am / faithful; save the / servant who / trusts in
2. joy to your servant, O / LORD, for to / you I / lift up my
3. heed, O LORD, to my / prayer and at - / tend to the / sound of my
4. gods there is none like you, O / LORD, nor / work to com - / pare with
5. great and do marvelous / deeds, / you who a - / lone are

6. Guide my / heart to / fear / your
7. love to me has been / great, you have / saved me from the depths / of the
8. you, O / LORD, they / pay / no
9. bounding in love and / truth, / turn and take / pity on
10. foes may see to their / shame that you con - / sole me and / give me your

1. you.   2. You are my
2. soul.   3. O
3. voice.   4. In the
4. yours.   5. All the
5. God.

6. name.   7. I will praise you,
7. grave.   8. The
8. heed.   9. But
9. me.   10. O give your
10. help.

Everlasting Is Your Love

Twenty-first Sunday in Ordinary Time, Song for the Word

Verse Tone

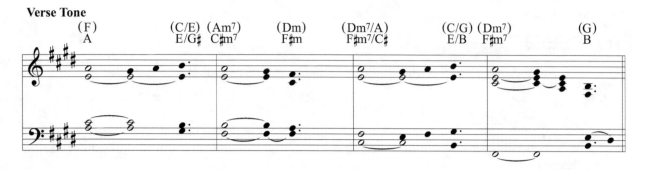

Psalm 138:1-3, 6, 8bc

1. I thank you, LORD, with <u>all</u> my heart,
   you have heard the words of <u>my</u> mouth.
   In the presence of the angels <u>I</u> will bless you.
   I will adore before your <u>ho</u>ly temple.

2. I thank you for your faithful<u>ness</u> and love
   which excel all we <u>ev</u>er knew of you.
   On the day I <u>called</u>, you answered;
   you increased the strength <u>of</u> my soul.

3. The LORD is high yet looks <u>on</u> the lowly
   and the haughty God knows from <u>a</u>far.
   Your love, O LORD, <u>is</u> eternal,
   discard not the work <u>of</u> your hands.

All Things Are from the Lord

Twenty-first Sunday in Ordinary Time, Song for the Table

Soprano Descant

All things are from the Lord, and for him.

Alto Descant

All things are for him.

Tenor Descant

All things are from the Lord . . .

Antiphon ♩ = 84

Capo 3: (A)   (Bm⁷)   (E)
C Dm^7 G

All things are from the Lord, through him and for him. All

All glo-ry be to Christ, A-men.

All glo-ry for e-ver, A-men.

All glo-ry be to Christ, A-men.

(A)   (G/B)   (A)
C $B\flat/D$ C

glo-ry be to Christ for e-ver, A-men.

Verse Tone

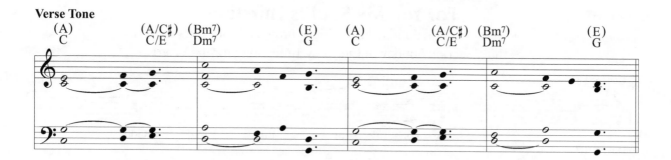

Psalm 104:1-2a, 13-15, 27-28, 29b-34

1. Bless the LORD, my soul!
   LORD God, how great you are,
   clothed in majesty and glory,
   wrapped in light as in a robe!

2. From your dwelling you water the hills;
   earth drinks its fill of your gift.
   You make the grass grow for the cattle
   and the plants to serve our needs.

3. May we bring forth bread from the earth
   and wine to cheer our hearts;
   oil to make our faces shine
   and bread to strengthen our hearts.

4. All things look to you
   to give them their food in due season.
   You give it, they gather it up;
   you open your hand, they have their fill.

5. You take back your spirit, they die,
   returning to the dust from which they came.
   You send forth your spirit, they are created;
   and you renew the face of the earth.

6. May the glory of the LORD last for ever!
   May the LORD rejoice in creation!
   God looks on the earth and it trembles;
   at God's touch, the mountains send forth smoke.

7. I will sing to the LORD all my life,
   make music to my God while I live.
   May my thoughts be pleasing to God.
   I find my joy in the LORD.

A-157 → Twenty-second Sunday in Ordinary Time, *Song for the Week, same as A-154*

A-158

For You My Soul Is Thirsting

Twenty-second Sunday In Ordinary Time, Song for the Word
Thirty-second Sunday In Ordinary Time, Song for the Word

Psalm 63:2-6, 8-9

1. O God, you are my God, for <u>you</u> I long;
   for you my <u>soul</u> is thirsting.
   My body <u>pines</u> for you
   like a dry, weary land <u>without</u> water.

2. So I gaze on you in the <u>sanctuary</u>
   to see your strength <u>and</u> your glory.
   For your love is <u>better</u> than life,
   my lips will <u>speak</u> your praise.

3. So I will bless you <u>all</u> my life,
   in your name I will lift <u>up</u> my hands.
   My soul shall be filled as with <u>a</u> banquet,
   my mouth shall praise <u>you</u> with joy.

4. For you have <u>been</u> my help;
   in the shadow of your wings <u>I</u> rejoice.
   My soul <u>clings</u> to you;
   your right hand <u>holds</u> me fast.

A-159 → Twenty-second Sunday In Ordinary Time, *Song for the Table, same as A-228*

With All My Heart I Cry

Twenty-third Sunday in Ordinary Time, Song for the Week

Psalm 119:145-152

1. I call with all my heart; LORD, <u>hear</u> me,   *answer me . . .*
   I will keep your <u>statutes</u>.   *answer me . . .*

2. I call upon you, <u>save</u> me   *(simile)*
   and I will do your <u>will</u>.

3. I rise before dawn and cry for <u>help</u>,
   I hope in your <u>word</u>.

4. My eyes watch through the <u>night</u>
   to ponder your <u>promise</u>.

5. In your love hear my voice, O LORD;
   give me life by your de<u>crees</u>.

6. Those who harm me unjustly draw <u>near</u>;
   they are far from your <u>law</u>.

7. But you, O LORD, are <u>close</u>,
   your commands are <u>truth</u>.

8. Long have I known that your <u>will</u>
   is established for <u>ever</u>.

Twenty-third Sunday in Ordinary Time, Song for the Word, *same as A-36* ← A-161

Where Two or Three Are Gathered

Twenty-third Sunday in Ordinary Time, Song for the Table

Verse Tone

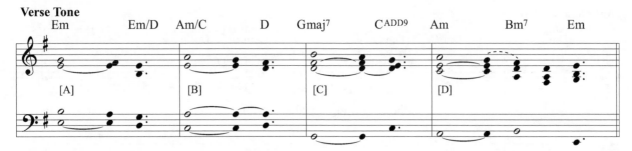

Em   Em/D Am/C   D   Gmaj⁷   C^ADD9   Am   Bm⁷   Em

Romans 12:1-2, 4-5, 9-17, 20ab, 21; 13:8, 9a, 9g-10; 14:8-9; 15:5-7

1. I appeal to you, brothers and sisters,
   by the mercies of God,
   to present your bodies as a living sacrifice,
   holy and acceptable to God.

2. Do not be conformed to this world,
   but be transformed by the renewing of your minds,
   so that you may discern what is the will of God,
   what is good and acceptable and perfect.

3. For as in one body we have many members,
   and not all the members have the same function,
   so we, who are many, are one body in Christ,
   and individually we are members of one another.

4. Let love be genuine; hate what is evil,
   hold fast to what is good;
   love one another with mutual affection:
   outdo one another in showing honor.

5. Do not lag in zeal,
   be ardent in spirit, serve the Lord.
   Rejoice in hope, be patient in suffering,
   persevere in prayer.
   [Repeat C-D]
   Contribute to the needs of the saints;
   extend hospitality to strangers.

6. Bless those who persecute you;
   bless and do not curse them.
   Rejoice with those who rejoice,
   weep with those who weep.

7. Live in harmony with one another;
   do not be haughty,
   but associate with the lowly;
   do not claim to be wiser than you are.
   [Repeat C-D]
   Do not repay anyone evil for evil,
   but take thought for what is noble in the sight of all.

8. If your enemies are hungry, feed them;
   if they are thirsty, give them something to drink.
   Do not be overcome by evil,
   but overcome evil with good.

9. Owe no one anything,
   except to love one another;
   for the one who loves another
   has fulfilled the law.

10. The commandments are summed up
    in this word:
    "Love your neighbor as yourself."
    Love does no wrong to a neighbor;
    therefore, love is the fulfilling of the law.

11. If we live, we live to the Lord,
    and if we die, we die to the Lord;
    so then, whether we live or whether we die,
    we are the Lord's.
    [Repeat C-D]
    To this end Christ died and lived again,
    so that he might be Lord of both
    the dead and the living.

12. May the God of steadfastness and
    encouragement
    grant you to live in harmony with one
    another,
    in accordance with Christ Jesus,
    so that together with one voice you may
    glorify the God and Father of our
    Lord Jesus Christ.

13. *[Omit A-B]*
    Welcome one another, therefore, just as
    Christ has welcomed you,
    for the glory of God.

A-163   Give Peace to Those Who Wait

Twenty-fourth Sunday in Ordinary Time, Song for the Week

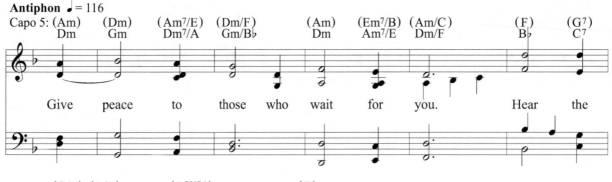

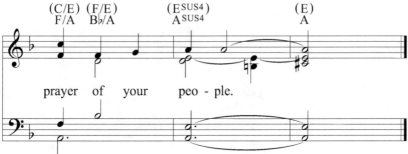

Verse Tone with Response

Sirach 36:1-7, 10, 18-22

1. Have mercy upon us, O God of all,
   and put all the nations in fear of you.
       Hear the prayer . . .

2. Lift up your hand against foreign nations
   and let them see your might.   *Hear the prayer . . .*

3. As you have used us to show your holiness to them,
   so use them to show your glory to us.   *(simile)*

4. Then they will know, as we have known
   that there is no God but you, O LORD.

5. Give new signs, and work other wonders;
   make your hand and your right arm glorious.

6. Hasten the day, and remember the appointed time,
   and let people recount your mighty deeds.

7. Have pity on the city of your sanctuary,
   Jerusalem, the place of your dwelling.

8. Fill Zion with your majesty,
   and your temple with your glory.

9. Bear witness to those whom you created
      in the beginning,
   and fulfill the prophecies spoken in your name.

10. Reward those who wait for you
    and let your prophets be found trustworthy.

11. Hear, O LORD, the prayer of your servants,
    according to your goodwill toward
       your people,

12. and all who are on the earth will know
    that you are the LORD, the God of the ages.

Merciful and Tender

Twenty-fourth Sunday in Ordinary Time, Song for the Word

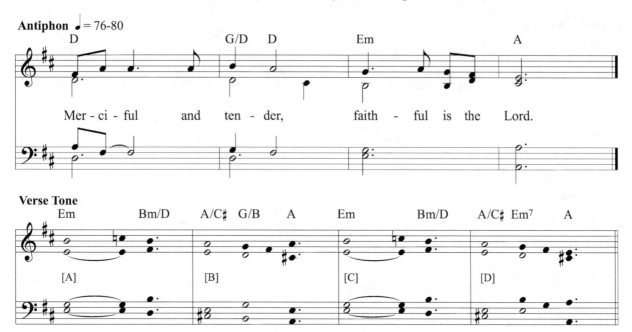

Psalm 103 [The Lectionary selections for the day are indicated by an asterisk.]

1. * My soul, give thanks to the LORD,
   * all my being, bless God's holy name.
   * My soul, give thanks to the LORD
   * and never forget all God's blessings.

2. * It is God who forgives all your guilt,
   * who heals every one of your ills,
   * who redeems your life from the grave,
   * who crowns you with love and compassion,
   [repeat C-D]
   who fills your life with good things,
   renewing your youth like an eagle's.

3. The LORD does deeds of justice,
   gives judgement for all who are oppressed.
   The LORD's ways were made known to Moses;
   the LORD's deeds to Israel's children.

4. The LORD is compassion and love,
   slow to anger and rich in mercy.
   * The LORD will not always chide,
   * will not be angry for ever.
   [repeat C-D]
   * God does not treat us according to our sins
   * nor repay us according to our faults.

5. * For as the heavens are high above the earth
   * so strong is God's love for the God-fearing;
   * as far as the east is from the west
   * so far does he remove our sins.

6. As parents have compassion on their children,
   the LORD has pity on those who are God-fearing
   for he knows of what we are made,
   and remembers that we are dust.

7. As for us, our days are like grass;
   we flower like the flower of the field;
   the wind blows and we are gone
   and our place never sees us again.

8. A But the love of the LORD is everlasting
   B upon those who fear the LORD.
   A God's justice reaches out to children's children
   B when they keep his covenant in truth,
   D when they keep his will in their mind.

9. A The LORD has set his throne in heaven
   B and his kingdom rules over all.
   A Give thanks to the LORD, all you angels,
   B mighty in power, fulfilling God's word,
   D who heed the voice of that word.

10. A Give thanks to the LORD, all you hosts,
    B you servants who do God's will.
    A Give thanks to the LORD, all his works,
    B in every place where God rules.
    D My soul, give thanks to the LORD!

A-165

If You Will Love Each Other

Twenty-fourth Sunday in Ordinary Time, Song for the Table

Verse Tone

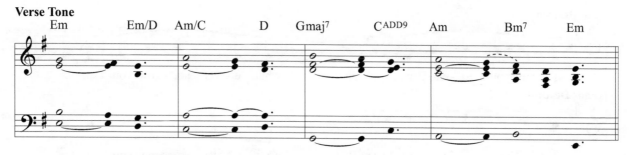

Romans 12:1-2, 4-5, 9-17, 20ab, 21; 13:8, 9a, 9g-10; 14:8-9; 15:5-7

1. I appeal to you, brothers <u>and</u> sisters,
   by the mercies <u>of</u> God,
   to present your bodies as a liv<u>ing</u> sacrifice,
   holy and accept<u>a</u>ble to God.

2. Do not be conformed to <u>this</u> world,
   but be transformed by the renewing of <u>your</u> minds,
   so that you may discern what is the will <u>of</u> God,
   what is good and accept<u>a</u>ble and perfect.

3. For as in one body we have ma<u>ny</u> members,
   and not all the members have the <u>same</u> function,
   so we, who are many, are one body <u>in</u> Christ,
   and individually we are members <u>of</u> one another.

4. Let love be genuine; hate what <u>is</u> evil,
   hold fast to what <u>is</u> good;
   love one another with mutual <u>af</u>fection:
   outdo one another <u>in</u> showing honor.

5. Do not lag <u>in</u> zeal,
   be ardent in spirit, serve <u>the</u> Lord.
   Rejoice in hope, be patient <u>in</u> suffering,
   per<u>se</u>vere in prayer.
   [Repeat C-D]
   Contribute to the needs of <u>the</u> saints;
   extend hospita<u>li</u>ty to strangers.

6. Bless those <u>who</u> persecute you;
   bless and do <u>not</u> curse them.
   Rejoice with those who re<u>joice</u>,
   weep <u>with</u> those who weep.

7. Live in harmony with one <u>another</u>;
   do not <u>be</u> haughty,
   but associate with <u>the</u> lowly;
   do not claim to be wis<u>er</u> than you are.
   [Repeat C-D]
   Do not repay anyone evil <u>for</u> evil,
   but take thought for what is noble in <u>the</u> sight of all.

8. If your enemies are hun<u>gry</u>, feed them;
   if they are thirsty, give them something <u>to</u> drink.
   Do not be overcome <u>by</u> evil,
   but overcome <u>evil</u> with good.

9. Owe no <u>one</u> anything,
   except to love one <u>another</u>;
   for the one who loves <u>another</u>
   has <u>ful</u>filled the law.

10. The commandments are summed up
    in <u>this</u> word:
    "Love your neighbor as <u>yourself</u>."
    Love does no wrong to <u>a</u> neighbor;
    therefore, love is the fulfil<u>ling</u> of the law.

11. If we live, we live to <u>the</u> Lord,
    and if we die, we die to <u>the</u> Lord;
    so then, whether we live or whether <u>we</u> die,
    we are____ the Lord's.
    [Repeat C-D]
    To this end Christ died and lived <u>again</u>,
    so that he might be Lord of both
    the <u>dead</u> and the living.

12. May the God of steadfastness and
    <u>en</u>couragement
    grant you to live in harmony with one
    <u>another</u>,
    in accordance with <u>Christ</u> Jesus,
    so that together with one voice you may
    glorify the God and Father of our
    <u>Lord</u> Jesus Christ.

13. *[Omit A-B]*
    Welcome one another, therefore, just as
    Christ <u>has</u> welcomed you,
    for the <u>glo</u>ry of God.

A-166

I Am Your Savior, My People

Twenty-fifth Sunday in Ordinary Time, Song for the Week

Verse Tone

Psalm 56

1. Have mercy on me, God, <u>foes</u> crush me;
   they fight me all day long and <u>oppress</u> me.
   My foes crush me all <u>day</u> long,
   for many fight proudly <u>against</u> me.

2. When I fear, I will trust <u>in</u> you,
   in God whose word <u>I</u> praise.
   In God I trust, I shall <u>not</u> fear;
   what can mere mor<u>tals</u> do to me?

3. All day long they distort <u>my</u> words,
   all their thought is <u>to</u> harm me.
   They band together <u>in</u> ambush,
   track me down and seek <u>my</u> life.

4. *A* Repay them, God, for <u>their</u> crimes;
   B in your anger, cast down <u>the</u> peoples.
   A You have kept an account of <u>my</u> wanderings;
   B you have kept a record of <u>my</u> tears;
   B (are they not written in <u>your</u> book?)
   C Then my foes will be put <u>to</u> flight
   D on the day that <u>I</u> call to you.

5. This I know, that God is on <u>my</u> side.
   In God, whose word <u>I</u> praise,
[repeat B]
      (in the LORD, whose word <u>I</u> praise,)
      in God I trust; I shall <u>not</u> fear;
      what can mere mor<u>tals</u> do to me?

6. I am bound by the vows I <u>have</u> made you.
   O God, I will offer <u>you</u> praise
[repeat A-B]
      for you rescued my soul <u>from</u> death,
      you kept my feet <u>from</u> stumbling
      that I may walk in the presence <u>of</u> God
      and enjoy the light of <u>the</u> living.

Performance Notes
The verses may be sung SATB.

Lord, You Are Close

Twenty-fifth Sunday in Ordinary Time, Song for the Word

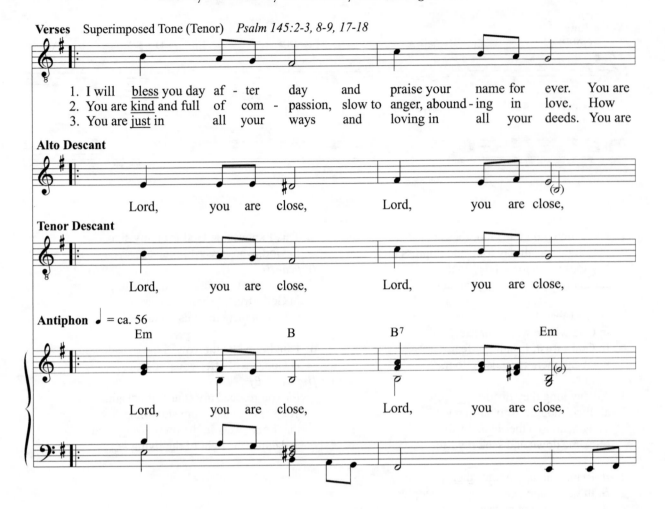

Verses Superimposed Tone (Tenor) *Psalm 145:2-3, 8-9, 17-18*

1. I will bless you day af - ter day and praise your name for ever. You are
2. You are kind and full of com - passion, slow to anger, abound - ing in love. How
3. You are just in all your ways and loving in all your deeds. You are

Alto Descant

Lord, you are close, Lord, you are close,

Tenor Descant

Lord, you are close, Lord, you are close,

Antiphon ♩ = ca. 56

Em · B · B⁷ · Em

Lord, you are close, Lord, you are close,

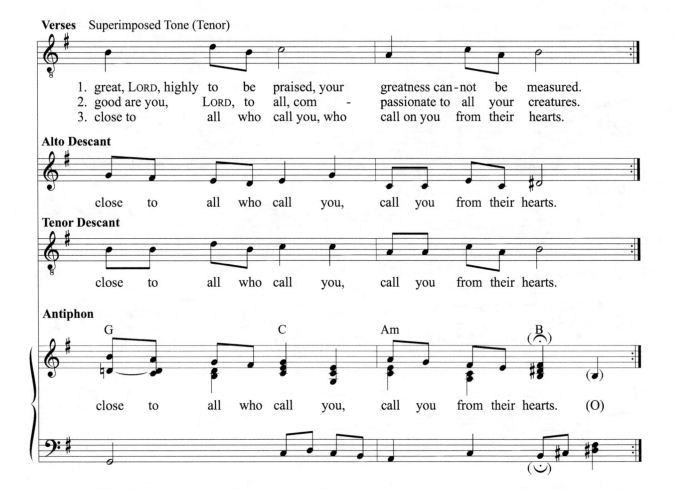

Verses   Superimposed Tone (Tenor)

1. great, LORD, highly to   be   praised, your   greatness can-not be   measured.
2. good are you,   LORD, to   all, com   -   passionate to all   your   creatures.
3. close to   all   who   call you, who   call on you   from their   hearts.

Alto Descant

close   to   all   who   call   you,   call   you   from their   hearts.

Tenor Descant

close   to   all   who   call   you,   call   you   from their   hearts.

Antiphon

G   C   Am   B

close   to   all   who   call   you,   call   you   from their   hearts.   (O)

Performance Notes

In measure 2, the cue-size notes in parentheses may be substituted if necessary.

The superimposed tone for a tenor cantor is intended as an alternative to the tenor descant - the two should not be sung concurrently.

The Antiphon melody is derived from the Gavotte in Bach's Suite #2 in B minor for flute and strings.

The Last Shall Be First

A-168

Twenty-fifth Sunday in Ordinary Time, Song for the Table

Alto Descant

such is the king - dom of God.

Tenor Descant

such is the king - dom of God.

Bass Descant

such is the king - dom of God.

Antiphon

Am   Em/B   B   Em

such is the king - dom of God.

Verse Tone

Em   A   D   A/C♯   B⁷/D♯   Em   Am   Am^ADD6/F♯   B

[A]   [B]   [C]

Ephesians 4:25-27, 29–5:2, 8-17, 18b-20; Philippians 2:1-5

1. Put away falsehood,
   speak the truth to your neighbors,
   for we are members of one another.

2. Be angry, but do not sin;
   do not let the sun go down on your anger,
   and do not make room for the devil.

3. Let no evil talk come out of your mouths,
   but only what is useful for building up,
       as there is need,
   so that your words may give grace
       to those who hear.

4. And do not grieve the Holy Spirit of God,
   with which you were marked
   with a seal for the day of redemption.

5. Put away from you all bitterness and wrath
   and anger and wrangling and slander,
   together with all malice.

6. Be kind to one another,
   tenderhearted, forgiving one another,
   as God in Christ has forgiven you.

Verse Tone

7. Therefore be imitators of God, as be<u>lov</u>ed children,
   and live in love, as Christ loved us
       and gave himself <u>up</u> for us,
   a fragrant offering and sa<u>cri</u>fice to God.

8. Once you were darkness, but now in the Lord
       <u>you</u> are light.
   Live as child<u>ren</u> of light —
   for the fruit of the light is found in all that is
       good <u>and</u> right and true.

9. Try to find out what is pleasing <u>to</u> the Lord.
   Take no part in the unfruitful <u>works</u> of darkness,
   but <u>in</u>stead expose them.

10. For it is shameful even to mention what such
        peo<u>ple</u> do secretly;
    but everything exposed by the light <u>be</u>comes
        visible,
    for everything that becomes vi<u>si</u>ble is light.

11. Therefore it says, "Sleep<u>er</u>, awake!
    Rise <u>from</u> the dead,
    and Christ <u>will</u> shine on you."

12. Be careful then <u>how</u> you live,
    not as unwise people <u>but</u> as wise,
    making the most of the time
        because <u>the</u> days are evil.

13. So do <u>not</u> be foolish,
    but understand what the will <u>of</u> the Lord is.
    Do not get drunk with wine,
        for <u>that</u> is debauchery.

14. Be filled <u>with</u> the Spirit,
    as you sing psalms and hymns and
        spiritual songs a<u>mong</u> yourselves,
    singing and making melody
        to the <u>Lord</u> in your hearts.

15. Give thanks to <u>God</u> the Father
    at all times <u>and</u> for everything
    in the name of our <u>Lord</u> Jesus Christ.

16. If there is any encourage<u>ment</u> in Christ,
    any consolation from love,
        any sharing <u>in</u> the Spirit,
    any com<u>pas</u>sion and sympathy,
[Repeat entire tone]
        make my <u>joy</u> complete:
    be of the same mind, hav<u>ing</u> the same love,
    being in full accord <u>and</u> of one mind.

17. Do nothing from selfish ambition <u>or</u> conceit,
[Omit B]
        but in humility regard others as bet<u>ter</u>
            than yourselves.

18. Let each of you look not to <u>your</u> own interests,
    but to the inte<u>rests</u> of others.
    Let the same mind be in you that
        <u>was</u> in Christ Jesus.

Blessed Are You, Lord

A-169

Twenty-sixth Sunday in Ordinary Time, Song for the Week

Daniel 2:20-23c; 4:3, 35, 37b

1. Blessed be the name of God
   from age to age;
   for wisdom and power are his.

2. He changes times and seasons,
   deposes kings and sets up kings;
   [repeat B]
   he gives wisdom to the wise
   *and knowledge to those who have understanding.

3. He reveals deep and hidden things;
   he knows what is in the darkness,
   and light dwells with him.

4. To you, O God of my ancestors,
   I give thanks and praise,
   *for you have given me wisdom and power.

5. How great are God's signs,
   how mighty his wonders!
   [repeat B]
   His kingdom is an everlasting kingdom,
   *and his sovereignty is from generation to generation.

6. All the inhabitants of the earth
   are accounted as nothing,
   [repeat B]
   and he does what he wills with the host of
   heaven
   and the inhabitants of the earth.

7. There is no one who can stay his hand
   [omit B]
   *or say to him: "What are you doing?"

8. All his works are truth
   and his ways are justice;
   [repeat B]
   and he is able to bring low
   those who walk in pride.

Performance Notes
In measure three of the Verse Tone, use the cue-size notes in lines marked with an asterisk.

A-170

Remember, Lord

Twenty-sixth Sunday in Ordinary Time, Song for the Word

Verses Superimposed Tone *Psalm 25:4-5b, 6, 7bc, 8-9*

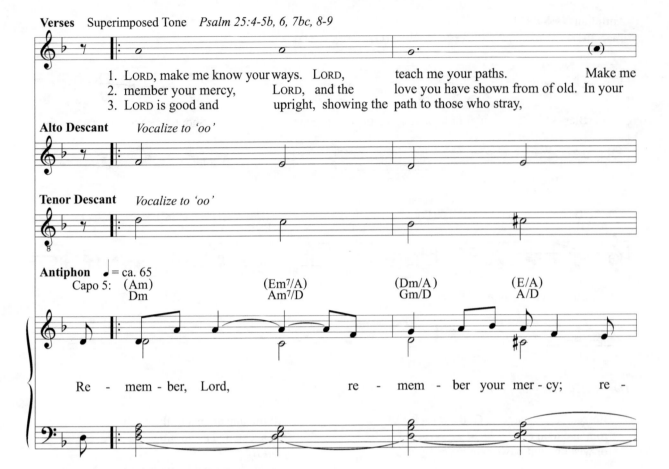

1. LORD, make me know your ways. LORD, teach me your paths. Make me
2. member your mercy, LORD, and the love you have shown from of old. In your
3. LORD is good and upright, showing the path to those who stray,

Alto Descant *Vocalize to 'oo'*

Tenor Descant *Vocalize to 'oo'*

Antiphon ♩ = ca. 65

Capo 5: (Am)   (Em7/A)   (Dm/A)   (E/A)
Dm   Am7/D   Gm/D   A/D

Re - mem - ber, Lord,   re - mem - ber your mer-cy;   re -

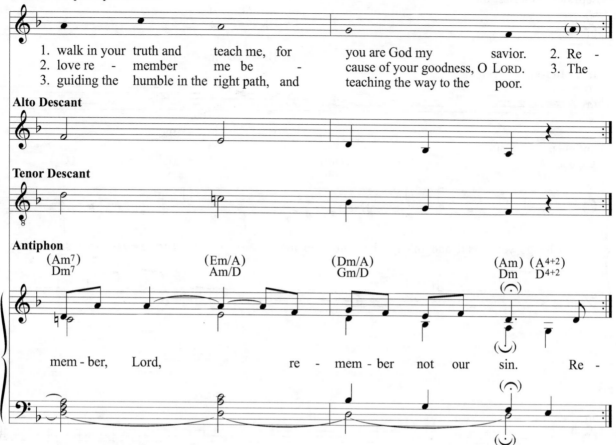

Change Your Heart and Mind

Twenty-sixth Sunday in Ordinary Time, Song for the Table: Option I

Verse Tone

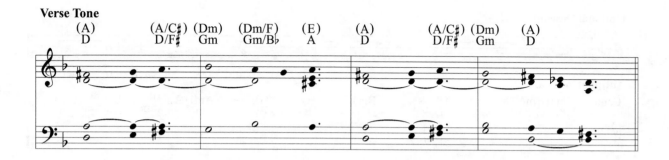

Psalm 119:33-48

1. Teach me the demands of your statutes
and I will keep them to the end.
Train me to observe your law,
to keep it with my heart.

2. Guide me in the path of your commands;
for there is my delight.
Bend my heart to your will
and not to love of gain.

3. Keep my eyes from what is false;
by your word, give me life.
Keep the promise you have made
to the servant who fears you.

4. Keep me from the scorn I dread,
for your decrees are good.
See, I long for your precepts;
then in your justice, give me life.

5. LORD, let your love come upon me,
the saving help of your promise.
And I shall answer those who taunt me
for I trust in your word.

6. Do not take the word of truth from my mouth
for I trust in your decrees.
I shall keep your law always
for ever and ever.

7. I shall walk in the path of freedom
for I seek your precepts.
I will speak of your will before the powerful
and not be abashed.

8. Your commands have been my delight;
these I have loved.
I will worship your commands and love them
and ponder your statutes.

Christ Laid Down His Life for Us

Twenty-sixth Sunday in Ordinary Time, Song for the Table: Option II

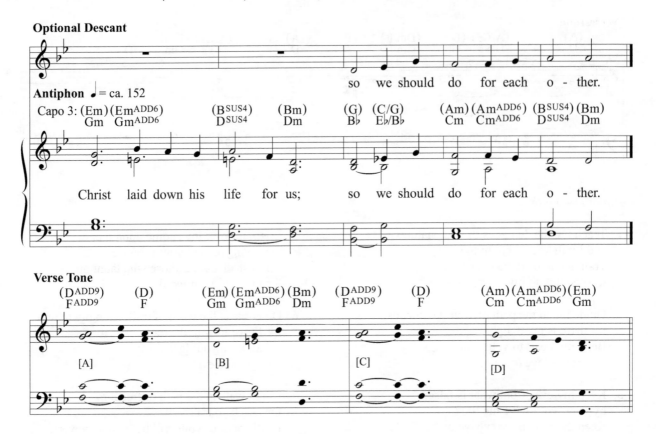

1 Peter 2:21-24; Philippians 2:6-11

1. To this you have <u>been</u> called,
   because Christ <u>suffered</u> for you,
   leaving you an <u>example</u>,
   so that you should follow <u>in</u> his steps.

2. He committed <u>no</u> sin,
   and no deceit was found <u>in</u> his mouth.
   When he was <u>abused</u>,
   he did not re<u>turn</u> abuse.

3. When <u>he</u> suffered,
   he <u>did</u> not threaten;
   but he entrusted <u>himself</u>
   to the one who <u>judges</u> justly.

4. He himself bore <u>our</u> sins
   in his body <u>on</u> the cross,
   so that, free from sins, we might live <u>for</u> righteousness;
   by his wounds you <u>have</u> been healed.

5. Christ Jesus, though he was in the form <u>of</u> God,
   did not regard equality with God as something
      to <u>be</u> exploited,
   but emptied himself, taking the form of <u>a</u> slave,
   being born in <u>human</u> likeness.

6. And being found in <u>human</u> form,
   he <u>humbled</u> himself
   and became obedient to the point <u>of</u> death—
   even death <u>on</u> a cross.

7. Therefore God also highly ex<u>alted</u> him
   and gave him the name that is above <u>every</u> name
   so that at the name of Jesus every knee <u>should</u>
      bend,
   in heaven and on earth and <u>under</u> the earth,
   A and every tongue <u>confess</u>
   B that Jesus <u>Christ</u> is Lord,
   D to the glory of <u>God</u> the Father.

The People of God Are the Vineyard

A-174

Twenty-seventh Sunday in Ordinary Time, Song for the Word

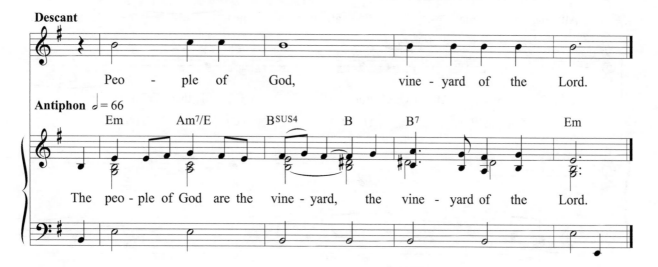

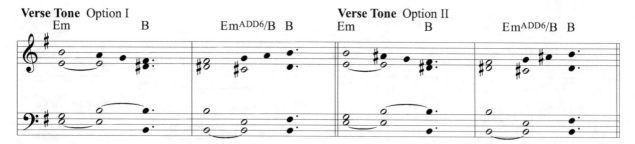

Psalm 80:9, 12-16, 19-20

1. You brought a vine <u>out</u> of Egypt;
   to plant it you drove <u>out</u> the nations.
   It stretched out its branches <u>to</u> the sea,
   to the Great River it stretched <u>out</u> its shoots.

2. Then why have you broken <u>down</u> its walls?
   It is plucked by all <u>who</u> pass by.
   It is ravaged by the boar <u>of</u> the forest,
   devoured by the beasts <u>of</u> the field.

3. God of hosts, turn again, <u>we</u> implore,
   look down from hea<u>ven</u> and see.
   Visit this vine <u>and</u> protect it,
   the vine your right <u>hand</u> has planted.

4. And we shall never forsake <u>you</u> again;
   give us life that we may call up<u>on</u> your name.
   God of hosts, <u>bring</u> us back;
   let your face shine on us and we <u>shall</u> be saved.

Performance Notes

The verse tone is sung twice for each stanza. For an increased Yiddish feel, use option II singing an A sharp (but retain G natural).

A-175

All That Is True

Twenty-seventh Sunday in Ordinary Time, Song for the Table

Verse Tone

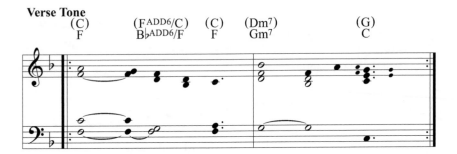

Psalm 122

1. I rejoiced when I heard them say:
   "Let us go to God's house."
   And now our feet are standing
   *within your gates, O Jerusalem.

2. Jerusalem is built as a city
   strongly compact.
   It is there that the tribes go up,
   the tribes of the LORD.

3. For Israel's law it is,
   *there to praise the LORD's name.
   There were set the thrones of judgement
   *of the house of David.

4. For the peace of Jerusalem pray:
   "Peace be to your homes!
   May peace reign in your walls,
   in your palaces, peace!"

5. For love of my fam'ly and friends
   *I say: "Peace upon you."
   For the love of the house of the LORD
   I will ask for your good.

Performance Notes

Use the small cue-size notes (second measure of the verse tone) on the verse lines marked with an asterisk.

The antiphon may be sung as suggested with the cantor leading and the assembly responding to each phrase. Another option is to divide the assembly into two groups, with one group leading and the other responding (women in one group, men in the other or right side of the church in one group, left side in the other).

The Antiphon melody is the old English folk melody "O Waly, Waly."

You Are Rich in Mercy

A-176

Twenty-eighth Sunday in Ordinary Time, Song for the Week

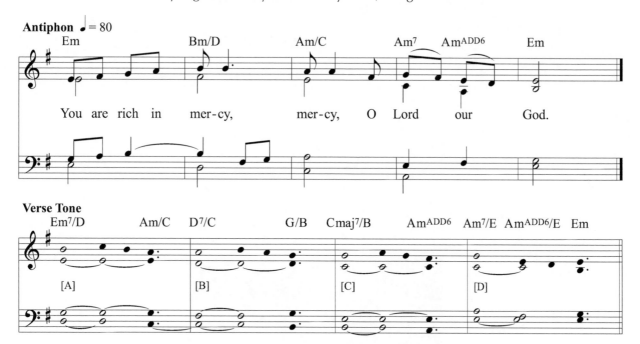

Isaiah 61:10–62:5

1. I will greatly rejoice in the Lord,
[Omit B-C]
   my whole being shall exult in my God.

2. He has clothed me with the garments of salvation,
   he has covered me with the robe of righteousness,
   as a bridegroom decks himself with a garland,
   and as a bride adorns herself with her jewels.

3. For as the earth brings forth its shoots,
   and as a garden causes what is sown in it to spring up,
   so the Lord God will cause righteousness and praise
   to spring up before all the nations.

4. For Zion's sake I will not keep silent,
   and for Jerusalem's sake I will not rest,
   until her vindication shines out like the dawn,
   and her salvation like a burning torch.

5. The nations shall see your vindication,
   and all the kings your glory;

   and you shall be called by a new name
   that the mouth of the Lord will give.

6. You shall be a crown of beauty in the
      hand of the Lord
   and a royal diadem in the hand of your God.
   You shall no more be termed Forsaken,
   and your land shall no more be termed Desolate;

7. but you shall be called My Delight Is in Her,
   and your land Married;
   for the Lord delights in you,
   and your land shall be married.

8. For as a young man marries a young woman,
   so shall your builder marry you,
   and as the bridegroom rejoices over the bride,
   so shall your God rejoice over you.

Performance Notes

The antiphon may be sung twice each time. If desired, the repetition could overlap on the final note, with "You are" being sung at the same time as "God."

I Shall Dwell in the House of the Lord

Twenty-eighth Sunday in Ordinary Time, Song for the Word

Psalm 23

1. LORD, you are <u>my</u> shepherd;
   there is nothing I shall want.
   Fresh and green are <u>the</u> pastures
   where you give <u>me</u> repose.

2. Near restful waters <u>you</u> lead me,
   to revive my drooping spirit.
   You guide me along the <u>right</u> path;
   you are true <u>to</u> your name.

3. If I should walk in the valley <u>of</u> darkness
   no__ evil would I fear.
   You are there with your crook and <u>your</u> staff;
   with these you <u>give</u> me comfort.

4. You have prepared a banquet <u>for</u> me
   in the sight__ of my foes.
   My head you have anointed <u>with</u> oil;
   my cup is <u>overflowing</u>.

5. Surely goodness and kindness <u>shall</u> follow me
   all the days__ of my life.
   In the LORD's own house shall <u>I</u> dwell
   for <u>ever</u> and ever.

Performance Notes

In measure 2 of the tone, extension lines in the text show where to observe the dotted slurs.

A-178

Finest Food! Choicest Wine!

Twenty-eighth Sunday in Ordinary Time, Song for the Table

Verse Tone

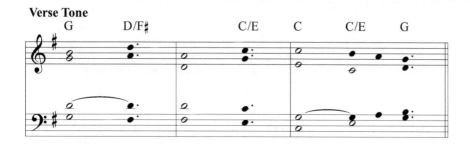

Psalm 125:1-4, 5c; 96:1-10

1. Those who put their trust in the LORD
   are like Mount Zion, that cannot be shaken,
   that stands for ever.

2. Jerusalem! The mountains surround her,
   so the LORD surrounds his people
   both now and for ever.

3. For the scepter of the wicked shall not rest
   over the land of the just
   for fear that the hands of the just should turn to evil.

4. Do good, LORD, to those who are good,
   to the upright of heart.
   On Israel, peace!

5. O sing a new song to the LORD,
   sing to the LORD all the earth.
   O sing to the LORD, bless his name.

6. Proclaim God's help day by day,
   tell among the nations his glory
   and his wonders among all the peoples.

7. The LORD is great and worthy of praise,
   to be feared above all gods;
   the gods of the heathens are naught.

8. It was the LORD who made the heavens.
   His are majesty and honor and power
   and splendor in the holy place.

9. Give the LORD, you families of peoples,
   give the LORD glory and power;
   give the LORD the glory of his name.

10. Bring an offering and enter God's courts,
    worship the LORD in the temple.
    O earth, stand in fear of the LORD.

11. Proclaim to the nations: "God is king."
    The world was made firm in its place;
    God will judge the peoples in fairness.

You Have Given Everything Its Place

Twenty-ninth Sunday in Ordinary Time, Song for the Week
Twenty-seventh Sunday in Ordinary Time, Song for the Week

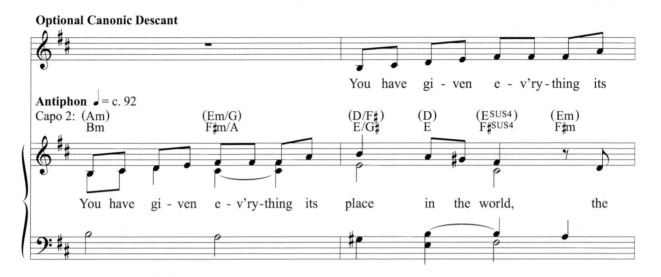

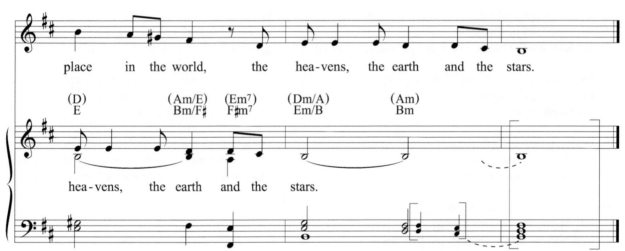

Cue-size notes and additional measure only if descant is used

Verse Tone with Response

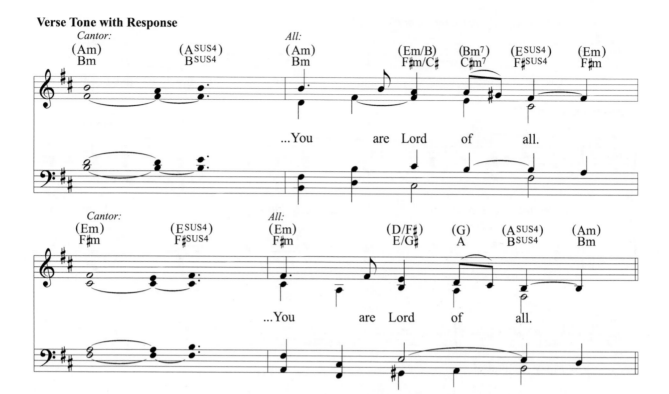

Psalm 8:2, 4-10

1. How great is your name, O LORD our God, through all the earth!   *You are Lord of all!*
   Your majesty is praised above the heavens.   *You are Lord of all!*

2. When I see the heavens, the work of your hands,   *(simile)*
   the moon and the stars which you arranged,

3. what are we that you should keep us in mind,
   mere mortals that you care for us?

4. Yet you have made us little less than gods;
   and crowned us with glory and honor.

5. You gave us power over the work of your hands,
   put all things under our feet.

6. All of them, sheep and cattle,
   yes, even the savage beasts,

7. birds of the air, and fish
   that make their way through the waters.

8. How great is your name, O LORD our God,
   through all the earth!

Give the Lord Power

Twenty-ninth Sunday in Ordinary Time, Song for the Word

Psalm 96:1, 3-5, 7-10a, 10c

1. O sing a new song to the LORD,
   sing to the LORD, all the earth.
   Tell among the nations God's glory
   and his wonders among all the peoples.

2. The LORD is great and worthy of praise,
   to be feared above all gods;
   the gods of the heathens are naught.
   It was the LORD who made the heavens.

3. Give the LORD, you families of peoples,
   give the LORD glory and power;
   give the LORD the glory of his name.
   Bring an offering and enter God's courts.

4. Worship the LORD in the temple.
   O earth, stand in fear of the LORD.
   Proclaim to the nations: "God is king."
   God will judge the peoples in fairness.

Performance Notes

The Antiphon is sung twice each time, with the Tenor descant added on the repeat.
Percussion is recommended for use with the Antiphon.

You Alone Are Lord

A-181

Twenty-ninth Sunday in Ordinary Time, Song for the Table

Psalm 33:10-22

1. The LORD foils the de<u>signs</u> of the <u>nations</u>,
   and defeats the plans <u>of</u> the peoples.
   The counsel of the <u>LORD</u> stands for <u>ev</u>er,
   the plans of God's heart from age <u>to</u> age.

2. They are happy, whose <u>God</u> is the <u>LORD</u>,
   the people who are chosen <u>as</u> his own.
   From the heavens the <u>LORD</u> looks <u>forth</u>
   and sees all the peoples of <u>the</u> earth.

3. From the heavenly <u>dwelling</u> God <u>gazes</u>
   on all the dwellers <u>on</u> the earth;
   God who shapes the <u>hearts</u> of them <u>all</u>
   and considers all <u>their</u> deeds.

4. A king is not <u>saved</u> by his <u>army</u>,
   nor a warrior preserved <u>by</u> his strength.

A vain hope for <u>safety</u> is the <u>horse</u>;
despite its power it can<u>not</u> save.

5. The LORD looks on <u>those</u> who <u>fear</u> him,
   on those who hope <u>in</u> his love,
   to rescue their <u>souls</u> from <u>death</u>,
   to keep them alive <u>in</u> famine.

6. Our soul is <u>waiting</u> for the <u>LORD</u>.
   The LORD is our help <u>and</u> our shield.
   Our hearts find <u>joy</u> in the <u>LORD</u>.
   We trust in God's ho<u>ly</u> name.

7. *[Omit A-B]*
   May your love be up<u>on</u> us, O <u>LORD</u>,
   as we place all our hope <u>in</u> you.

A-182   Seek the Lord! Long for the Lord!
Thirtieth Sunday in Ordinary Time, Song for the Week

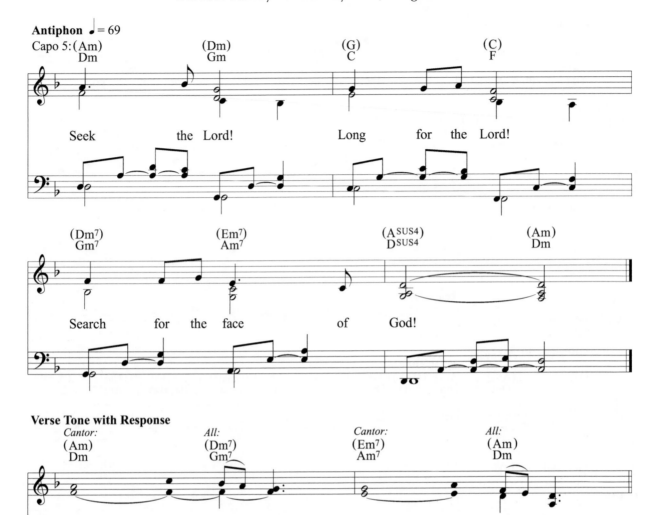

Psalm 105:1-5

1. Give thanks and acclaim God's <u>name</u> *al-ways*,
   make known God's deeds among the peo<u>ples</u> *al-ways*.

2. O sing to the LORD, sing <u>praise</u> *al-ways*;
   tell all his wonderful <u>works</u> *al-ways*!

3. Be proud of God's holy <u>name</u> *al-ways*,
   let the hearts that seek the LORD re<u>joice</u> *al-ways*.

4. Consider the LORD, who is <u>strong</u> *al-ways*;
   constantly seek his <u>face</u> *al-ways*.

5. Remember the wonders of the LORD *al-ways*,
   the miracles and judgements pro<u>nounced</u> *al-ways*.

Performance Notes
Descants for the antiphon are available at A-32.

I Love You, Lord

Thirtieth Sunday in Ordinary Time, Song for the Word

Psalm 18:2-4, 47, 51ab

1. I love you, LORD, my strength,
   my rock, my for<u>tress</u>, my savior.

2. God, you are the rock where <u>I</u> take refuge;
   my shield, my mighty <u>help</u>, my stronghold.

3. LORD, you are worthy <u>of</u> all praise,

   when I call I am saved <u>from</u> my foes.

4. Long life to you, LORD, my rock!
   Praise to you, <u>God</u>, who saves me.

5. You have given great victories <u>to</u> your king
   and shown your love for <u>your</u> anointed.

The Strong Lord Sets Me Free

Thirtieth Sunday in Ordinary Time, Song for the Table: Option I
Eighth Sunday in Ordinary Time, Song for the Week

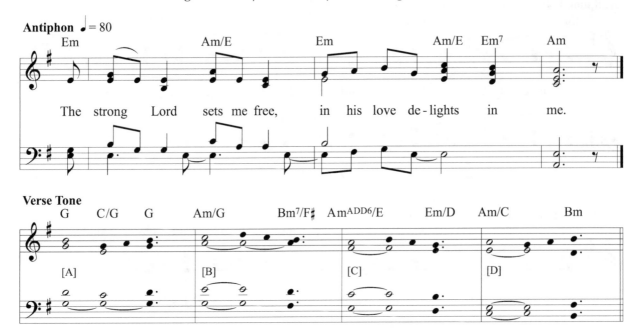

Psalm 18

1. I love you, LORD, my strength,
   my rock, my for<u>tress</u>, my savior.
   God, you are the rock where <u>I</u> take refuge;
   my shield, my mighty <u>help</u>, my stronghold.
   [repeat A and D]
   LORD, you are worthy <u>of</u> all praise,
   when I call I am saved <u>from</u> my foes.

2. The waves of death <u>rose</u> about me;
   the torrents of destruc<u>tion</u> assailed me;
   the snares of the <u>grave</u> entangled me;
   the traps of <u>death</u> confronted me.

3. In my anguish I called <u>to</u> you, LORD;
   I cried to you, <u>God</u>, for help.
   From your temple you <u>heard</u> my voice;
   my cry came <u>to</u> your ears.

4. Then the earth reeled and rocked;
   the mountains were shaken <u>to</u> their base,
   they reeled at your ter<u>rible</u> anger.
   Smoke came forth from your nostrils
   and scorching fire <u>from</u> your mouth,
   coals were set ablaze <u>by</u> its heat.

5. You lowered the heavens <u>and</u> came down,
   a black cloud un<u>der</u> your feet.
   You came enthroned <u>on</u> the cherubim,
   you flew on the wings <u>of</u> the wind.

6. You made the dark<u>ness</u> your covering,
   the dark waters of the <u>clouds</u>, your tent.
   A brightness shone <u>out</u> before you
   with hailstones and flash<u>es</u> of fire.

7. LORD, you thundered <u>in</u> the heavens,
   Most High, you let your <u>voice</u> be heard.
   You shot your arrows, scat<u>tered</u> the foe,
   flashed your lightnings and put <u>them</u> to flight.

8. The bed of the ocean <u>was</u> revealed;
   the foundations of the world <u>were</u> laid bare
   at the thunder of your <u>threat</u>, O LORD,
   at the blast of the breath <u>of</u> your anger.

9. From on high you reached <u>down</u> and seized me;
   you drew me out of the <u>mighty</u> waters.
   You snatched me from my po<u>werful</u> foe,
   from my enemies whose strength I <u>could</u> not match.

10. They assailed me in the day of <u>my</u> misfortune,
    but you, LORD, were <u>my</u> support.
    You brought me forth <u>into</u> freedom,
    you saved me be<u>cause</u> you loved me.

11. You rewarded me because <u>I</u> was just,
    repaid me, for my <u>hands</u> were clean,
    for I have kept your <u>way</u>, O LORD,
    and have not fallen a<u>way</u> from you.

Verse Tone

12. Your judgements are all before me;
    I have never neglected your commands.
    I have always been upright before you;
    I have kept myself from guilt.

13. You repaid me because I was just
    and my hands were clean in your eyes.
    You are loving with those who love you,
    you show yourself perfect with the perfect.

14. With the sincere you show yourself sincere,
    but the cunning you outdo in cunning.
    For you save a humble people
    but humble the eyes that are proud.

15. You, O Lord, are my lamp,
    my God who lightens my darkness.
    With you I can break through any barrier,
    with my God I can scale any wall.

16. Your ways, O God, are perfect;
    your word, O Lord, is purest gold.
    You indeed are the shield
    of all who make you their refuge.

17. For who is God but you, Lord?
    Who is a rock but you, my God?
    You who gird me with strength
    and make the path safe before me.

18. My feet you made swift as the deer's,
    you have made me stand firm on the heights.
    You have trained my hands for battle
    and my arms to bend the heavy bow.

19. You gave me your saving shield;
    you upheld me, trained me with care.
    You gave me freedom for my steps;
    my feet have never slipped.

20. I pursued and overtook my foes,
    never turning back till they were slain.
    I smote them so they could not rise;
    they fell beneath my feet.

21. You girded me with strength for battle,
    you made my enemies fall beneath me,
    you made my foes take flight;
    those who hated me I destroyed.

22. They cried, but there was no one to save them;
    they cried to you, Lord, but in vain.
    I crushed them fine as dust before the wind;
    trod them down like dirt in the streets.

23. You saved me from the feuds of the people
    and put me at the head of the nations.
    People unknown to me served me;
    when they heard of me they obeyed me.

24. Foreign nations came to me cringing,
    foreign nations faded away.
    [omit C]
    They came trembling out of their strongholds.

25. Long life to you, Lord, my rock!
    Praise to you, God, who saves me,
    the God who gives me redress
    and subdues people under me.

26. *A* You saved me from my furious foes.
    B You set me above my assailants.
    A You saved me from violent hands,
    B so I will praise you, Lord, among the nations;
    D I will sing a psalm to your name.

27. You have given great victories to your king
    and shown your love for your anointed,
    [omit C]
    for David and his line for ever.

Love the Lord Your God

Thirtieth Sunday in Ordinary Time, Song for the Table: Option II
Seventh Sunday in Ordinary Time, Song for the Table

Alto Descant

Love, and you shall live.

Bass Descant

Love, and you shall live.

Verse Tone with Response

Cantor:

D Dmaj7 Em/D G/A A D *All:* G A7/G D/F♯ Bm Asus4 A

...Do this and you shall live.

Psalm 119:1-8

1. They are happy whose <u>life</u> is blameless,
   who fol<u>low</u> God's law! *Do this . . .*

2. They are happy who <u>do</u> God's will,
   seeking God with <u>all</u> their hearts. *Do this . . .*

3. They never do a<u>ny</u>thing evil
   but walk <u>in</u> God's ways. *(simile)*

4. You have laid <u>down</u> your precepts
   to be o<u>beyed</u> with care.

5. May my foot<u>steps</u> be firm
   to o<u>bey</u> your statutes.

6. Then I shall not be <u>put</u> to shame
   as I heed <u>your</u> commands.

7. I will thank you with an <u>upright</u> heart
   as I learn <u>your</u> decrees.

8. I will o<u>bey</u> your statutes;
   do <u>not</u> forsake me.

A-186 From the East and West, from the North and South

Thirty-first Sunday in Ordinary Time, Song for the Week

The Antiphon melody is adapted from the first half of the anonymous English carol tune NOEL, traditionally sung in England to "It came upon the midnight clear."

Psalm 104:10, 12-15, 27-28, 29bc-31, 33-34

1. You make springs gush forth in <u>the</u> valleys;   *we will . . .*
   they flow in between <u>the</u> hills.   *where the greatest . . .*

2. On their banks dwell the birds <u>of</u> heaven;   *(simile)*
   from the branches they sing <u>their</u> song.

3. From your dwelling you water <u>the</u> hills;
   earth drinks its fill of <u>your</u> gift.

4. You make the grass grow for <u>the</u> cattle
   and the plants to serve <u>our</u> needs,

5. that we may bring forth bread from <u>the</u> earth
   and wine to cheer <u>our</u> hearts;

6. oil, to make our fa<u>ces</u> shine
   and bread to strengthen <u>our</u> hearts.

7. All of these look <u>to</u> you
   to give them their food in <u>due</u> season.

8. You give it, they gather <u>it</u> up;
   you open your hand, they have <u>their</u> fill.

9. You take back your spirit, <u>they</u> die,
   returning to the dust from which <u>they</u> came.

10. You send forth your spirit, they are <u>created</u>;
    and you renew the face of <u>the</u> earth.

11. May the glory of the LORD last <u>for</u> ever!
    May the LORD rejoice in <u>creation</u>!

12. I will sing to the LORD all <u>my</u> life,
    make music to my God while <u>I</u> live.

13. May my thoughts be pleasing <u>to</u> God.
    I find my joy in <u>the</u> LORD.

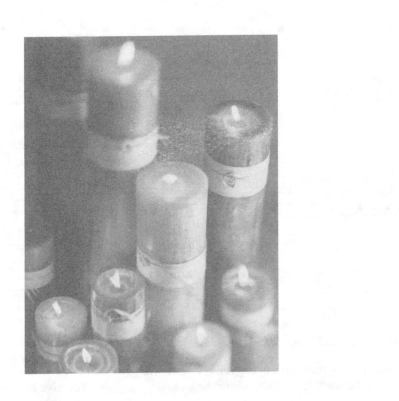

Keep My Soul in Peace

Thirty-first Sunday in Ordinary Time, Song for the Word

Psalm 131

1. O Lord, my heart is not proud
   nor haughty my eyes.
   I have not gone after things too great
   nor marvels beyond me.

2. Truly I have set my soul
   in silence and peace.

A weaned child on its mother's breast,
even so is my soul.

3. *[Omit A-B]*
   O Israel, hope in the Lord
   both now and for ever.

The Word of God at Work in Us
Thirty-first Sunday in Ordinary Time, Song for the Table

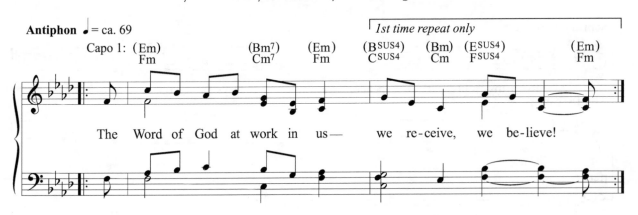

The Word of God at work in us— we re-ceive, we be-lieve!

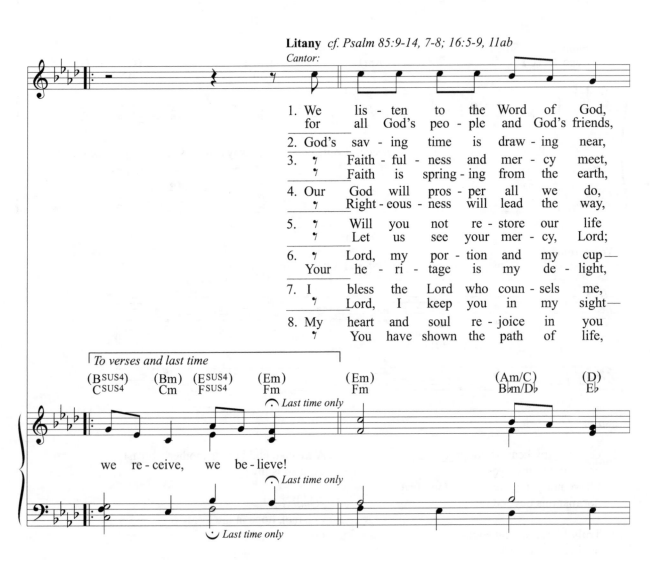

Litany *cf. Psalm 85:9-14, 7-8; 16:5-9, 11ab*

Cantor:

1. We lis - ten to the Word of God,
   for all God's peo - ple and God's friends,
2. God's sav - ing time is draw - ing near,
3. Faith - ful - ness and mer - cy meet,
   Faith is spring - ing from the earth,
4. Our God will pros - per all we do,
   Right - eous - ness will lead the way,
5. Will you not re - store our life
   Let us see your mer - cy, Lord;
6. Lord, my por - tion and my cup—
   Your he - ri - tage is my de - light,
7. I bless the Lord who coun - sels me,
   Lord, I keep you in my sight—
8. My heart and soul re - joice in you
   You have shown the path of life,

we re-ceive, we be-lieve!

Cantor:

1., 2.   *1st time to repeat, 2nd time to response below*

1. a   voice   that   speaks   of   love   and   peace,
   for those   who   turn   their   hearts   to   God.
2. God's glo - ry   dwell - ing   in   our   land. *
3. ⅄ peace   and   just - ice   have   em - braced.
   ⅄ hea - ven's   just - ice   rain - ing   down.
4. ⅄ and   our   earth   shall   yield   its   fruit.
   and   peace   shall   fol - low   in   its   path.
5. ⅄ that   your   peo - ple   may   re - joice?
   ⅄ may   we   know   your   sav - ing   help.
6. ⅄ it   is   you   who   are   my   prize.
   ⅄ and   the   lot   marked   out   for   me.
7. ⅄ who   at   night   di - rects   my   heart.
   with   you   be - side   me,   I   stand   firm.
8. ⅄ and   my   bo - dy   safe - ly   rests.
   ⅄ in   your   pre - sence   on - ly   joy!

All:

(B♭SUS4) (B♭m) (E♭SUS4) (E♭m)   (E♭m)   (C♭maj7)   (D♭)
C♭SUS4   C♭m   F♭SUS4   F♭m   F♭m   D♭maj7   E♭

We re - ceive,   we be - lieve!

Repeat omitted

All: To antiphon

(B♭SUS4) (B♭m) (E♭SUS4) (E♭m)
C♭SUS4   C♭m   F♭SUS4   F♭m

We re - ceive,   we be - lieve!

Let My Prayer Come Before You, Lord

Thirty-second Sunday in Ordinary Time, Song for the Week: Option I

Verse Tone with Response

...lis - ten and an - swer.

Psalm 88:2-5, 7-19

1. LORD my God, I call for <u>help</u> by day,
    Listen and answer.
   I cry at <u>night</u> before you.
    Listen and answer.
   Let my prayer come in<u>to</u> your presence.
    Listen and answer.
   O turn your ear <u>to</u> my cry.
    Listen and answer.

2. For my soul is <u>filled</u> with evils;   *(simile)*
   my life is on the brink <u>of</u> the grave.
   I am reckoned as one <u>in</u> the tomb;
   I have reached the end <u>of</u> my strength.

3. You have laid me in the depths <u>of</u> the tomb,
   in places that are dark, <u>in</u> the depths.
   Your anger weighs <u>down</u> upon me;
   I am drowned be<u>neath</u> your waves.

4. You have taken a<u>way</u> my friends
   and made me hateful <u>in</u> your sight.
   Imprisoned, I can<u>not</u> escape;
   my eyes are sunk<u>en</u> with grief.

5. I call to you, LORD, all <u>the</u> day long;
   to you I stretch <u>out</u> my hands.
   Will you work your wonders <u>for</u> the dead?
   Will the shades <u>stand</u> and praise you?

6. Will your love be told <u>in</u> the grave
   or your faithfulness a<u>mong</u> the dead?
   Will your wonders be known <u>in</u> the dark
   or your justice in the land <u>of</u> oblivion?

7. As for me, LORD, I call to <u>you</u> for help;
   in the morning my prayer <u>comes</u> before you.
   LORD, why do <u>you</u> reject me?
   Why do you <u>hide</u> your face?

8. Wretched, close to death <u>from</u> my youth,
   I have borne your trials; <u>I</u> am numb.
   Your fury has swept <u>down</u> upon me;
   your terrors have utter<u>ly</u> destroyed me.

9. They surround me all the day <u>like</u> a flood,
   they assail me <u>all</u> together.
   Friend and neighbor you have ta<u>ken</u> away;
   my one compan<u>ion</u> is darkness.

Thirty-second Sunday in Ordinary Time, Song for the Week: Option II, *same as A-141* ← **A-190**

Thirty-second Sunday in Ordinary Time, Song for the Word, *same as A-158* ← **A-191**

Behold, the Bridegroom Is Here

Thirty-second Sunday in Ordinary Time, Song for the Table

Be - hold, the bride - groom is here: keep watch, stay a - wake.

Verse Tone with Response

...keep watch, stay a - wake.

Psalm 37:1, 3-5, 7ab, 8, 11, 18, 27, 29a, 31b, 34abc, 39a, 40

1. Do not fret because of the wicked:
   keep watch . . .
2. Do not envy those who do evil: *(simile)*
3. Trust in the LORD and do good:
4. Live in the land and be secure:
5. If you find your delight in the LORD:
6. The LORD will grant your heart's desire:
7. Commit your life to the LORD:
8. Be confident, and God will act:
9. Be still before the LORD and wait in patience:
10. Do not fret at those who prosper:
11. Calm your anger and forget your rage:
12. Do not fret, it only leads to evil:
13. The humble shall own the land:
14. The humble shall enjoy the fullness of peace:
15. God protects the lives of the upright:
16. The heritage of the upright will last for ever:
17. Turn away from evil and do good:
18. You shall have a home for ever:
19. The just shall inherit the land:
20. The steps of the just shall be saved from stumbling:
21. Wait for the LORD, keep to God's way:
22. It is God who will free you from the wicked:
23. God will raise you up to possess the land:
24. The salvation of the just comes from the LORD:
25. The LORD helps the just and delivers them:
26. The refuge of the just is in God:

Performance Notes

Since the psalm verses are fairly short, it is recommended that the Antiphon only be sung after every fourth verse.

My Plans for You Are Peace

Thirty-third Sunday in Ordinary Time, Song for the Week

Soprano / Alto Descants

My plans are peace.

Antiphon ♩ = ca. 88

My plans for you are peace, not af - flic - tion, says the Lord.

On - ly cry and I will bring you home.

On - ly cry to me, and I will bring you home.

Verse Tone

Psalm 126

1. When the LORD delivered Zion from bondage,
   it seemed like a dream.
   Then was our mouth filled with laughter,
   on our lips there were songs.

2. The heathens themselves said: "What marvels
   the LORD worked for them!"
   What marvels the Lord worked for us!
   Indeed we were glad.

3. Deliver us, O LORD, from our bondage
   as streams in dry land.
   Those who are sowing in tears
   will sing when they reap.

4. They go out, they go out, full of tears,
   carrying seed for the sowing;
   they come back, they come back, full of song,
   carrying their sheaves.

How Happy Are You

A-194

Thirty-third Sunday in Ordinary Time, Song for the Word
Holy Family, Song for the Word

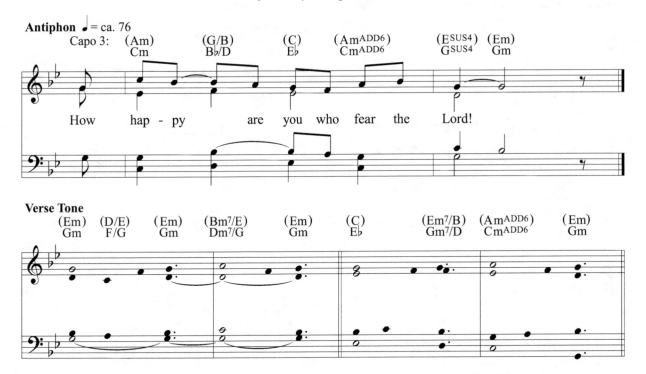

Psalm 128

1. O blessed are you who fear the LORD
   and walk in God's ways!

2. By the labor of your hands you shall eat.
   You will be happy and prosper.

3. Your wife like a fruitful vine
   in the heart of your house;

4. your children like shoots of the olive,
   around your table.

5. Indeed thus shall be blessed
   those who fear the LORD.

6. May the LORD bless you from Zion
   all the days of your life!

7. May you see your children's children
   in a happy Jerusalem!
   On Israel, peace!

Performance Notes
Two accompaniments for the two-measure Verse Tone are provided for the sake of variety.

Come, All You Good and Faithful Servants

Thirty-third Sunday in Ordinary Time, Song for the Table

Verses 1–7 *Psalm 34:1-15*

1. I will bless the LORD at all times, God's praise always on my lips;
   In the LORD my soul shall make its boast; the humble shall hear and be glad.
2. Glorify the LORD with me. Together let us praise God's name.
   I sought the LORD and was heard; from all my terrors set free.
3. Look towards God and be radiant; let your faces not be a - bashed.
   When the poor cry out the LORD hears them and rescues them from all their dis - tress.
4. The angel of the LORD is en - camped around those who fear God, to rescue them.
   Taste and see that the LORD is good. They are happy who seek refuge in God.
5. Revere the LORD, you saints. They lack nothing, who revere the LORD.
   Strong lions suffer want and go hungry but those who seek the LORD lack no blessing.
6. Come, children, and hear me that I may teach you the fear of the LORD.
   Who are those who long for life and many days, to enjoy their pros - perity?
7. Keep your tongue from evil and your lips from speaking de - ceit.
   Turn aside from evil and do good; seek and strive af - ter peace.

Verse Tone with Response

(D) (Dmaj⁷) (Em⁷) (A)
F Fmaj⁷ Gm⁷ C

1. To repeat | 2. To antiphon

Soprano Descant

share in the joy, the joy of the Lord. share in the joy of the Lord.

Tenor /Alto Descant

share in the joy, the joy of the Lord. share in the joy of the Lord.

Response (melody)

(D) (G) (A) (D) (Am⁷) (D)
F Bb C F Cm⁷ F

share in the joy, the joy of the Lord. share in the joy of the Lord.

Verses 8–14   *Psalm 34:16-23; 73:23-26, 28*

8. The eyes of the LORD are toward the just and his ears toward their ap - peal.
The face of the LORD rebuffs the wicked to destroy their remembrance from the earth.
9. They call and the LORD hears and rescues them in all their dis - tress.
The LORD is close to the bro - ken - hearted; those whose spirit is crushed God will save.
10. Many are the trials of the upright but the LORD will come to rescue them,
keeping guard over all their bones, not one of their bones shall be broken.
11. Evil brings death to the wicked; those who hate the good are doomed.
The LORD ransoms the souls of the faithful. None who trust in God shall be con - demned.
12. I was always in your presence; you were holding me by my right hand.
You will guide me by your counsel and so you will lead me to glory.
13. What else have I in heaven but you? Apart from you I want nothing on earth.
My body and my heart faint for joy; God is my possession for ever.
14. To be near God is my happiness. I have made the LORD God my refuge.
I will tell of all your works at the gates of the city of Zion.

Verse Tone with Response

Soprano Descant

share in the joy, the joy of the Lord.   share in the joy of the Lord.

Tenor /Alto Descant

share in the joy, the joy of the Lord.   share in the joy of the Lord.

Response (melody)

share in the joy, the joy of the Lord.   share in the joy of the Lord.

Worthy Is the Lamb Who Was Slain

Christ the King, Song for the Week

Descant

Worth - y is the Lamb, worth - y, worth-y of glo - ry.

Antiphon ♩. = ca. 72

Capo 5: (G)   (Gmaj⁷/B)   (C)   (Gmaj⁷/B) (Am⁷)   (G/B)   (C)   (D)
C   Cmaj⁷/E   F   Cmaj⁷/E   Dm⁷   C/E   F   G

Worth - y is the Lamb who was slain, worth-y of power, worth-y of glo - ry.

Worth - y is the Lamb, worth - y of wis-dom and might.

(G)   (Gmaj⁷/B)   (C)   (Gmaj⁷/B)   (C)   (Dm⁷/G)   (G)
C   Cmaj⁷/E   F   Cmaj⁷/E   F   Gm⁷/C   C

Worth - y is the Lamb who was slain, worth-y of wis-dom and might.

Verse Tone with Response *Psalm 24:7; 72:5-6, 8, 18-19*

Cantor: *All:*

(G)   (Gmaj⁷/B)   (C)   (Gmaj⁷/B) (Am⁷)   (G/B)   (C)   (D)
C   Cmaj⁷/E   F   Cmaj⁷/E   Dm⁷   C/E   F   G

1. Lift your heads, O an - cient doors: *worth-y of pow'r,   worth-y of glo-ry.*
2. May he live as long as the sun:
3. May he be like rain on the grass:
4. May he rule from sea to sea:
5. Bless the God of Is - ra - el:
6. Bles - sed be God's glo - ri - ous name:

Verse Tone with Response

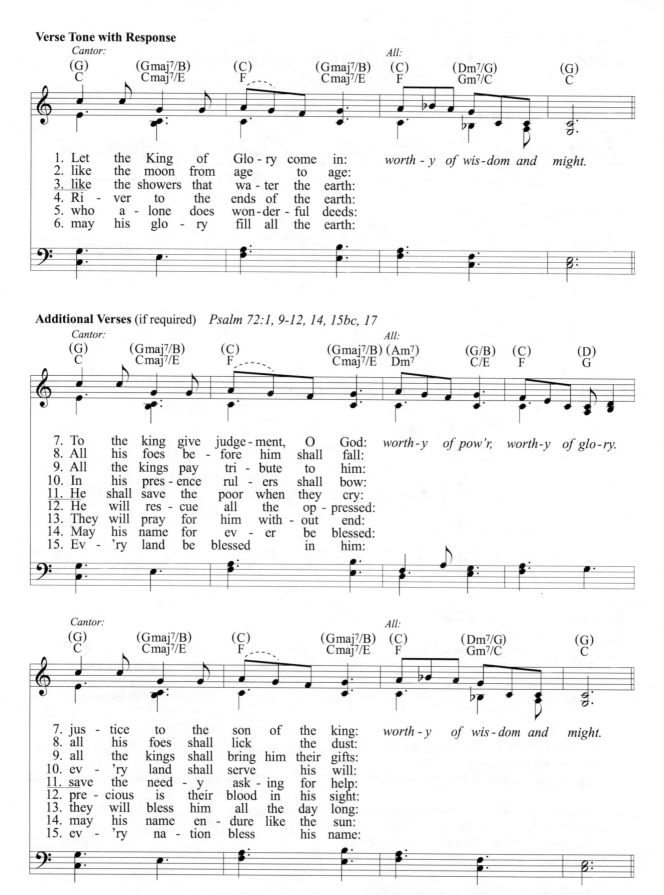

1. Let the King of Glo - ry come in: worth - y of wis-dom and might.
2. like the moon from age to age:
3. like the showers that wa - ter the earth:
4. Ri - ver to the ends of the earth:
5. who a - lone does won-der - ful deeds:
6. may his glo - ry fill all the earth:

Additional Verses (if required) *Psalm 72:1, 9-12, 14, 15bc, 17*

7. To the king give judge-ment, O God: worth-y of pow'r, worth-y of glo-ry.
8. All his foes be - fore him shall fall:
9. All the kings pay tri - bute to him:
10. In his pres - ence rul - ers shall bow:
11. He shall save the poor when they cry:
12. He will res - cue all the op - pressed:
13. They will pray for him with - out end:
14. May his name for ev - er be blessed:
15. Ev - 'ry land be blessed in him:

7. jus - tice to the son of the king: worth - y of wis - dom and might.
8. all his foes shall lick the dust:
9. all the kings shall bring him their gifts:
10. ev - 'ry land shall serve his will:
11. save the need - y ask - ing for help:
12. pre - cious is their blood in his sight:
13. they will bless him all the day long:
14. may his name en - dure like the sun:
15. ev - 'ry na - tion bless his name:

A-198   # Listen, Listen to the Voice of Jesus
Christ the King, Song for the Table

Isaiah 58:6-8b, 9ab, 10-11ab,11def

1. Is not this the fast <u>that</u> I choose:
to loose the bonds <u>of</u> injustice,
to undo the thongs <u>of</u> the yoke,
to let the oppressed go free, and to break <u>eve</u>ry yoke?

2. Is it not to share your bread <u>with</u> the hungry,
and bring the homeless poor <u>in</u>to your house;
when you see the na<u>ked</u>, to cover them,
and not to hide yourself from <u>your</u> own kin?

3. Then your light shall break forth <u>like</u> the dawn,
and your healing shall <u>spring</u> up quickly.
Then you shall call and the <u>LORD</u> will answer;
you shall cry for help, and he will say, <u>Here</u> I am.

4. If you offer your food <u>to</u> the hungry
and satisfy the needs of <u>the</u> afflicted,
then your light shall rise <u>in</u> the darkness
and your gloom be <u>like</u> the noonday.

5. The LORD will guide <u>you</u> continually,
and satisfy your needs <u>in</u> parched places.
and you shall be like a <u>wa</u>tered garden,
like a spring of water, whose waters <u>nev</u>er fail.

You Have Shown You Love Us

A-199

The Most Holy Trinity, Song for the Week

Antiphon ♩ = 92-96

You have shown you love us, Fa-ther, Son and Spi-rit.

Bless'd are you, O God, the God of faith-ful love.

Verse Tone

Omit for doxology

Psalm 113

1. Praise, O servants of the LORD,
   praise the name of the LORD!
   May the name of the LORD be blessed
   both now and for evermore!
   From the rising of the sun to its setting
   praised be the name of the LORD!

2. High above all nations is the LORD,
   above the heavens God's glory.
   Who is like the LORD, our God,
   the one enthroned on high,
   who stoops from the heights to look down,
   to look down upon heaven and earth?

3. From the dust God lifts up the lowly,
   from the dungheap God raises the poor
   to set them in the company of rulers,
   yes, with the rulers of the people.
   To the childless wife God gives a home
   and gladdens her heart with children.

Trinitarian doxology (for Trinity Sunday):

Sing praise to the Abba of Jesus,
through the Spirit poured into our hearts.
By the Spirit, the Water and the Blood
we are saved and share in their love.

For Ever, For Ever, We Praise You For Ever

The Most Holy Trinity, Song for the Word

Alto Descant

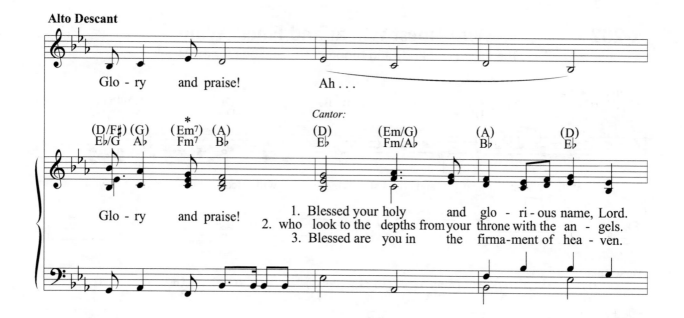

Cantor:

Glory and praise!   Ah . . .

Glory and praise!

1. Blessed your holy   and glo - ri - ous name, Lord.
2. who look to the depths from your throne with the an - gels.
3. Blessed are you in the firma-ment of hea - ven.

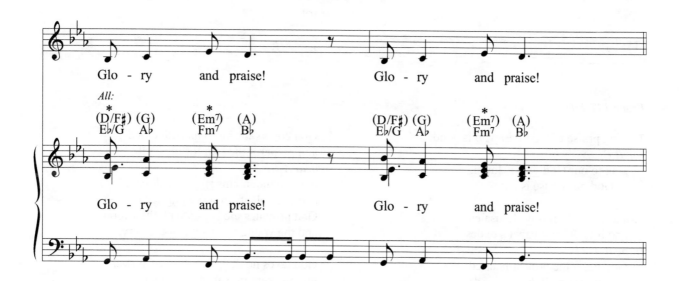

All:

Glo - ry   and praise!   Glo - ry   and praise!

Glo - ry   and praise!   Glo - ry   and praise!

Perfomance Notes

A variety of styles possible here, from a detached Gospel style to a smoother and more relaxed rendition. The tempo may be faster or slower than that indicated.

The verses are sung in a roughly metrical way.

Asterisked guitar chords may be omitted.

A-201 ➔ The Most Holy Trinity, Song for the Table, *same as A-92*

A-202 **With Finest Wheat and Finest Wine**

The Most Holy Body and Blood of Christ, Song for the Week

Psalm 147:1-11

1. Sing praise to the LORD <u>who</u> is good;
[omit B]

   sing to our God <u>who</u> is loving:
   to God our <u>praise</u> is due.

2. The LORD builds <u>up</u> Jerusalem
   and brings back <u>Israel's</u> exiles,
[repeat A-B]

   God heals the <u>broken</u>-hearted,
   and binds up all <u>their</u> wounds.
   God fixes the number <u>of</u> the stars;
   and calls each one <u>by</u> its name.

3. Our LORD is great <u>and</u> almighty;
   God's wisdom can never <u>be</u> measured.
[repeat A-B]

   The LORD rais<u>es</u> the lowly,
   and humbles the wicked to <u>the</u> dust.
   O sing to the LORD, <u>giving</u> thanks;
   sing psalms to our God <u>with</u> the harp.

4. God covers the heav<u>ens</u> with clouds,
   and prepares the rain for <u>the</u> earth;
[repeat A-B]

   making mountains <u>sprout</u> with grass
   and with plants to serve <u>our</u> needs.
   God provides the beasts <u>with</u> their food
   and the young ravens <u>when</u> they cry.

5. God takes no delight in <u>horses'</u> power
   nor pleasure in war<u>riors'</u> strength.
   The LORD delights in those <u>who</u> revere him,
   in those who wait <u>for</u> his love.

O Praise the Lord, Jerusalem

The Most Holy Body and Blood of Christ, Song for the Word

Verse Tone with Response Superimposed Tone *Psalm 147B:13-20*

Cantor:

All:

* 1. God has strengthened the bars of your gates,
* 2. and has blessed the child - ren with - in you;
* 3. has e - stablished peace on your borders,
* 4. and feeds you with fin - est wheat.
* 5. God sends out word to the earth
* 6. and swiftly runs the com - mand.
  7. God showers down snow white as wool,
  8. and scatters hoar - frost like ashes.
  9. God hurls down hail - stones like crumbs,
  10. and causes the wa - ters to freeze.
  11. God sends forth a word and it melts them:
  12. at the breath of God's mouth the wa - ters flow.
* 13. God makes his word known to Jacob,
* 14. to Israel his laws and de - crees.
* 15. God has not dealt thus with o - ther nations;
* 16. has not taught them di - vine de - crees.

Zi-on, praise your God.

Alto Descant (verses only - *hum on first two measures*)

Alto Descant (antiphon only)

Zi-on, praise your God.

O praise the Lord, Je - ru-sa-lem: Zi-on, praise your God.

Antiphon ♩ = 96

Capo 3: (A⁴⁺²) (A) (C/A) (A) (A/C♯) (Em⁷) (A)
C⁴⁺² C E♭/C C C/E Gm⁷ C

O praise the Lord, Je - ru-sa-lem: Zi-on, praise your God.

Performance Notes

The Lectionary selections for the day are indicated by an asterisk.

The Most Holy Body and Blood of Christ, Song for the Table, *same as A-50* ← **A-204**

The Most Sacred Heart of Jesus, Song for the Day, *same as A-49* ← **A-205**

The Most Sacred Heart of Jesus, Song for the Word, *same as A-111* ← **A-206**

A-208   You Are Rich in Mercy

Ash Wednesday, Song for the Day

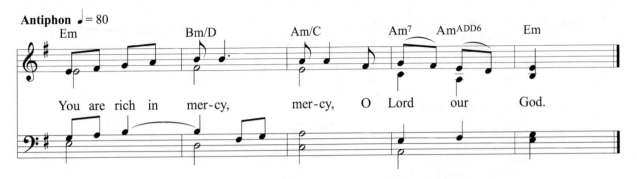

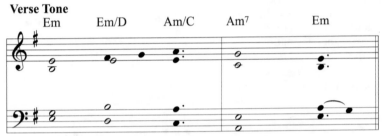

Wisdom 11:21–12:2

1. O LORD, it is always in your power to <u>show</u> great strength,
   and who can withstand the might of your <u>arm</u>?

2. Because the whole world before you is like a speck that <u>tips</u> the scales,
   and like a drop of morning dew that falls on the <u>ground</u>.

3. But you are merciful to all, for you can <u>do</u> all things,
   and you overlook people's sins, so that they may re<u>pent</u>.

4. For you love all things that exist, and detest none of the things that <u>you</u> have made,
   for you would not have made anything if you had <u>hated</u> it.

5. How would anything have endured if you <u>had</u> not willed it?
   Or how would anything not called forth by you have been pre<u>served</u>?

6. You spare all things for they are yours, O LORD, you who <u>love</u> the living.
   For your immortal spirit is in <u>all</u> things.

7. Therefore you correct little by little those who trespass,
   and you remind and warn them of the things through <u>which</u> they sin,
   so that they may be freed from wickedness, and put their trust in you, O <u>LORD</u>.

Performance Notes

The Antiphon may be sung twice each time. If desired, the repetition could overlap on the final note, with "You are" being sung at the same time as "God."

Give: Your Father Sees

A-210

Ash Wednesday, Song for the Table

Matthew 5:3-10

1. Blessed are the <u>poor</u> in spirit,
   for theirs is the king<u>dom</u> of heaven.
   Blessed are <u>those</u> who mourn,
   for they <u>will</u> be comforted.

2. Blessed <u>are</u> the meek,
   for they will in<u>her</u>it the earth.
   Blessed are those who hunger
      and <u>thirst</u> for righteousness,
   for they <u>will</u> be filled.

3. Blessed <u>are</u> the merciful,
   for they will re<u>ceive</u> mercy.
   Blessed are the <u>pure</u> in heart,
   for they <u>will</u> see God.

4. Blessed <u>are</u> the peacemakers,
   for they will be called chil<u>dren</u> of God.
   Blessed are those who are persecuted
      for right<u>eous</u>ness' sake,
   for theirs is the king<u>dom</u> of heaven.

Christ Is the Light

Presentation of the Lord (February 2), Introductory Rites

Alto Descant

Christ is the light, light of the na-tions, glo-ry of Is-ra-el, glo-ry for all.

Tenor Descant

Christ is the light, light of the na-tions, glo-ry of Is-ra-el, glo-ry for all.

Antiphon ♩. = 65

Capo 2:

Christ is the light, light of the na-tions, glo-ry of Is-ra-el, glo-ry for all.

...glo-ry of Is-ra-el, glo-ry for all.

...glo-ry of Is-ra-el, glo-ry for all.

Verse Tone with Response

Cantor:

All:

...glo-ry of Is-ra-el, glo-ry for all.

Verse Tone with Response

...glo-ry of Is-ra-el,   glo-ry for all.

Verses for the Gathering and Kindling of Candles

Luke 2:29-32

1. At last, all-powerful <u>Mas</u>ter,
   you give leave to <u>your</u> servant   *glory of Israel . . .*
   to go in <u>peace</u>,
   according to <u>your</u> promise.   *glory of Israel . . .*

2. For my eyes have seen your sal<u>va</u>tion
   which you have prepared for <u>all</u> nations,   *(simile)*
   the light to enlighten the <u>Gen</u>tiles,
   and give glory to Israel, <u>your</u> people.

Verses for the Entrance Procession of Candles

Psalm 122

1. I rejoiced when I heard them <u>say</u>:
   "Let us go to <u>God</u>'s house."   *glory of Israel . . .*
   And now our feet are <u>stand</u>ing
   within your gates, O <u>Je</u>rusalem.   *glory of Israel . . .*

2. Jerusalem is built as a <u>ci</u>ty
   strongly com<u>pact</u>.   *(simile)*
   It is there that the tribes go <u>up</u>,
   the tribes of <u>the</u> LORD.

3. For Israel's law it <u>is</u>,
   there to praise the <u>LORD</u>'s name.
   There were set the thrones of <u>judge</u>ment
   of the house <u>of</u> David.

4. For the peace of Jerusalem <u>pray</u>:
   "Peace be to <u>your</u> homes!
   May peace reign in your <u>walls</u>,
   in your pala<u>ces</u>, peace!"

5. For love of my family and <u>friends</u>
   I say: "Peace up<u>on</u> you."
   For love of the house of the <u>LORD</u>
   I will ask for <u>your</u> good.

A-213

Christ Is the Light

Presentation of the Lord (February 2), Song for the Table

Verse Tone with Response

...glo-ry of Is - ra - el, glo-ry for all.

Psalm 145

1. *[For this verse only, omit the tone repeat.]*
   I will give you glory, O God my <u>king</u>,
   I will bless your name <u>for</u> ever. *glory of Israel . . .*

2. I will bless you day after <u>day</u>
   and praise your name <u>for</u> ever. *glory of Israel . . .*
   You are great, LORD, highly to be <u>praised</u>,
   your greatness cannot <u>be</u> measured. *glory of Israel . . .*

3. Age to age shall proclaim your <u>works</u>,
   shall declare your might<u>y</u> deeds, *(simile)*
   shall speak of your splendor and <u>glory</u>,
   tell the tale of your wonder<u>ful</u> works.

4. They will speak of your terrible <u>deeds</u>,
   recount your greatness <u>and</u> might.
   They will recall your abundant <u>goodness</u>;
   age to age shall ring out <u>your</u> justice.

5. You are kind and full of compassion,
   slow to anger, abounding <u>in</u> love.
   How good you are, LORD, to <u>all</u>,
   compassionate to all <u>your</u> creatures.

6. All your creatures shall thank you, O <u>LORD</u>,
   and your friends shall repeat <u>their</u> blessing.
   They shall speak of the glory of your <u>reign</u>
   and declare your might, <u>O</u> God,

7. to make known to all your mighty <u>deeds</u>
   and the glorious splendor of <u>your</u> reign.
   Yours is an everlasting <u>kingdom</u>;
   your rule lasts from age <u>to</u> age.

8. You are faithful in all your <u>words</u>
   and loving in all <u>your</u> deeds.
   You support all those who are <u>falling</u>
   and raise up all who are <u>bowed</u> down.

9. The eyes of all creatures look to <u>you</u>
   and you give them their food in <u>due</u> season.
   You open wide your <u>hand</u>,
   grant the desires of all <u>who</u> live.

10. You are just in all your <u>ways</u>
    and loving in all <u>your</u> deeds.
    You are close to all who <u>call</u> you,
    who call on you from <u>their</u> hearts.

11. You grant the desires of those who <u>fear</u> you,
    you hear their cry and <u>you</u> save them.
    LORD, you protect all who <u>love</u> you;
    but the wicked you will utterly <u>destroy</u>.

12. Let me speak your praise, O <u>LORD</u>,
    let all peoples bless your hol<u>y</u> name,
    for <u>ever</u>,
    for ages <u>unending</u>.

A-214
John Was Sent from God
The Nativity of Saint John the Baptist (June 24), Song for the Day

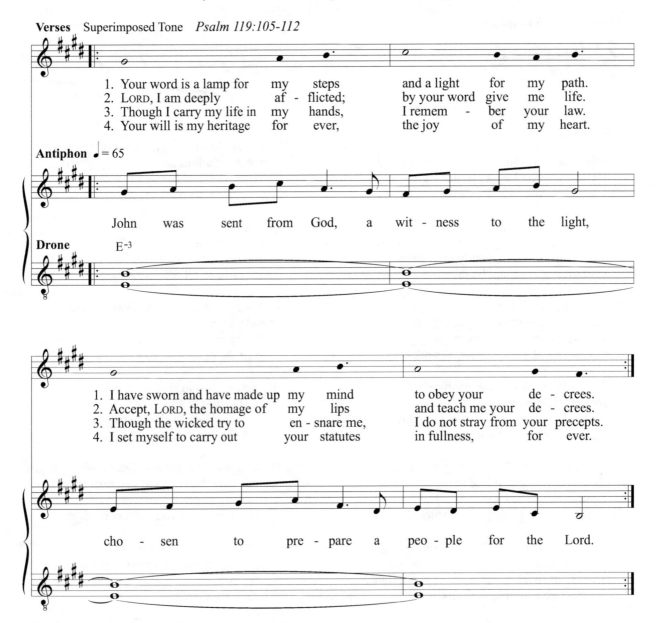

Verses Superimposed Tone *Psalm 119:105-112*

1. Your word is a lamp for my steps and a light for my path.
2. LORD, I am deeply af - flicted; by your word give me life.
3. Though I carry my life in my hands, I remem - ber your law.
4. Your will is my heritage for ever, the joy of my heart.

Antiphon ♩ = 65

John was sent from God, a wit - ness to the light,

Drone E⁻³

1. I have sworn and have made up my mind to obey your de - crees.
2. Accept, LORD, the homage of my lips and teach me your de - crees.
3. Though the wicked try to en - snare me, I do not stray from your precepts.
4. I set myself to carry out your statutes in fullness, for ever.

cho - sen to pre - pare a peo - ple for the Lord.

Performance Notes

The drone is preferably hummed (to an 'n' sound rather than an 'm' sound), but may also be sustained on the organ or played by guitars strumming an E chord without the 3rd on the first beat of every measure only.

I Will Praise You, I Will Thank You

A-215

The Nativity of Saint John the Baptist (June 24), Song for the Word

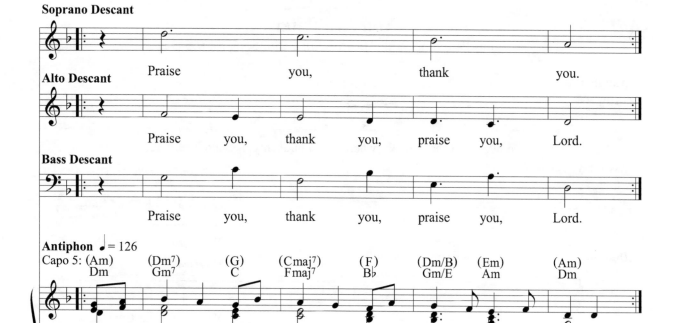

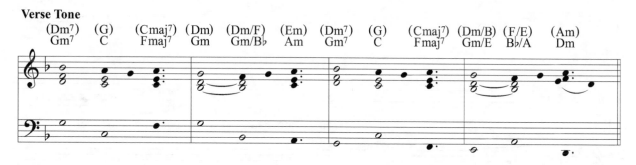

Psalm 139:1-3, 13-15

1. O LORD, you search me <u>and</u> you know me,
   you know my resting and my rising,
      you discern my purpose <u>from</u> afar.
   You mark when I walk <u>or</u> lie down,
   all my ways lie <u>o</u>pen to you.

2. For it was you who cre<u>at</u>ed my being,
   knit me together in my <u>mo</u>ther's womb.

I thank you for the wonder <u>of</u> my being,
for the wonders of all <u>your</u> creation.

3. Already you <u>knew</u> my soul,
   my body held no se<u>cret</u> from you
   when I was being <u>fa</u>shioned in secret
   and molded in the depths <u>of</u> the earth.

Performance Notes

In the first two full measures of the Antiphon, the accompaniment bass clef and alto/bass descant rhythms could be sung and played as two dotted quarter notes (as in the third full measure) instead of half note followed by quarter note.

A-216 → The Nativity of Saint John the Baptist (June 24), Song for the Table, *same as A-6*

A-217

You Are Peter

Saints Peter and Paul, Apostles (June 29), Song for the Day

Verse Tone

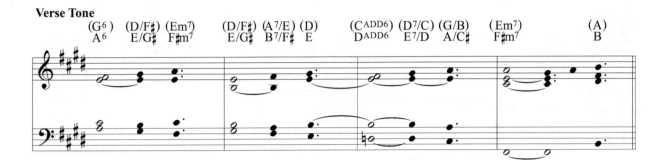

Psalm 116:10-19

1. I trusted, even when I said:
   "I am sorely afflicted,"
   and when I said in my alarm:
   "There is no one I can trust."

2. How can I repay the LORD
   for his goodness to me?
   The cup of salvation I will raise;
   I will call on the LORD's name.

3. My vows to the LORD I will fulfill
   before all the people.
   O precious in the eyes of the LORD
   is the death of the faithful.

4. Your servant, LORD, your servant am I;
   you have loosened my bonds.
   A thanksgiving sacrifice I make;
   I will call on the LORD's name.

5. My vows to the LORD I will fulfill
   before all the people,
   in the courts of the house of the LORD,
   in your midst, O Jerusalem.

Performance Notes

In the Antiphon, the assembly sings the full-size notes, imitating the cantor's melody, while choir members may add the descant part in cue-size notes. If by chance the assembly becomes confused and sings the descant part instead of the main melody at any point, this does not matter: a built-in congregational mistake that still fits! It would even be possible for the assembly to sing all their sections of the Antiphon to the same melody.

I Called in My Distress

A-218

Saints Peter and Paul, Apostles (June 29), Song for the Word

Psalm 34:2-9

1. I will bless the LORD <u>at</u> all times,
   God's praise always <u>on</u> my lips;
   God set me free.
   In the LORD my soul shall <u>make</u> its boast.
   The humble shall hear <u>and</u> be glad.
   God set me free.

2. Glorify the <u>LORD</u> with me.
   Together let us <u>praise</u> God's name.
   God set me free.
   I sought the LORD <u>and</u> was heard;
   from all my te<u>rrors</u> set free.
   God set me free.

3. Look towards God <u>and</u> be radiant;
   let your faces not <u>be</u> abashed.
   God set me free.
   When the poor cry out <u>the</u> LORD hears them
   and rescues them from all <u>their</u> distress.
   God set me free.

4. The angel of the LORD <u>is</u> encamped
   around those who fear <u>God</u>, to rescue them.
   God set me free.
   Taste and see that the <u>LORD</u> is good.
   They are happy who seek re<u>fuge</u> in God.
   God set me free.

Psalm text: The Grail (England), © 1963, 1986, 1993, 2000, The Grail, GIA Publications, Inc., agent. All rights reserved. Used with permission.
Music and antiphon text: © 2005, The Collegeville Composers Group. All rights reserved. Published and administered by the Liturgical Press, Collegeville, MN 56321.

If You Love Me, Feed My Lambs

Saints Peter and Paul, Apostles (June 29), Song for the Table

Psalm 80:2ac, 3bc, 9-12, 15-16, 18-19

1. O shepherd of Israel, <u>hear</u> us,
   shine forth from your cheru<u>bim</u> throne.
   O Lord, rouse up <u>your</u> might,
   O Lord, come to <u>our</u> help.

2. You brought a vine out <u>of</u> Egypt;
   to plant it you drove out <u>the</u> nations.
   Before it you cleared <u>the</u> ground;
   it took root and spread through <u>the</u> land.

3. The mountains were covered with <u>its</u> shadow,
   the cedars of God with <u>its</u> boughs.

It stretched out its branches to <u>the</u> sea,
to the Great River it stretched out <u>its</u> shoots.

4. God of hosts, turn again, we <u>implore</u>,
   look down from heaven <u>and</u> see.
   Visit this vine and <u>protect</u> it,
   the vine your right hand <u>has</u> planted.

5. May your hand be on the one you <u>have</u> chosen,
   the one you have given <u>your</u> strength.
   And we shall never forsake you <u>again</u>;
   give us life that we may call upon <u>your</u> name.

Performance Notes *The Antiphon may be sung SATB.*

The Lord Is King

A-221

The Transfiguration of the Lord (August 6), Song for the Word

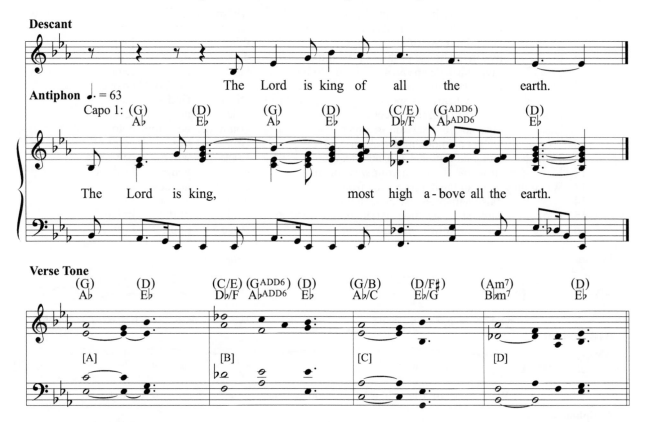

Psalm 97:1-6, 9

1. The LORD is king, let earth rejoice,
   let all the coastlands be glad.
   Surrounded by cloud and darkness;
   justice and right, God's throne.

2. A fire prepares the way;
   it burns up foes on every side.
   God's lightnings light up the world,
   the earth trembles at the sight.

3. The mountains melt like wax
   before the LORD of all the earth.
   The skies proclaim God's justice;
   all peoples see God's glory.

4. For you indeed are the LORD
   most high above all the earth,
   [Omit C]
   exalted far above all spirits.

A-222

We Shall Be Like You

The Transfiguration of the Lord (August 6), Song for the Table

Verses Superimposed Tone *Psalm 27:1, 4, 7-14*

1. The	LORD is my light and my help;	whom shall I	fear?
2. The	LORD is the stronghold of my life; before	whom shall I	shrink?
3. There is	one thing I ask of the LORD, for	this I	long,
4. to	live in the house of the LORD, all the	days of my	life,
5. to	savor the sweetness of the LORD, to be —	hold his	temple.
6. O	LORD, hear my voice when I call; have	mer - cy and	answer.
7. Of	you my heart has spoken:	"Seek God's	face."
8. It is your	face, O LORD, that I seek;	hide not your	face.
9. Dis -	miss not your servant in anger;	you have been my	help.
10.	Do not abandon or forsake me, O	God my	help!
11. Though	father and mother forsake me, the	LORD will re -	ceive me.
12. In -	struct me, LORD, in your way; on an	e - ven path	lead me.
13. When they	lie in ambush, protect me from my	e - nemies'	greed.
14.	False witnesses rise against me,	breath - ing out	fury.
15. I am	sure I shall see the LORD's goodness in the	land of the	living.
16. In the	LORD, hold firm and take heart.	Hope in the	LORD!

Descant

you are re-vealed.

Canon

We shall be like you when

Bass Descant

We shall be like you when you are re-vealed.

Antiphon ♩ = ca. 63

Capo 4: (Dm) (DmADD6/F) (Am) (F) (Dm) (Fmaj7) (ASUS4) (Am)
F♯m F♯mADD6/A C♯m A F♯m Amaj7 C♯SUS4 C♯m

We shall be like you when you are re-vealed.

A Woman Clothed with the Sun

Assumption of the Blessed Virgin Mary (August 15), Song for the Day

Song of Songs 2:13b-14; 4:8ab; 5:9; 6:1; 7:6

1. Arise, my love, my fair one, and <u>come</u> away.
   O my dove, in the clefts of the rock, in the covert <u>of</u> the cliff.

2. Let me see your face, let me <u>hear</u> your voice;
   for your voice is sweet, and your <u>face</u> is lovely.

3. Come with me from Leba<u>non</u>, my bride;
   come with <u>me</u> from Lebanon.

4. What is your beloved more than an<u>other</u> beloved,
   O fai<u>rest</u> of women?

5. Where has your beloved gone, O fai<u>rest</u> of women?
   Which way has your beloved turned, that we may seek <u>him</u> with you?

6. How fair and plea<u>sant</u> you are,
   O loved one, delec<u>ta</u>ble maiden!

A-224

Rise Up, O Lord

Assumption of the Blessed Virgin Mary (August 15), Song for the Word

Psalm 132:6-7, 9-10, 13-14

1. At Ephrata we heard of the ark;
   we found it in the plains of Yearim.
   "Let us go to the place of God's dwelling;
   let us go to kneel at God's footstool."

2. Your priests shall be clothed with holiness;
   your faithful shall ring out their joy.
   For the sake of David your servant
   do not reject your anointed.

3. For the LORD has chosen Zion;
   has desired it for a dwelling:
   "This is my resting-place for ever,
   here have I chosen to live."

My Soul Rejoices in God

Assumption of the Blessed Virgin Mary (August 15), Song for the Table
The Immaculate Conception of the Blessed Virgin Mary (December 8), Song for the Table

Luke 1:46-55

1. My soul glorifies the Lord, *My soul rejoices . . .*
   my spirit rejoices in God, my Savior. *All my being . . .*

2. He looks on his servant in her lowliness; *(simile)*
   henceforth all generations will call me blessed.

3. The Almighty works marvels for me.
   Holy his name!

4. His mercy is from age to age
   on those who fear him.

5. He puts forth his arm in strength
   and scatters the proud-hearted.

6. He casts the mighty from their thrones
   and raises the lowly.

7. He fills the starving with good things,
   sends the rich away empty.

8. He protects Israel his servant,
   remembering his mercy,

9. the mercy promised to our fathers,
   for Abraham and his children for ever.

A-227   # Rise Up and Tell All Your Children

Exaltation of the Holy Cross (September 14), Song for the Word

Psalm 78:1-2, 34-38

1. Give heed, my people, <u>to</u> my teaching;
   turn your ear to the words <u>of</u> my mouth.
   Do not forget . . .
   I will open my mouth <u>in</u> a parable
   and reveal hidden lessons <u>of</u> the past.
   Do not forget . . .

2. When God slew them <u>they</u> would seek him,
   return and seek <u>him</u> in earnest. *(simile)*
   They remembered that God <u>was</u> their rock,
   God, the Most High, <u>their</u> redeemer.

3. But the words they spoke <u>were</u> mere flattery;
   they lied to God <u>with</u> their lips.
   For their hearts were not tru<u>ly</u> sincere;
   they were not faithful <u>to</u> the covenant.

4. Yet the one who is full <u>of</u> compassion
   forgave them their <u>sin</u> and spared them.
   So often God held <u>back</u> the anger
   that might have been stirred <u>up</u> in rage.

Lose Your Life and Save It

Exaltation of the Holy Cross (September 14), Song for the Table
Thirteenth Sunday in Ordinary Time, Song for the Table
Twenty-second Sunday in Ordinary Time, Song for the Table

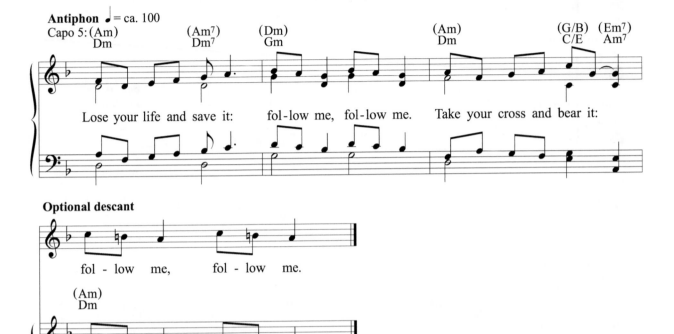

Lose your life and save it: fol-low me, fol-low me. Take your cross and bear it:

fol - low me, fol - low me.

fol - low me, fol - low me.

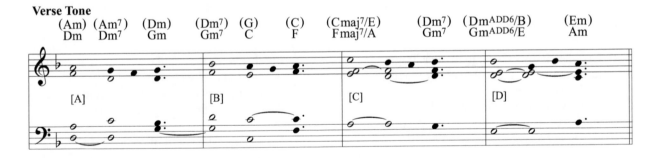

Psalm 116:1-9 (10-19)

1. I love the LORD, for the LORD has heard
   the cry of <u>my</u> appeal.
   The LORD was att<u>entive</u> to me
   in the day <u>when</u> I called.

2. They surrounded me, the <u>snares</u> of death,
   with the anguish <u>of</u> the tomb;
   they caught me, sorrow <u>and</u> distress.
   I called on the LORD's name.
      O LORD my <u>God</u>, deliver me!

3. How gracious is the <u>LORD</u>, and just;
   our God <u>has</u> compassion.
   The LORD protects the <u>simple</u> hearts;
   I was helpless <u>so</u> God saved me.

4. Turn back, my soul, <u>to</u> your rest
   for the LORD <u>has</u> been good,
   and has kept my <u>soul</u> from death,
   my eyes from tears, my <u>feet</u> from stumbling.

5. *A* I will walk in the presence <u>of</u> the LORD
   D in the land <u>of</u> the living.

Verse Tone

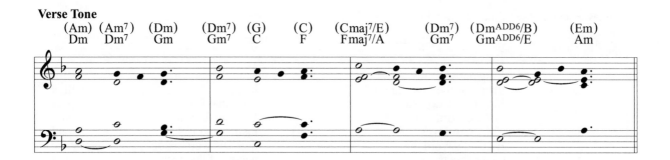

Additional verses if required (Psalm 116:10-19)

6. I trusted, even <u>when</u> I said:
   "I am sore<u>ly</u> afflicted,"
   and when I said in <u>my</u> alarm:
   "There is no one <u>I</u> can trust."

7. How can I re<u>pay</u> the LORD
   for his good<u>ness</u> to me?
   The cup of salvation <u>I</u> will raise;
   I will call <u>on</u> the LORD's name.

8. My vows to the LORD I <u>will</u> fulfill
   before <u>all</u> the people.
   O precious in the eyes <u>of</u> the LORD
   is the death <u>of</u> the faithful.

9. Your servant, LORD, your ser<u>vant</u> am I;
   you have loos<u>ened</u> my bonds.
   A thanksgiving sacri<u>fice</u> I make;
   I will call <u>on</u> the LORD's name.

10. My vows to the LORD I <u>will</u> fulfill
    before <u>all</u> the people,
    in the courts of the house <u>of</u> the LORD,
    in your midst, <u>O</u> Jerusalem.

Rejoice in the Lord on This Feast of the Saints

All Saints (November 1), Song for the Day

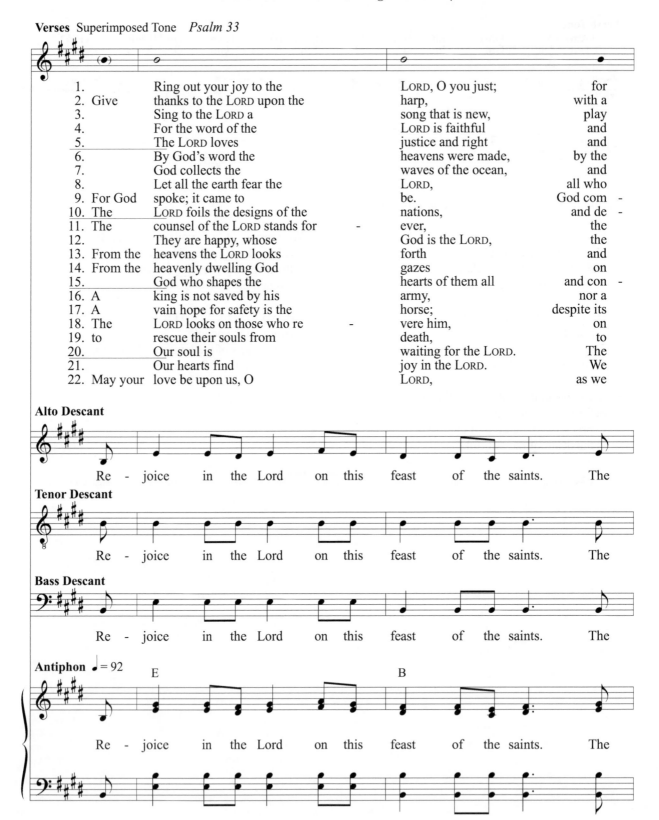

Verses Superimposed Tone   *Psalm 33*

#			
1.		Ring out your joy to the	LORD, O you just;	for
2.	Give	thanks to the LORD upon the	harp,	with a
3.		Sing to the LORD a	song that is new,	play
4.		For the word of the	LORD is faithful	and
5.		The LORD loves	justice and right	and
6.		By God's word the	heavens were made,	by the
7.		God collects the	waves of the ocean,	and
8.		Let all the earth fear the	LORD,	all who
9.	For God	spoke; it came to	be.	God com -
10.	The	LORD foils the designs of the	nations,	and de -
11.	The	counsel of the LORD stands for - ever,	the
12.		They are happy, whose	God is the LORD,	the
13.	From the	heavens the LORD looks	forth	and
14.	From the	heavenly dwelling God	gazes	on
15.		God who shapes the	hearts of them all	and con -
16.	A	king is not saved by his	army,	nor a
17.	A	vain hope for safety is the	horse;	despite its
18.	The	LORD looks on those who re - vere him,	on
19.	to	rescue their souls from	death,	to
20.		Our soul is	waiting for the LORD.	The
21.		Our hearts find	joy in the LORD.	We
22.	May your	love be upon us, O	LORD,	as we

Alto Descant

Re - joice in the Lord on this feast of the saints. The

Tenor Descant

Re - joice in the Lord on this feast of the saints. The

Bass Descant

Re - joice in the Lord on this feast of the saints. The

Antiphon ♩ = 92   E   B

Re - joice in the Lord on this feast of the saints. The

Verses Superimposed Tone

1. praise is fitting for loyal hearts.
2. ten-stringed lute play your songs.
3. loudly with all your skill.
4. all his works done in truth.
5. fills the earth with his love.
6. breath of his mouth all the stars.
7. stores up the depths of the sea.
8. live in the world stand in awe.
9. manded; it sprang into being.
10. feats the plans of the peoples.
11. plans of God's heart from age to age.
12. people who are chosen as his own.
13. sees all the peoples of the earth.
14. all the dwellers on the earth;
15. siders all their deeds.
16. warrior preserved by his strength.
17. power it cannot save.
18. those who hope in his love,
19. keep them alive in famine.
20. LORD is our help and our shield.
21. trust in God's holy name.
22. place all our hope in you.

Alto Descant

an - gels re - joice and give praise to the Son.

Tenor Descant

an - gels re - joice and give praise to the Son.

Bass Descant

an - gels re - joice and give praise to the Son.

Antiphon

an - gels re - joice and give praise to the Son.

Lord, This Is the People

All Saints (November 1), Song for the Word

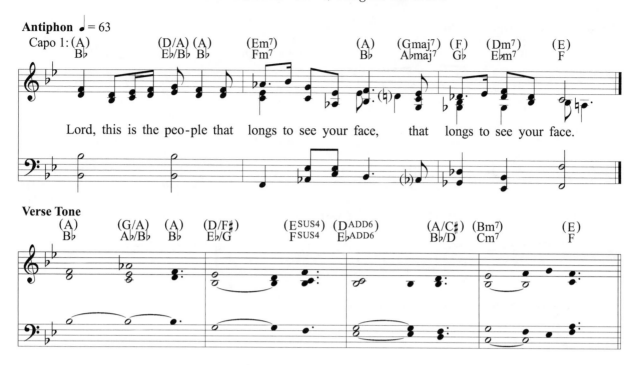

Psalm 24:1-6

1. The LORD's is the earth and its fullness,
   the world and all its peoples.
   It is God who set it on the seas,
   who made it firm on the waters.

2. Who shall climb the mountain of the LORD?
   Who shall stand in God's holy place?
   Those with clean hands and pure hearts,
   who desire not worthless things.

3. They shall receive blessings from the LORD
   and reward from the God who saves them.
   These are the ones who seek,
   seek the face of the God of Jacob.

The Spirit and the Bride Say "Come!"

All Saints (November 1), Song for the Table

Matthew 5:3-10; Isaiah 66:10-14a

1. Blessed are the poor in spirit,
   for theirs is the kingdom of heaven.
   Blessed are those who mourn,
   for they will be comforted.

2. Blessed are the meek,
   for they will inherit the earth.
   Blessed are those who hunger and
      thirst for righteousness,
   for they will be filled.

3. Blessed are the merciful,
   for they will receive mercy.
   Blessed are the pure in heart,
   for they will see God.

4. Blessed are the peacemakers,
   for they will be called children of God.
   Blessed are those who are persecuted for
      righteousness' sake,
   for theirs is the kingdom of heaven.

5. Rejoice with Jerusalem,
   and be glad for her, all you who love her;
   rejoice with her in joy,
   all you who mourn over her—

6. that you may nurse and be satisfied
   from her consoling breast;
   that you may drink deeply with delight
   from her glorious bosom.

Verse Tone

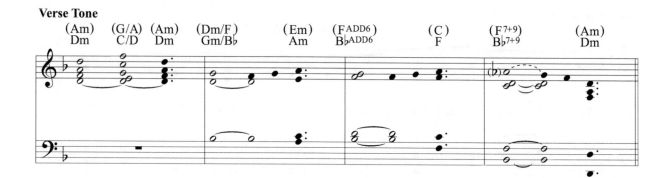

7. For thus <u>says</u> the L<small>ORD</small>:
   I will extend prosperity to her <u>like</u> a river,
   and the wealth <u>of</u> the nations
   like an over<u>flow</u>ing stream;

8. and you shall nurse and be <u>carried</u> on her <u>arm</u>,
   and dandled <u>on</u> her knees.
   As a mother com<u>forts</u> her child,
   so I will <u>com</u>fort you.

9. You shall be <u>comforted</u> in Je<u>ru</u>salem.
   You shall see, and your heart <u>shall</u> rejoice;
   your bo<u>dies</u> shall flourish
   <u>like</u> the grass.

10. And it <u>shall</u> be <u>known</u>
    that the hand of the L<small>ORD</small> is <u>with</u> his servants,
    and his <u>indignation</u>
    is a<u>gainst</u> his enemies.

Verse Tone (alternate setting)

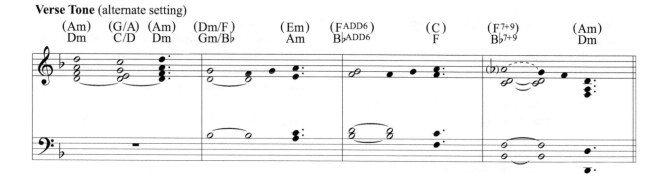

Performance Notes

In both Antiphon and tone, the A-naturals with flats in parentheses indicate optional "blue notes."
The double underlined word "like" in verse nine is sung over the slurred notes.

God, Who Raised Jesus from the Dead

All Souls (November 2), Song for the Day

Antiphon ♩ = ca. 92

God, who raised Je-sus from the dead will give our bo-dies life by the Spi-rit with-in.

[A] [B]

Verse Tone

Psalm 16:1-2, 5-11

1. Preserve me, God, I take refuge in you.
[Repeat A]
   I say to you, LORD: "You are my God.
   My happiness lies in you alone."

2. O LORD, it is you who are my portion and cup,
   it is you yourself who are my prize.

3. The lot marked out for me is my delight,
   welcome indeed the heritage that falls to me!

4. I will bless you, LORD, you give me counsel,
   and even at night direct my heart.

5. I keep you, LORD, ever in my sight;
   since you are at my right hand, I shall stand firm.

6. And so my heart rejoices, my soul is glad;
   even my body shall rest in safety.

7. For you will not leave my soul among the dead,
   nor let your beloved know decay.

8. You will show me the path of life,
   the fullness of joy in your presence,
[Repeat B]
   at your right hand happiness for ever.

My Shepherd Is the Lord

All Souls (November 2), Song for the Word: Option I

Psalm 23

1. Fresh and green are the pastures *there is . . .*
   where you give me repose. *my God . . .*
   Near restful waters you lead me *there is . . .*
   to revive my drooping spirit. *my God . . .*

2. You guide me along the right path; *(simile)*
   you are true to your name.
   If I should walk in the valley of darkness
   no evil would I fear.
   You are there with your crook and your staff;
   with these you give me comfort.

3. You have prepared a banquet for me
   in the sight of my foes.
   My head you have anointed with oil;
   my cup is overflowing.

4. Surely goodness and kindness shall follow me
   all the days of my life.
   In the LORD's own house shall I dwell
   for ever and ever.

A-234

Lord, Listen to My Prayer
All Souls (November 2), Song for the Word: Option II

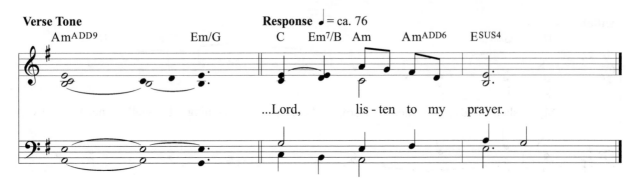

Psalm 143   *[The Lectionary selections for the day are indicated by an asterisk.]*

1. * Lord, turn your ear to <u>my</u> appeal: *Lord, listen . . .*
2. * You are faithful, you are <u>just</u>; give answer: *(simile)*
3. Do not call your ser<u>vant</u> to judgement:
4. No one is just <u>in</u> your sight:
5. The enemy pur<u>sues</u> my soul:
6. The enemy has crushed my life <u>to</u> the ground:
7. The enemy has made me <u>dwell</u> in darkness:
8. The enemy has made me like the dead, <u>long</u>-forgotten:
9. Therefore my <u>spirit</u> fails:
10. My heart is <u>numb</u> within me:
11. * I remember the days <u>that</u> are past:
12. * I ponder <u>all</u> your works:
13. * I muse on what your <u>hand</u> has wrought:
14. * To you I stretch <u>out</u> my hands:
15. * Like a parched land my soul <u>thirsts</u> for you:
16. * Lord, make <u>haste</u> and answer:
17. * My spirit <u>fails</u> within me:
18. Do not <u>hide</u> your face:
19. Do not let me become like those <u>in</u> the grave:
20. * In the morning let me <u>know</u> your love:
21. * I put my <u>trust</u> in you:
22. Make me know the way <u>I</u> should walk:
23. To you I lift <u>up</u> my soul:
24. Rescue me, Lord, <u>from</u> my enemies:
25. I have fled to <u>you</u> for refuge:
26. * Teach me to <u>do</u> your will:
27. * You, O Lord, <u>are</u> my God:
28. * Let your good <u>spirit</u> guide me:
29. * Lead me in ways that are le<u>vel</u> and smooth:
30. For your name's sake, Lord, <u>save</u> my life:
31. In your justice save my soul <u>from</u> distress:
32. In your love make an end <u>of</u> my foes:
33. Destroy all those <u>who</u> oppress me:
34. I am your <u>servant</u>, Lord:

How I Thirst for You

A-235

All Souls (November 2), Song for the Word: Option III

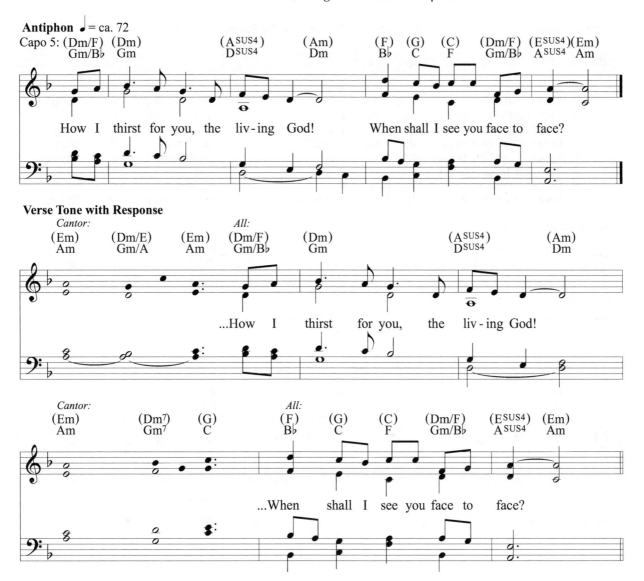

Psalm 42:2-3, 5cdef; 43:3-5

1. Like the deer that yearns for <u>running</u> streams   *How I thirst . . .*
   so my soul is yearning for <u>you</u>, my God.   *When shall I see . . .*

2. My soul is thirsting for God, the God <u>of</u> my life;   *(simile)*
   when can I enter and see the <u>face</u> of God?

3. I would lead the rejoicing crowd into the <u>house</u> of God,
   amid cries of gladness and thanksgiving, the throng <u>wild</u> with joy.

4. O send forth your light and your truth; let these <u>be</u> my guide.
   Let them bring me to your holy mountain, to the place <u>where</u> you dwell.

5. And I will come to your altar, O God, the God <u>of</u> my joy.
   My redeemer, I will thank you on the harp, O <u>God</u>, my God.

6. Why are you cast down, my soul, why <u>groan</u> within me?
   Hope in God; I will praise yet again my savior <u>and</u> my God.

Eat My Flesh and Drink My Blood

All Souls (November 2), Song for the Table

Verses   Superimposed Tone   *cf. John 11:25-26; 2 Esdras 2:35, 34; Psalm 27:1, 4, 6c-10, 13-14*

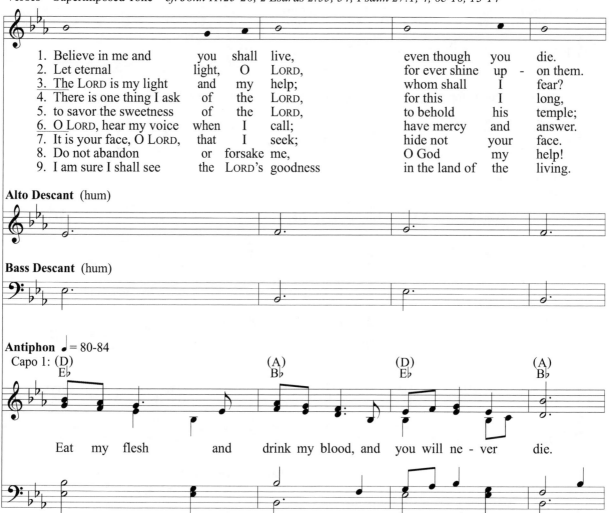

1. Believe in me and you shall live, even though you die.
2. Let eternal light, O LORD, for ever shine up - on them.
3. The LORD is my light and my help; whom shall I fear?
4. There is one thing I ask of the LORD, for this I long,
5. to savor the sweetness of the LORD, to behold his temple;
6. O LORD, hear my voice when I call; have mercy and answer.
7. It is your face, O LORD, that I seek; hide not your face.
8. Do not abandon or forsake me, O God my help!
9. I am sure I shall see the LORD's goodness in the land of the living.

Alto Descant (hum)

Bass Descant (hum)

Antiphon ♩ = 80-84

Capo 1: (D)

Eat my flesh and drink my blood, and you will ne - ver die.

Verses   Superimposed Tone

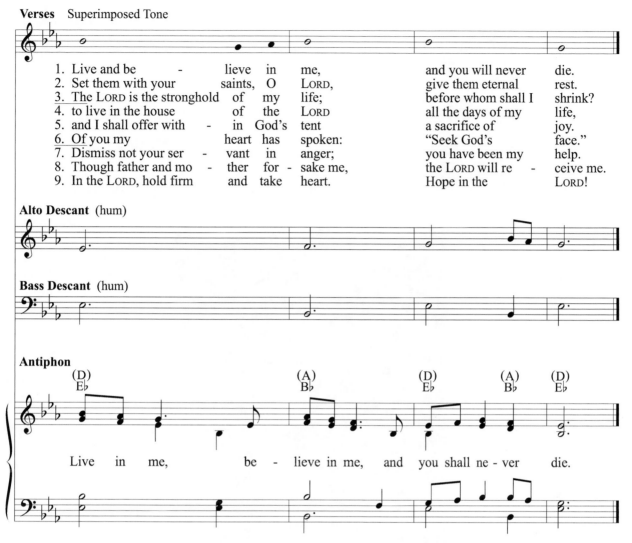

1. Live and be - lieve in me,   and you will never die.
2. Set them with your saints, O LORD,   give them eternal rest.
3. The LORD is the stronghold of my life;   before whom shall I shrink?
4. to live in the house of the LORD   all the days of my life,
5. and I shall offer with - in God's tent   a sacrifice of joy.
6. Of you my heart has spoken: "Seek God's face."
7. Dismiss not your ser - vant in anger;   you have been my help.
8. Though father and mo - ther for - sake me,   the LORD will re - ceive me.
9. In the LORD, hold firm and take heart.   Hope in the LORD!

Alto Descant (hum)

Bass Descant (hum)

Antiphon

(D)   (A)   (D)   (A)   (D)
Eb   Bb   Eb   Bb   Eb

Live in me,   be - lieve in me,   and you shall ne - ver die.

I Will Dwell with You

A-237

Dedication of the Lateran Basilica (November 9), Song for the Day

Verses Superimposed Tone *Revelation 21:1a, 2-5ab, 6; 22:17*

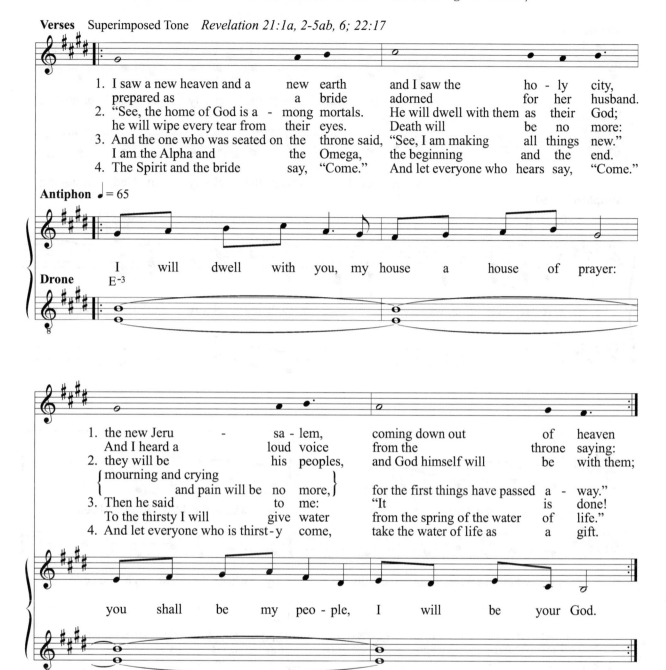

1. I saw a new heaven and a new earth and I saw the ho - ly city,
prepared as a bride adorned for her husband.
2. "See, the home of God is a - mong mortals. He will dwell with them as their God;
he will wipe every tear from their eyes. Death will be no more:
3. And the one who was seated on the throne said, "See, I am making all things new."
I am the Alpha and the Omega, the beginning and the end.
4. The Spirit and the bride say, "Come." And let everyone who hears say, "Come."

Antiphon ♩ = 65

Drone E⁻³

I will dwell with you, my house a house of prayer:

1. the new Jeru - sa - lem, coming down out of heaven
And I heard a loud voice from the throne saying:
2. they will be his peoples, and God himself will be with them;
{ mourning and crying
and pain will be no more, } for the first things have passed a - way."
3. Then he said to me: "It is done!
To the thirsty I will give water from the spring of the water of life."
4. And let everyone who is thirst - y come, take the water of life as a gift.

you shall be my peo - ple, I will be your God.

Performance Notes

The drone is preferably hummed (to an 'n' sound rather than an 'm' sound), but may also be sustained on the organ or played by guitars strumming an E chord without the 3rd on the first beat of every measure only.
Note the correct accentuation of "Omega" in verse 3, with the stress on the first and not the second syllable.

A River Flows

A-238

Dedication of the Lateran Basilica (November 9), Song for the Word

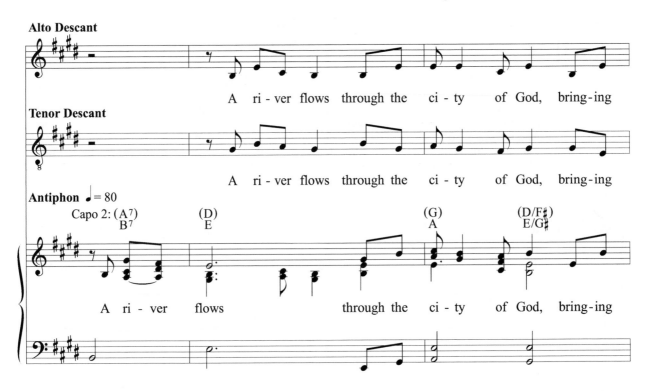

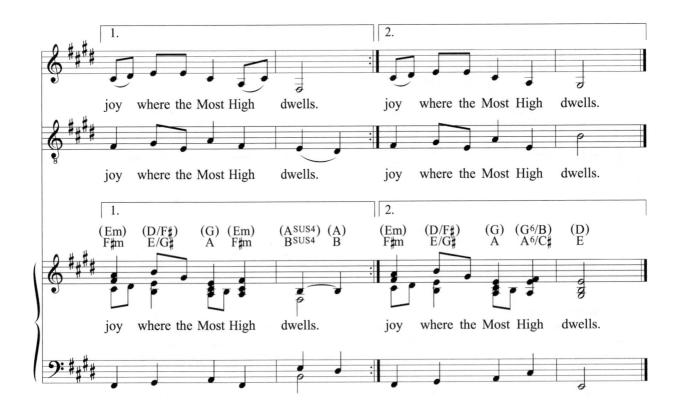

Verse Tone

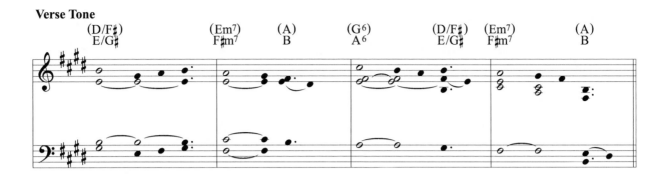

Psalm 46:2-3, 5-6, 11-12

1. God is for us a re<u>fuge</u> and strength,
   a helper close at hand, in time of dis<u>tress</u>,
   so we shall not fear though the <u>earth</u> should rock,
   though the mountains fall into the depths <u>of</u> the sea.

2. The waters of a river give joy <u>to</u> God's city,
   the holy place where the Most <u>High</u> dwells.
   God is within, it can<u>not</u> be shaken;
   God will help it at the dawning <u>of</u> the day.

3. "Be still and know that <u>I</u> am God,
   supreme among the nations, supreme on <u>the</u> earth!"
   The LORD of <u>hosts</u> is with us;
   the God of Jacob <u>is</u> our stronghold.

Ask and Receive

Dedication of the Lateran Basilica (November 9), Song for the Table

A-239

Psalms 133; 134; 135:1-4, 13-14

1. How good and how pleasant it <u>is</u>,
[omit B-C]
    when people <u>live</u> in unity.

2. It is like precious oil upon the <u>head</u>,
    running down upon the <u>beard</u>,
    running down upon <u>Aa</u>ron's beard,
    upon the collar <u>of</u> his robes.

3. It is like the dew of <u>Her</u>mon
    which falls on the heights of <u>Zi</u>on.
    For there the Lord gives <u>bless</u>ing,
    <u>life</u> for ever.

4. O come, bless the <u>Lord</u>,
    all you who serve the <u>Lord</u>,
    who stand in the house <u>of</u> the Lord,
    in the courts of the house <u>of</u> our God.

5. Lift up your hands to the <u>ho</u>ly place
    and bless the Lord through the <u>night</u>.
    May the Lord bless <u>you</u> from Zion,
    God who made both hea<u>ven</u> and earth.

6. Alleluia! Praise the name of the <u>Lord</u>,
    praise, you servants of the <u>Lord</u>,
    who stand in the house <u>of</u> the Lord,
    in the courts of the house <u>of</u> our God.

7. Praise the Lord, for the Lord is <u>good</u>.
    Praise God's name; God is <u>gra</u>cious.
    For Jacob has been chosen <u>by</u> the Lord;
    Israel for God's <u>own</u> possession.

8. Lord, your name stands for <u>ev</u>er,
    unforgotten from age to <u>age</u>,
    for the Lord does justice <u>for</u> his people;
    the Lord takes pity <u>on</u> his servants.

A-240 **As a Bridegroom Rejoices**

The Immaculate Conception of the Blessed Virgin Mary (December 8), Song for the Day

Descant 2

...and your God will re - joice, will re - joice o - ver you.

Verse Tone with Response

Cantor:
C   Cmaj⁷/E   Dm⁷   G

All:
F/A   Cmaj⁷/E   Dm⁷ Gˢᵁˢ⁴   C

...and your God will re - joice, will re - joice o - ver you.

Isaiah 61:10–62:5

1. *[For this verse only, omit the tone repeat.]*
   I will greatly rejoice in the LORD,
   my whole being shall exult in my God.
   and your God will rejoice . . .

2. He has clothed me with the garments of salvation,
   he has covered me with the robe of righteousness,
   and your God will rejoice . . .
   as a bridegroom decks himself with a garland,
   and as a bride adorns herself with her jewels.
   and your God will rejoice . . .

3. For as the earth brings forth its shoots,
   and as a garden causes what is sown in it
      to spring up,   *(simile)*
   so the LORD God will cause righteousness
      and praise
   to spring up before all the nations.

4. For Zion's sake I will not keep silent,
   and for Jerusalem's sake I will not rest,
   until her vindication shines out like the dawn,
   and her salvation like a burning torch.

5. The nations shall see your vindication,
   and all the kings your glory;
   and you shall be called by a new name
   that the mouth of the LORD shall give.

6. You shall be a crown of beauty
      in the hand of the LORD
   and a royal diadem in the hand of your God.
   You shall no more be termed Forsaken,
   and your land shall no more be termed Desolate;

7. but you shall be called My Delight Is in Her,
   and your land Married;
   for the LORD delights in you,
   and your land shall be married.

8. For as a young man marries a young woman,
   so shall your builder marry you,
   and as the bridegroom rejoices over the bride,
   so shall your God rejoice over you.

The Immaculate Conception of the Blessed Virgin Mary (December 8), Song for the Word,

same as A-79 ← **A-241**

The Immaculate Conception of the Blessed Virgin Mary (December 8), Song for the Table,

same as A-225 ← **A-242**

A-244 Happy Are They Who Dwell in Your House

Anniversary of the Dedication of a Church, Song for the Word: Option I

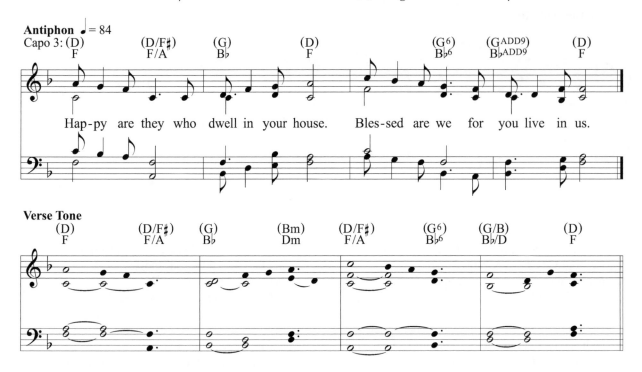

Psalm 84:3-12   *[The Lectionary selections for the day are indicated by an asterisk.]*

1. * My soul is longing and yearning,
   * is yearning for the courts of the LORD.
   * My heart and my soul ring out their joy
   * to God, the living God.

2. * The sparrow herself finds a home
   * and the swallow a home for her brood;
   * she lays her young by your altars,
   * LORD of hosts, my king and my God.

3. * They are happy, who dwell in your house,
   * for ever singing your praise.
   They are happy, whose strength is in you,
   in whose hearts are the roads to Zion.

4. As they go through the Bitter Valley
   they make it a place of springs.
   They walk with ever-growing strength,
   they will see the God of gods in Zion.

5. O LORD God of hosts, hear my prayer,
   give ear, O God of Jacob.
   * Turn your eyes, O God, our shield,
   * look on the face of your anointed.

6. * One day within your courts
   * is better than a thousand elsewhere.
   * The threshold of the house of God
   * I prefer to the dwellings of the wicked.

7. For the LORD God is a rampart, a shield.
   The LORD will give us favor and glory.
   The LORD will not refuse any good
   to those who walk without blame.

Venite, Adoremus

Anniversary of the Dedication of a Church, Song for the Word: Option II
Fifth Sunday in Ordinary Time, Song for the Week

A-245

Verses Superimposed Tone *Psalm 95:1-9*

*1. Come,   ring out our joy to the LORD;   hail the rock who saves us.
*2. Let us   come before God, giving thanks,   with   songs let us hail the LORD.
*3. A   mighty God is the LORD,   a   great king above all gods,
*4. in God's hands are the depths of the earth;   the   heights of the mountains as well.
*5. The   sea belongs to God, who made it   and the dry land shaped by his hands.
*6. Come   in; let us bow and bend low;   let us kneel before the God who made us
*7. for   this is our God and we   the   people who belong to his pasture,
*8.   we are the flock   that is led by God's hand.
 9.   O that today you would   listen to God's voice!
10. "Harden not your hearts as at Meribah,   as on that day at Massah in the desert;
11.   harden not your hearts   as when your ancestors put me to the test;
12.   harden not your hearts   as when your ancestors tried me, though they saw my work."

Performance Notes

Stanzas 1–8 are the Lectionary verses for the Anniversary of the Dedication of a Church.

The Antiphon can be used as an ostinato chant, or with psalm verses. When using the psalm, the Antiphon should be established before the cantor begins to chant the psalm verses. As the verses are chanted, the first half of the Antiphon can be sung quietly underneath with its text, or simply hummed. The second half of the Antiphon (with its text) then becomes a refrain at the end of each verse.

A-247

You Are God's Temple

Anniversary of the Dedication of a Church, Song for the Table

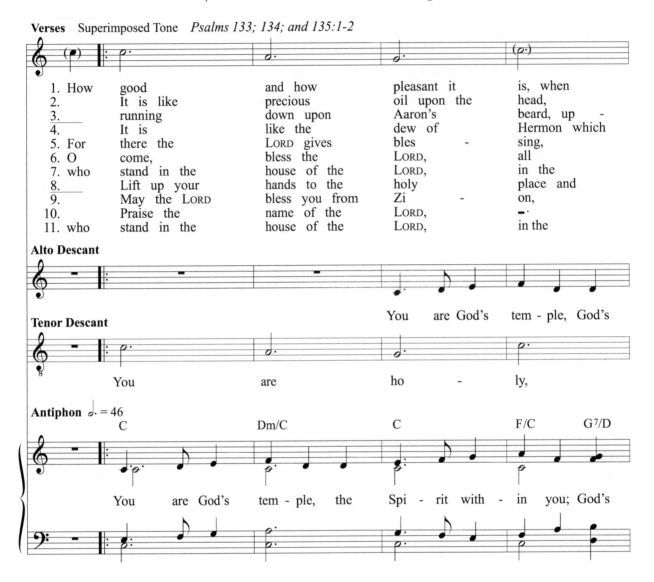

Verses   Superimposed Tone   *Psalms 133; 134; and 135:1-2*

1. How	good	and how	pleasant it	is, when
2.	It is like	precious	oil upon the	head,
3.	running	down upon	Aaron's	beard, up -
4.	It is	like the	dew of	Hermon which
5. For	there the	LORD gives	bles -	sing,
6. O	come,	bless the	LORD,	all
7. who	stand in the	house of the	LORD,	in the
8.	Lift up your	hands to the	holy	place and
9.	May the LORD	bless you from	Zi -	on,
10.	Praise the	name of the	LORD,	-
11. who	stand in the	house of the	LORD,	in the

Alto Descant

You   are God's   tem - ple, God's

Tenor Descant

You   are   ho - ly,

Antiphon ♩. = 46

C   Dm/C   C   F/C   G⁷/D

You   are God's   tem - ple, the   Spi - rit with - in   you; God's

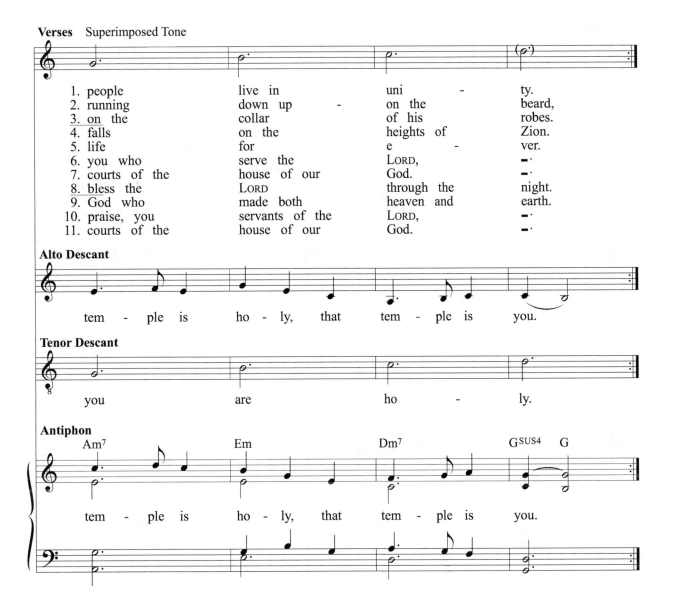

Verses Superimposed Tone

1. people   live in   uni   -   ty.
2. running   down up   -   on the   beard,
3. on the   collar   of his   robes.
4. falls   on the   heights of   Zion.
5. life   for   e   -   ver.
6. you who   serve the   LORD,   -.
7. courts of the house of our God.   -.
8. bless the   LORD   through the   night.
9. God who   made both   heaven and   earth.
10. praise, you servants of the LORD,   -.
11. courts of the house of our God.   -.

Alto Descant

tem - ple is   ho - ly,   that   tem - ple is   you.

Tenor Descant

you   are   ho   -   ly.

Antiphon

Am⁷   Em   Dm⁷   G^SUS4   G

tem - ple is   ho - ly,   that   tem - ple is   you.

Performance Notes

The Tenor Descant should not be sung while the cantor is singing the Superimposed Verses, but only when the Antiphon is sung independently of the Verses.

Sing and Make Music

Thanksgiving Day, Song for the Day

Verse Tone

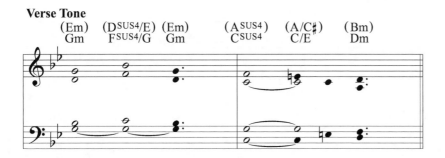

Psalm 147

1. Alleluia, alleluia!
   Sing praise to the LORD who is good.

2. Sing to our God who is loving:
   to God our praise is due.

3. The LORD builds up Jerusalem
   and brings back Israel's exiles.

4. God heals the broken-hearted,
   and binds up all their wounds.

5. God fixes the number of the stars;
   and calls each one by its name.

6. Our LORD is great and almighty;
   God's wisdom can never be measured.

7. The LORD raises the lowly;
   and humbles the wicked to the dust.

8. O sing to the LORD, giving thanks;
   sing psalms to our God with the harp.

9. God covers the heavens with clouds,
   and prepares the rain for the earth.

10. God makes mountains sprout with grass
    and with plants to serve our needs.

11. God provides the beasts with their food
    and the young ravens when they cry.

12. God takes no delight in horses' power
    nor pleasure in warriors' strength.

13. The LORD delights in those who revere him,
    in those who wait for his love.

14. O praise the LORD, Jerusalem!
    Zion, praise your God!

15. God has strengthened the bars of your gates,
    and has blessed the children within you.

16. God has established peace on your borders,
    and feeds you with finest wheat.

17. God sends out word to the earth
    and swiftly runs the command.

18. God showers down snow white as wool,
    and scatters hoarfrost like ashes.

19. God hurls down hailstones like crumbs,
    and causes the waters to freeze.

20. God sends forth a word and it melts them:
    at the breath of God's mouth the waters flow.

21. God makes his word known to Jacob,
    to Israel his laws and decrees.

22. God has not dealt thus with other nations;
    has not taught them divine decrees. Alleluia!

A-249

Our God Has Blessed Us

Thanksgiving Day, Song for the Word

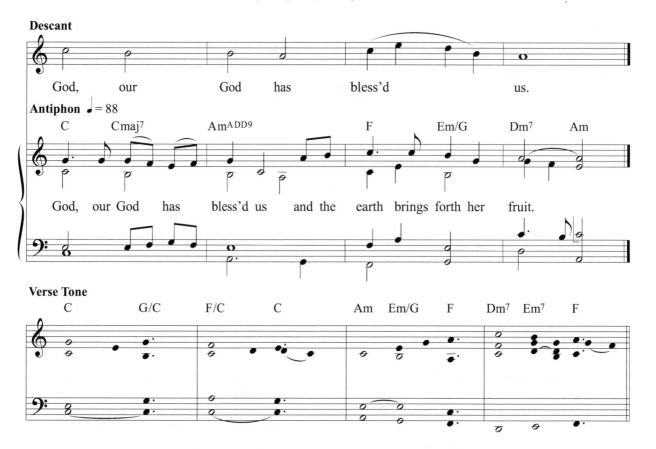

Psalm 67

1. O God, be gracious <u>and</u> bless us
   and let your face shed its light <u>up</u>on us.
   So will your ways be known <u>up</u>on earth
   and all nations learn your <u>sav</u>ing help.

2. Let the nations be glad and <u>ex</u>ult
   for you rule the world <u>with</u> justice.
   With fairness you <u>rule</u> the peoples,
   you guide the <u>nations</u> on earth.

3. The earth has yielded <u>its</u> fruit
   for God, our God, <u>has</u> blessed us.
   May God still <u>give</u> us blessing
   till the ends of the earth <u>stand</u> in awe.

4. Let the peoples praise you, <u>O</u> God;
   let all the <u>peoples</u> praise you.
   Let the peoples praise <u>you</u>, O God,
   let all the <u>peoples</u> praise you.

May God Grant Us Joy of Heart

Thanksgiving Day, Song for the Table

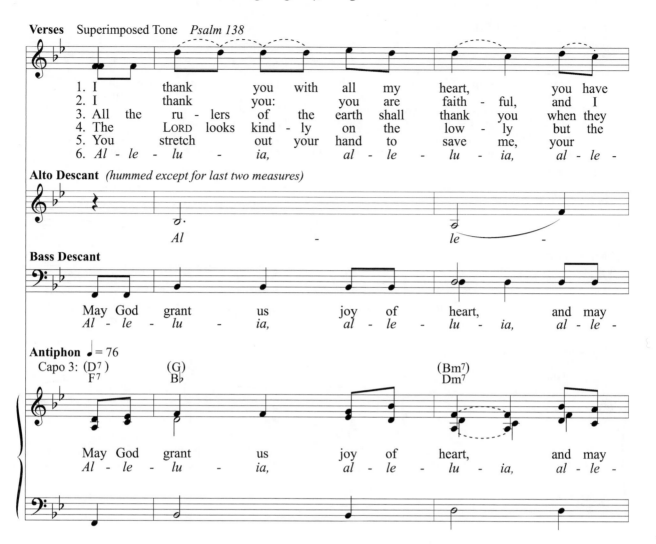

Verses Superimposed Tone *Psalm 138*

1. I thank you with all my heart, you have
2. I thank you: you are faith - ful, and I
3. All the ru - lers of the earth shall thank you when they
4. The LORD looks kind - ly on the low - ly but the
5. You stretch out your hand to save me, your
6. *Al - le - lu - ia, al - le - lu - ia, al - le -*

Alto Descant *(hummed except for last two measures)*

Al - le -

Bass Descant

May God grant us joy of heart, and may
Al - le - lu - ia, al - le - lu - ia, al - le -

Antiphon ♩ = 76

Capo 3: (D⁷)   (G)   (Bm⁷)
         F⁷   B♭   Dm⁷

May God grant us joy of heart, and may
Al - le - lu - ia, al - le - lu - ia, al - le -

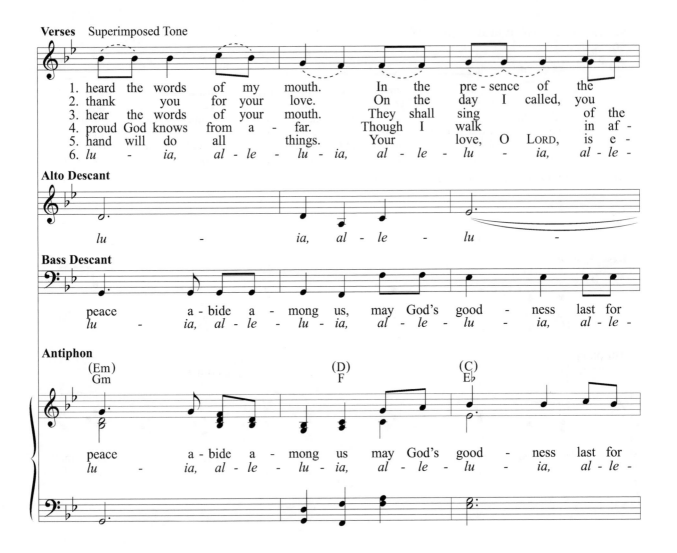

Verses Superimposed Tone

1. heard the words of my mouth. In the pre - sence of the
2. thank you for your love. On the day I called, you
3. hear the words of your mouth. They shall sing of the
4. proud God knows from a - far. Though I walk in af -
5. hand will do all things. Your love, O Lord, is e -
6. *lu - ia, al - le - lu - ia, al - le - lu - ia, al - le -*

Alto Descant

lu - ia, al - le - lu -

Bass Descant

peace a - bide a - mong us, may God's good - ness last for
lu - ia, al - le - lu - ia, al - le - lu - ia, al - le -

Antiphon

(Em)   (D)   (C)
Gm   F   E♭

peace a - bide a - mong us may God's good - ness last for
lu - ia, al - le - lu - ia, al - le - lu - ia, al - le -

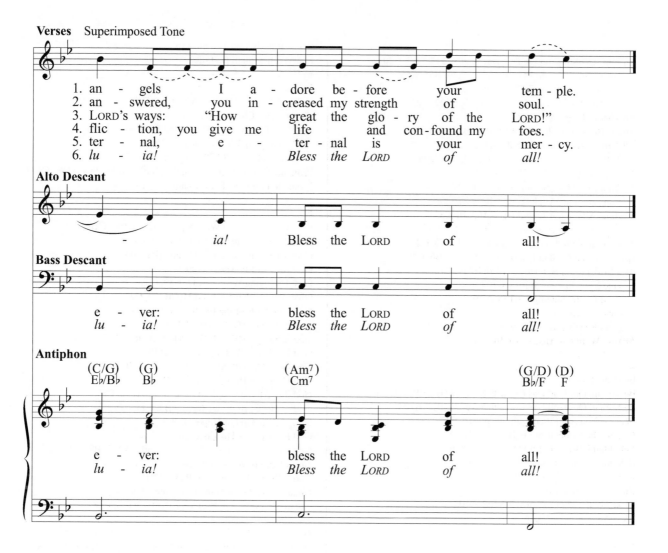

Verses   Superimposed Tone

1. an - gels   I a - dore be - fore   your   tem - ple.
2. an - swered,   you in - creased my strength   of   soul.
3. LORD's ways: "How   great the glo - ry of the LORD!"
4. flic - tion, you give me   life   and con - found my foes.
5. ter - nal,   e -   ter - nal is   your   mer - cy.
6. *lu - ia!*   *Bless the LORD*   *of*   *all!*

Alto Descant

- *ia!* Bless the LORD   of   all!

Bass Descant

e - ver: bless the LORD   of   all!
lu - ia!   *Bless the LORD   of   all!*

Antiphon

(C/G) (G)   (Am⁷)   (G/D) (D)
Eb/Bb Bb   Cm⁷   Bb/F F

e - ver: bless the LORD   of   all!
lu - ia!   *Bless the LORD   of   all!*

Performance Notes

At the end of the piece, the Antiphon may be repeated using the Alleluias in italics instead of the usual text or
humming.

A

A Light Will Shine on Us This Day – A13, B13, C13, C20
A New Commandment I Give to You – A49, B55, C55
A River Flows – A238, B237, C239
A Woman Clothed with the Sun – A223, B222, C224
All That Is True – A175
All the Ends of the Earth – A14, B14, B87, C14, C179
All Things Are from the Lord – A156
All Who Labor, Come to Me – A133, B204, C206
All You Nations – A128, B131, C131
All Your Sins Have Been Forgiven – C127
Alleluia, Alleluia, Alleluia! (I) – B75, C75
Alleluia, Alleluia, Alleluia! (II) – A62, B68, C68
Alleluia, Send Out Your Spirit – A93, B96, C96
Arise, Jerusalem, Look to the East – A23, B23, C23
Arise, Jerusalem, Stand on the Height – A4, B6, C4
As a Bridegroom Rejoices – A240, B239, C100
As One Body in Your Spirit – C103
As Seed for the Sowing – A136, A139
Ask and Receive (I) – A143
Ask and Receive (II) – A239, B238, C146, C240
At Your Word Our Hearts Are Burning – A75

B

Be Patient, Beloved – A9
Be Strong, Our God Has Come to Save Us (I) – B9, C9
Be Strong, Our God Has Come to Save Us (II) – B164
Because You Are Filled with the Spirit – B173
Behold, the Bridegroom Is Here (I) – B118
Behold, the Bridegroom Is Here (II) – A192, B3
Behold the Lamb of God! – A97, B100
Bless the Lord, My Soul – C27
Blessed Are You, Lord – A169, B171
Blest Are the Poor in Spirit – A102, A103
Blest Are You Who Weep – C112

C

Cast Out into the Deep – C109
Change Your Heart and Mind – A171
Chosen in Christ, Blessed in Christ – B139
Christ Is the Light – A211, A213, B210, B212, C212, C214
Christ Laid Down His Life for Us – A172, B170
Christ, Our Pasch – A67, B70, C70
Christ the Lord Is Risen Again – A65, B71, C71
Clothed in Christ, One in Christ – A28, B28, B69, C69
Come, All You Good and Faithful Servants – A195
Come, Come to the Banquet – A146, C43
Come, Lord, and Save Us – A8
Come, My Children – B176
"Come," Says My Heart – B92, C92
Come to Me and Drink – A94, B97, C97
Come to Me and You Shall Never Hunger – A147, B148
Courage! Get Up! – B185

D

Do Not Abandon Me, Lord! – B186, C188
Do Not Store Up Earthly Treasures – C149, C171
Don't Be Afraid – A150, B133, C152, C196

E

Eat My Flesh and Drink My Blood – A236, B235, C237

Everlasting Is Your Love – A155
Every Valley Shall Be Filled – C6

F

Father, into Your Hands – A51, B57, C57
Finest Food! Choicest Wine! – A178
For Ever, For Ever, We Praise You For Ever – A200
For You My Soul Is Thirsting – A158, C129
Forgive, and You Will Be Forgiven – C115
From the East and West, from the North and South – A186, C158
From the Fullness of Our Hearts – C118

G

Give Peace to Those Who Wait – A163, B165, C166
Give Thanks to the Lord, Alleluia (I) – A70
Give Thanks to the Lord, Alleluia (II) – B129
Give the Lord Power – A180
Give Us Living Water – A37, B39, C39
Give: Your Father Sees – A210, B209, C211
Go to the Ends of the Earth – C120
God, Come to My Aid (I) – C154
God, Come to My Aid (II) – A144, B146, C147
God Feeds Us, God Saves Us – A115, C183
God Goes Up with Shouts of Joy – A87, B90, C90
God Heals the Broken – B109, C173
God, Let All the Peoples Praise You – A152, C87
God of Hosts, Bring Us Back – B2, C11
God of Life, God of Hope – C193
God Remembers His Covenant For Ever – B18
God, Who Raised Jesus from the Dead – A232, B231, C233
God's Love is Revealed to Us – A15, B15, C28
God's Tender Mercy – A6, B215, C217
Great In Our Midst Is the Holy One – C8
Guard Me as the Apple of Your Eye! – B180, C181

H

Happy Are They Who Dwell in Your House – A244, B38, C18
Happy Are They Who Follow – A108
Happy Are They Whose God Is the Lord – B199, C151
Heal Me in Your Mercy – B112
Heal My Soul – B114
Heaven and Earth Will Fade Away – A109, B194
Here I Am – A96, B99, C107
Here in Your Presence – B121
Here Is My Servant, Here Is My Son – A34, B26, B34, C26
Home for the Lonely – B143, C144, C161
Hosanna, Hosanna, Hosanna in the Highest – A44, B50, C50
How Happy Are You – A194, B175
How I Thirst for You – A235, B234, C236
How Wonderful Your Name, O Lord – C201

I

I Am the Resurrection – A43, B49, C49
I Am the Way: Follow Me – A81
I Am With You – C30
I Am Your Savior, My People – A166, B168, C169
I Called in My Distress – A218, B217, C219
I Know I Shall See the Goodness of the Lord – A90
I Love You, Lord – A183
I Loved Wisdom More Than Health or Beauty – A141, B179, C163

I Shall Dwell in the House of the Lord – A177
I Thank You, Lord, with All My Heart – C180
I Will Dwell with You – A237, B236, C238
I Will Praise You, I Will Thank You – A215, B214, C216
I Will Praise You, Lord – A56, B62, C62, C78
I Will Praise Your Name For Ever (I) – C84
I Will Praise Your Name For Ever (II) – A132, C189
I Will See You Again – A88, B91, C91
I Will Show God's Salvation – A120
I Will Sing For Ever of Your Love – A129, B11
I Will Walk in the Presence of the Lord – B33, B166
If I Must Drink This Cup – A46, B52, C52
If You Love Me, Feed My Lambs (I) – C79
If You Love Me, Feed My Lambs (II) – A219, B218, C220
If You Will Love Each Other – A165
In Every Age, O Lord, You Have Been Our Refuge – C164
In God Alone Is My Soul at Rest – A114
In the Presence of the Angels – C108
In Your Abundant Love – A126
It Is Good to Give You Thanks – B126, C117

J

Jesus Christ, the Same Today, Yesterday and Evermore – A22,
    B22, C22
Jesus, Mighty Lord, Come Save Us – A12
John Was Sent from God – A214, B213, C215
Joyfully You Will Draw Water – A57, B27, B205, C63
Justice Shall Flourish – A5

K

Keep My Soul in Peace – A187
Keep These Words in Your Heart and Soul – A118
Keep Us in Your Name – B127, C94

L

Laughter Fills Our Mouths – B184, C5
Lead Me, Guide Me – A107, B110, C110
Let All the Earth Adore and Praise You – A73, B98, C77
Let All the Earth Cry Out Your Praises – A73, B77, C77
Let My Prayer Come Before You, Lord – A189, B189, C191
Let the King of Glory Come In – A11, B211, C213
Let the Word Make a Home in Your Heart – A19, B161
Let Us Go Rejoicing – A2, B245, C198
Let Your Love Be Upon Us, O Lord – A33, A80, B181
Lift Up Your Heads, Stand and Believe – C3
Light of the World – A100, A106
Like a Deer That Longs for Running Streams – A59, B65, C65
Like Newborn Children – A69, B74, C74
Listen: I Stand at the Door and Knock – A140, C143
Listen! Listen! Open Your Hearts! – A36, B37, C37
Listen, Listen to the Voice of Jesus – A198, B197
Listen, Listen to the Words of Jesus – A148
Live on in My Love – A85, A91, B88, B94, C88
Look on My Toil – A116, B119, C119
Lord, Cleanse My Heart – A61, B46, C67
Lord, Listen to My Prayer – A234, B233, C235
Lord, This Is the People – A230, B229, C231
Lord, You Are Close – A167
Lose Your Life and Save It – A228, B167, B227, C130, C165
Love Bears All Things – C106
Love Is My Desire – A121
Love the Lord Your God – A112, A185, C140

M

May God Bless Us in Mercy – A21, B21, C21
May God Grant Us Joy of Heart – A250, B249, C251
Merciful and Tender – A111, A164, B117, C36, C114, C187
My God, My God – A45, B51, C51
My God, My Strength, Defend My Cause – A41, B45, C45
My Grace Is Enough – B136
My Lips Will Tell of Your Justice – C105
My Plans for You Are Peace – A193, B192, C194
My Portion and My Cup – A54, B60, B193, C60, C132
My Sheep I Will Pasture – C208
My Shepherd Is the Lord – A39, A233, B42, B82, B141, B191,
    B232, C82, C207, C234
My Soul Rejoices in God – A225, B8, B224, C12, C226

N

Not on Bread Alone Are We Nourished – A31, C31
Now Is the Hour – A3

O

O Let My Tongue Cleave to My Mouth – B41
O Praise the Lord, Jerusalem – A203, B151
One Thing I Seek – A122, B125, C125
Open, You Skies: Rain Down the Just One – A10, B10, C10
Open Your Hand, Lord – B145
Our City Has No Need of Sun or Moon – A25, B25, C25
Our Cup of Blessing – A48, B54, C54
Our Glory and Pride is the Cross of Jesus Christ – A47, B53, C53,
    C227
Our God Has Blessed Us – A249, B248, C250
Our Help Shall Come from the Lord – C182
Our Shelter and Our Help – C124

P

People of God, Flock of the Lord – A123, C81
Planted Like a Tree – C111
Praise the Lord, Alleluia! – B108
Praise to God Who Lifts Up the Poor – C170
Proclaim the Wonders God Has Done – C99
Put Your Hand Here, Thomas – A72, B76, C76

R

Raise the Cup of Salvation – B202
Rejoice in the Lord, Again Rejoice! – A7, B7, C7
Rejoice in the Lord on This Feast of the Saints – A229, B228,
    C230
Rejoice, Rejoice, All You Who Love Jerusalem! – A38, B40, C40
Rejoice, Your Names Are Written in Heaven – C136
Remember, Lord – A170
Ring Out Your Joy – B120
Rise Up and Tell All Your Children – A227, B226, C228
Rise Up, O Lord – A224, B223, C225

S

Salvation Has Come to This House – C190
Save Me, O Lord – A117
Save Us, Lord – A125, B128, B142, C128
Seek the Lord! Long for the Lord! – A32, A101, A182, B32, C32
Send Out Your Spirit – A52, B58, C58
Set the Earth on Fire – C155
Shine Out, O Lord; You Are My God – B106
Shine Your Face on Us, Lord – B78

Genesis

1:2 — Send Out Your Spirit – A52, B58, C58

Exodus

15:1b — Sing to the Lord – A55, B61, C61

19:5-6 — You Shall Be a Royal Priesthood – A124

Numbers

11:29 — Because You Are Filled with the Spirit – B173

Deuteronomy

8:3 — Not on Bread Alone Are We Nourished – A31, C31

11:18 — Keep These Words in Your Heart and Soul – A118

1 Kings

19:12 — Listen, Listen to the Words of Jesus – A148

Esther

13:10-11 — You Have Given Everything Its Place – A179, B174, C175

2 Maccabees

7:14 — God of Life, God of Hope – C193

Psalms

4:7 — Shine Your Face on Us, Lord – B78

8:2a — How Wonderful Your Name, O Lord – C201

9:1-2 — With All My Heart I Praise You – B115

13:6 — Your Mercy Is My Hope – A110, B113, C113

15:1 — Those Who Do Justice – A151, B160, C142

16:5, 9 — My Portion and My Cup – A54, B60, B193, C60, C132

16:11 — You Will Show Me the Path of Life – B188

16:11 — You Will Show Us the Path of Life – A74

17:8 — Guard Me as the Apple of Your Eye! – B180, C181

17:15 — To Gaze on Your Glory – A134, B137

18:2 — I Love You, Lord – A183

18:19-20 — The Strong Lord Sets Me Free – A184, B116, C116

19:4 — The Message Goes Forth – A98, B101

22:2a — My God, My God – A45, B51, C51

22:26a — You Are My Praise – B84

23:1-3 — My Shepherd Is the Lord – A39, A233, B42, B82, B141, B191, B232, C82, C207, C234

23:1-3 — You Are the Shepherd – A78

23:6bc — I Shall Dwell in the House of the Lord – A177

24:6 — Lord, This Is the People – A230, B229, C231

24:7c, 10b — Let the King of Glory Come In – A11, B211, C213

25:1-2 — To You, O Lord, I Lift My Soul – A1, B1, C2

25:4-5 — Teach Me Your Path – B30

25:6a — Remember, Lord – A170

25:4, 18 — Look on My Toil – A116, B119, C119

27:1 — The Lord Is My Light – A99, B122, C33, C122

27:4 — One Thing I Seek – A122, B125, C125

27:7-9 — "Come," Says My Heart – B92, C92

27:13 — I Know I Shall See the Goodness of the Lord – A90

28:9 — Save Us, Lord – A125, B128, B142, C128

29:11b — The Lord Will Bless His People – A27

30:2a — I Will Praise You, Lord – A56, B62, C62, C78

31:2b, 3a, 3b — Save Me, O Lord – A117

31:2b, 3a, 3b — Lead Me, Guide Me – A107, B110, C110

31:14, 16 — Shine Out, O Lord; You Are My God – B106

32:7 — You Are My Hiding-place, O Lord – C48

32:7 — Turn to the Lord – B111, C126

33:5-6 — The Earth Is Full of the Goodness of God – A53, A76, B59, B80, C59, C80

33:12 — Happy Are They Whose God Is the Lord – B199, C151

33:14, 19 — God Feeds Us, God Saves Us – A115, C183

33:22 — Let Your Love Be Upon Us, O Lord – A33, A80, B181

34:5 — I Called in My Distress – A218, B217, C219

34:8 — The Goodness of the Lord – B150, C41

34:8 — Behold the Lamb of God! – A97, B100

34:9 — When the Poor Cry Out – C185

38:22-23 — From the East and West, from the North and South – A186, C158

38:22-23 — Do Not Abandon Me, Lord! – B186, C188

40:8a — Here I Am – A96, B99, C107

41:5b — Heal My Soul – B114

42:2 — Like a Deer That Longs for Running Streams – A59, B65, C65

42:3 — How I Thirst for You – A235, B234, C236

43:1 — My God, My Strength, Defend My Cause – A41, B45, C45

46:5 — A River Flows – A238, B237, C239

47:1 — All You Nations – A128, B131, C131

47:6 — God Goes Up with Shouts of Joy – A87, B90, C90

48:10 — Within Your Temple – A131, B134, C134

50:23b — I Will Show God's Salvation – A120

51:3 — We Have Sinned, Lord – A30, B208, C167

51:10 — Lord, Cleanse My Heart – A61, B46, C67

54:4 — You Alone Are My Help – A137, B140, C141

62:6a — In God Alone Is My Soul at Rest – A114

63:2 — For You My Soul Is Thirsting – A158, C129

66:1-2 — Let All the Earth Cry Out Your Praises – A73, B77, C77

66:4 — Let All the Earth Adore and Praise You – A73, B98, C77

67:2a — May God Bless Us in Mercy – A21, B21, C21

67:4 — God, Let All the Peoples Praise You – A152, C87

67:7 — Our God Has Blessed Us – A249, B248, C250

68:6-7, 35 — Home for the Lonely – B143, C144, C161

69:14c — In Your Abundant Love – A126

70:2, 6 — God, Come to My Aid (II) – A144, B146, C147

72:7 — Justice Shall Flourish – A5

72:11 — They Shall Adore You – A24, B24, C24

74:16, 19, 21 — Yours Is the Day – B149, C150

78a, c — Rise Up and Tell All Your Children – A227, B226, C228

80:19 — God of Hosts, Bring Us Back – B2, C11

81:1-2	Ring Out Your Joy – B120	128:1	How Happy Are You – A194, B175
81:17	With Finest Wheat and Finest Wine – A202, B201, C203	130:7	There Is Mercy in the Lord – A42, B47, C47
84:4	Happy Are They Who Dwell in Your House – A244, B38, C18	131:2	Keep My Soul in Peace – A187
		132:7	Rise Up, O Lord – A224, B223, C225
85:1-3	Turn to Me, Answer Me – A154, B156, C156	137:6	O Let My Tongue Cleave to My Mouth – B41
85:7	Show Us, Lord, Your Kindness – A149, B5	138:1, 2b, 3z	I Thank You, Lord, with All My Heart – C180
86:5a	You Are Good and Forgiving – A138	138:1-3, 6-8	In the Presence of the Angels – C108
88:1-2	Let My Prayer Come Before You, Lord – A189, B189, C191	138:8bc	Everlasting Is Your Love – A155
89:1	I Will Sing For Ever of Your Love – A129, B11	139:14	I Will Praise You, I Will Thank You – A215, B214, C216
90:1	In Every Age, O Lord, You Have Been Our Refuge – C164	140:14b, 18d	God, Come to My Aid (I) – C154
		143:4a	Lord, Listen to My Prayer – A234, B233, C235
90:14	When You Fill Us with Your Word – B178, C148	145:1	I Will Praise Your Name For Ever – A132, C84, C189
91:14-15	Those Who Love Me, I Will Deliver – A29, B29, C38, C29	145:15-16	Open Your Hand, Lord – B145
91:15	I Am With You – C30	145:16	You Open Your Hand – A127, B144
92:1	It Is Good to Give You Thanks – B126, C117	145:18a	Lord, You Are Close – A167
93:1a	The Lord Is King (II) – B196	146:1b	Praise the Lord, Alleluia! – B108
95:6	Venite, Adoremus – A245, B107, C246	146:3	God Heals the Broken – B109, C173
96:7b, 4a	Give the Lord Power – A180	147:3	God Heals the Broken – B109, C173
95:7b-8a	Listen! Listen! Open Your Hearts! – A36, B37, C37	147:5	Praise the Lord, Alleluia! – B108
		147:12	O Praise the Lord, Jerusalem – A203, B151
97:1a, 9a	The Lord Is King (I) – A221, B220, C93		
98:1-2	Sing to God a New Song – A79, B83, C83	**Wisdom**	
98:3c	All the Ends of the Earth – A14, B14, B87, C14, C179	9	I Loved Wisdom More Than Health or Beauty – A141, B179, C163
100:3c	People of God, Flock of the Lord – A123, C81	**Sirach**	
103:3b	Heal Me in Your Mercy – B112	28:2	If You Will Love Each Other – A165
103:3b	If You Will Love Each Other – A165	35:21	The Prayer of Our Hearts – C186
103:8	Merciful and Tender – A111, A164, B117, C36, C114, C187	36:18	Give Peace to Those Who Wait – A163, B165, C166
104:1-2	Bless the Lord, My Soul – C27	50:23	May God Grant Us Joy of Heart – A250, B249, C251
104:28b	You Open Your Hand – A127, B144		
104:30	Send Out Your Spirit – A52, B58, C58	**Isaiah**	
104:30	Alleluia, Send Out Your Spirit – A93, B96, C96	2:3, 4	Now Is the Hour – A3
		5:7a	The People of God Are the Vineyard – A174
105:4	Seek the Lord! Long for the Lord! – A32, A101, A182, B32, C32	9:2, 6	A Light Will Shine on Us This Day – A13, B13, C13, C20
105:7a, 8a	God Remembers His Covenant For Ever – B18	12:3	Joyfully You Will Draw Water – A57, B27, B205, C63
107:1b	Give Thanks to the Lord, Alleluia (II) – B129	12:6	Great In Our Midst Is the Holy One – C8
109:26	Heal Me in Your Mercy – B112	25:6b	Finest Food! Choicest Wine! – A178
110:4b	You Are a Priest For Ever – C204	35:4	Come, Lord, and Save Us – A8
112:4a	Those Who Fear the Lord – A105	35:4, 6	Be Strong, Our God Has Come to Save Us – B9, B164, C9
113:1, 7b	Praise to God Who Lifts Up the Poor – C170	40:4-5	Every Valley Shall Be Filled – C6
116:9	I Will Walk in the Presence of the Lord – B33, B166	45:5	You Alone Are Lord – A181
116:13	Raise the Cup of Salvation – B202	45:8	Open, You Skies: Rain Down the Just One – A10, B10, C10
117:1	Speak Your Word, O Lord – C121	48:20	Shout to the Ends of the Earth – A89, B86, C86
118:22	The Stone Which the Builders Rejected – B81	55:11	As Seed for the Sowing – A136, A139
118:24	This Is the Day – A66, B72, C72	56:7	I Will Dwell with You – A237, B236, C238
118:24	Give Thanks to the Lord, Alleluia (I) – A70	62:5	As a Bridegroom Rejoices – A240, B239, C100
119:1	Happy Are They Who Follow – A108	66:10-11	Rejoice, Rejoice, All You Who Love Jerusalem! – A38, B40, C40
119:145a	With All My Heart I Cry (I) – A160, B162		
119:145a, 97a	With All My Heart I Cry (II) – A142	**Jeremiah**	
121:2	Our Help Shall Come from the Lord – C182	29:11, 12, 14	My Plans for You Are Peace – A193, B192, C194
122:1	Let Us Go Rejoicing – A2, B245, C198		
123:2cd	We Look to You, O Lord – B135	33:14, 16	The Days Are Coming, Surely Coming – C1
126:2	Laughter Fills Our Mouths – B184, C5		

Baruch

5:5, 4:46	Arise, Jerusalem, Look to the East – A23, B23, C23
5:5, 4:46	Arise, Jerusalem, Stand on the Height – A4, B6, C4

Ezekiel

18:27	Change Your Heart and Mind – A171
34:11, 12, 14, 16	My Sheep I Will Pasture – C208
36:26-27	Turn Our Hearts from Stone to Flesh – A35, B35, C35
36:28	I Will Dwell with You – A237, B236, C238

Daniel

3:23	To Gaze on Your Glory – C137
3:26, 42, 43	Blessed Are You, Lord – A169, B171
3:52b	For Ever, For Ever, We Praise You For Ever – A200
9:19	To Gaze on Your Glory – C137

Matthew

1:21, 23	Jesus, Mighty Lord, Come Save Us – A12
4:4b	Not on Bread Alone Are We Nourished – A31, C31
5:3	Blest Are the Poor in Spirit – A102, A103
5:14	Light of the World – A100, A106
6:3-4, 5-6, 17-18	Give: Your Father Sees – A210, B209, C211
7:7a	Ask and Receive – A143, A239, B238, C240
7:21	Keep These Words in Your Heart and Soul – A118
9:13, 9	Love Is My Desire – A121
10:6-7	You Shall Be a Royal Priesthood – A124
11:28-29	All Who Labor, Come to Me – A133, B204, C206
13:44	Ask and Receive (I) – A143
16:16, 18	You Are Peter – A217, B216, C218
18:20	Where Two or Three Are Gathered – A162
18:35	If You Will Love Each Other – A165
20:16	The Last Shall Be First – A168
21:31-32	Change Your Heart and Mind – A171
22:4	Finest Food! Choicest Wine! – A178
22:21b	You Alone Are Lord – A181
25:21	Come, All You Good and Faithful Servants – A195
26:5	Behold, the Bridegroom Is Here – A192, B3, B118
26:42	If I Must Drink This Cup – A46, B52, C52

Mark

1:11	Here Is My Servant, Here Is My Son – A34, B26, B34, C26
1:15, 17	Walk in My Ways – B31, B103
2:19, 22	Behold, the Bridegroom Is Here (I) – B118
2:26-28	Here in Your Presence – B121
3:35	Those Who Do the Will of God – B124
4:41	Who Can This Be – B130
5:36, 34	Don't Be Afraid – A150, B133, C152, C196
6:6	My Grace Is Enough – B136
8:34-35	Lose Your Life and Save It – A228, B167, B227, C130, C165
9:7	Here Is My Servant, Here Is My Son – A34, B26, B34, C26
9:39-41	Because You Are Filled with the Spirit – B173
10:14	Come, My Children – B176
10:43, 39, 45	The Greatest Among You – B182

10:49, 51	Courage! Get Up! – B185
13:31	Heaven and Earth Will Fade Away – A109, B194
13:33, 37	Behold, the Bridegroom Is Here (II) – A192, B3

Luke

1:17	John Was Sent from God – A214, B213, C215
1:46-47, 49	My Soul Rejoices in God – A225, B8, B224, C12, C226
1:78-79	God's Tender Mercy – A6, B215, C217
2:32	Christ Is the Light – A211, A213, B210, B212, C212, C214
7:48, 59	All Your Sins Have Been Forgiven – C127
8:8	The Seed That Falls on Good Ground – A135
9:61	We Will Follow You, Lord – C133
10:9, 20	Rejoice, Your Names Are Written in Heaven – C136
10:27-28	Love the Lord Your God – A112, A185, C140
11:9	Ask and Receive (II) – C146
12:21	Do Not Store Up Earthly Treasures – C149, C171
12:49	Set the Earth on Fire – C155
15:23, 31	Come, Come to the Banquet – A146, C43
17:7, 8	Take Your Place at the Table – C177
18:13	The Prayer of Our Hearts – C186
19:9	Salvation Has Come to This House – C190
20:38	God of Life, God of Hope – C193
21:27-28	Lift Up Your Heads, Stand and Believe – C3
23:46	Father, into Your Hands – A51, B57, C57
24:32, 35	At Your Word Our Hearts Are Burning – A75

John

1:6-7	John Was Sent from God – A214, B213, C215
1:14, 16, 17	We Receive from Your Fullness – A16, B16, C16
1:35, 39	Behold the Lamb of God! – A97, B100
1:39, 43	Here I Am – A96, B99, C107
3:19-21	You Are Light in the Lord – A40, B44, C44
4:10, 14, 23	Give Us Living Water – A37, B39, C39
6:33	This Is the Bread – B147, B155
6:35	Come to Me and You Shall Never Hunger – A147, B148
6:35	Touch Me and See – A71, B79
6:54	Eat My Flesh and Drink My Blood – A236, B235, C237
6:68	Your Word Is Life, Lord – A58, B36, B64, B158, C64
7:37-38	Come to Me and Drink – A94, B97, C97
8:12	Light of the World – A100, A106
11:25	I Am the Resurrection – A43, B49, C49
11:26	Eat My Flesh and Drink My Blood – A236, B235, C237
12:24	Unless a Grain of Wheat – B48
13:34	A New Commandment I Give to You – A49, B55, C55
14: 6, 12	I Am the Way: Follow Me – A81
15:5	I Am the Way: Follow Me – A81
15:5	You Are the Vine – A82, B85
15:9	Live on in My Love – A85, A91, B88, B94, C88
16:22	I Will See You Again – A88, B91, C91

17:11	Keep Us in Your Name – B127, C94
20:27	Put Your Hand Here, Thomas – A72, B76, C76
21:12	Touch Me and See – A71, B79
21:15-17, 19	If You Love Me, Feed My Lambs (II) – A219, B218, C220
21:19	I Am the Way: Follow Me – A81

Acts
11:1	Why Stare into the Sky? – A86, B89, C89

Romans
5:5	The Love of God – A92, B95, B200, C95
8:11	God, Who Raised Jesus from the Dead – A232, B231, C233
8:11	The Love of God – A92, B95, B200, C95
11:32	The Mercy of God Is for All – A153
11:36	All Things Are from the Lord – A156
13:11	Now Is the Hour – A3

1 Corinthians
3:9c, 17d, 16b	You Are God's Temple – A247, B246, C248
5:7b	Christ, Our Pasch – A67, B70, C70
10:16	Our Cup of Blessing – A48, B54, C54
11:24-25	This Is My Body – A50, B56, C56
13:7	Love Bears All Things – C106

2 Corinthians
12:9	My Grace Is Enough – B136

Galatians
3:27	Clothed in Christ, One in Christ – A28, B28, B69, C69
4:16	Our Glory and Pride is the Cross of Jesus Christ – A47, B53, C53, C227

Ephesians
1:4, 3, 12	Chosen in Christ, Blessed in Christ – B139
2:4	You Are Rich in Mercy – A68, A208, A176, B43, B177, B207, C178, C209
5:19-20	Sing and Make Music – A248, B247, C249

Philippians
1:21	The Last Shall Be First – A168
2:5	Change Your Heart and Mind – A171
4:4-5	Rejoice in the Lord, Again Rejoice! – A7, B7, C7
4:8-9	All That Is True – A175
4:19	Finest Food! Choicest Wine! – A178

Colossians
3:1	Do Not Store Up Earthly Treasures – C149, C171

3:16	Let the Word Make a Home in Your Heart – A19, B161

1 Thessalonians
1:4	You Alone Are Lord – A181
2:13	The Word of God at Work in Us – A188

2 Thessalonians
3:5	God of Life, God of Hope – C193

1 Timothy
6:12, 14	Take Hold of Eternal Life – C174

Hebrews
2:4	Take Your Place at the Table – C177
12:2	Set the Earth on Fire – C155
13:8	Jesus Christ, the Same Today, Yesterday and Evermore – A22, B22, C22

James
1:21	Let the Word Make a Home in Your Heart – A19, B161
5:7a, 8b	Be Patient, Beloved – A9

1 Peter
2:2	Like Newborn Children – A69, B74, C74

1 John
3:2	We Shall Be Like You – A222, B221, C223
3:16	Christ Laid Down His Life for Us – A172, B170
4:9	God's Love Is Revealed to Us – A15, B15, C28

Revelation
1:6	Worthy Is the Lamb Who Was Slain – A196, B195, C197
1:8	Listen, Listen to the Voice of Jesus – A198, B197
3:20	Listen, Listen to the Voice of Jesus – A198, B197
3:20	Listen: I Stand at the Door and Knock – A140, C143
5:12	Worthy Is the Lamb Who Was Slain – A196, B195, C197
12:1	A Woman Clothed with the Sun – A223, B222, C224
19:9	The Spirit and the Bride Say "Come!" – A231, B230, C232
21:3b	I Will Dwell with You – A237, B236, C238
21:23	Our City Has No Need of Sun or Moon – A25, B25, C25
22:17	The Spirit and the Bride Say "Come!" – A231, B230, C232

Advent

Arise, Jerusalem, Stand on the Height – A4, B6, C4
Be Patient, Beloved – A9
Be Strong, Our God Has Come to Save Us (I) – B9, C9
Behold, the Bridegroom Is Here (II) – B3
Come, Lord, and Save Us – A8
Every Valley Shall Be Filled – C6
God of Hosts, Bring Us Back – B2, C11
God's Tender Mercy – A6
Great In Our Midst Is the Holy One – C8
I Will Sing For Ever of Your Love – B11
Jesus, Mighty Lord, Come Save Us – A12
John Was Sent from God – A214, B213, C215
Justice Shall Flourish – A5
Laughter Fills Our Mouths – C5
Let the King of Glory Come In – A11
Let Us Go Rejoicing – A2
Lift Up Your Heads, Stand and Believe – C3
My Soul Rejoices in God – A225, B8, B224, C12, C226
Now Is the Hour – A3
Open, You Skies: Rain Down the Just One – A10, B10, C10
Our Shelter and Our Help – C124
Rejoice in the Lord, Again Rejoice! – A7, B7, C7
Show Us, Lord, Your Kindness – B5
The Days Are Coming, Surely Coming – C1
To You, O Lord, I Lift My Soul – A1, B1, C2

Christmas

A Light Will Shine on Us This Day – A13, B13, C13, C20
All the Ends of the Earth – A14, B14, B87, C14, C179
God Remembers His Covenant For Ever – B18
God's Love Is Revealed to Us – A15, B15, C28
Happy Are They Who Dwell in Your House – C18
How Happy Are You – A194
Jesus Christ, the Same Today, Yesterday and Evermore – A22, B22, C22
Let the Word Make a Home in Your Heart – A19
May God Bless Us in Mercy – A21, B21, C21
Sing to God a New Song – A79, B83, C83
We Receive from Your Fullness – A16, B16, C16

Epiphany / Baptism of the Lord

A Light Will Shine on Us This Day – A13, B13, C13, C20
All the Ends of the Earth – A14, B14, B87, C14, C179
Arise, Jerusalem, Look to the East – A23, B23, C23
Behold the Lamb of God! – B100
Bless the Lord, My Soul – C27
Clothed in Christ, One in Christ – A28, B28
God's Love Is Revealed to Us – A15, B15, C28
Here I Am – B99, C107
Here Is My Servant, Here Is My Son – A34, B26, B34, C26
Joyfully You Will Draw Water – A57, B27, B205, C63
Let All the Earth Adore and Praise You – B98
Our City Has No Need of Sun or Moon – A25, B25, C25
Sing to God a New Song – A79, B83, C83
The Lord Will Bless His People – A27
The Message Goes Forth – B101
They Shall Adore You – A24, B24, C24

Lent

All Your Sins Have Been Forgiven – C127
Come, Come to the Banquet – C43
For You My Soul Is Thirsting – A158, C129
Forgive, and You Will Be Forgiven – C115
Give Us Living Water – A37, B39, C39
Give: Your Father Sees – A210, B209, C211

Happy Are They Who Dwell in Your House – B38
Here Is My Servant, Here Is My Son – A34, B26, B34, C26
I Am the Resurrection – A43, B49, C49
I Am With You – C30
I Will Walk in the Presence of the Lord – B33, B166
Laughter Fills Our Mouths – C5
Let Your Love Be Upon Us, O Lord – A33
Listen! Listen! Open Your Hearts! – A36, B37, C37
Lord, Cleanse My Heart – A61, B46, C67
Lose Your Life and Save It – C130, C165
Merciful and Tender – C36, C114, C187
My God, My Strength, Defend My Cause – A41, B45, C45
My Sheep I Will Pasture – C208
My Shepherd Is the Lord – A39, A233, B42, B82, B141, B191, B232, C82, C207, C234
Not on Bread Alone Are We Nourished – A31, C31
O Let My Tongue Cleave to My Mouth – B41
Rejoice, Rejoice, All You Who Love Jerusalem! – A38, B40, C40
Save Us, Lord – C128
Seek the Lord! Long for the Lord! – A32, A182, B32, C32
Teach Me Your Path – B30
The Goodness of the Lord – C41
The Lord Is My Light – C33
The Prayer of Our Hearts – C186
There Is Mercy in the Lord – A42, B47, C47
Those Who Love Me, I Will Deliver – A29, B29, C29, C38
Turn Our Hearts from Stone to Flesh – A35, B35, C35
Turn to the Lord – C126
Unless a Grain of Wheat – B48
Walk in My Ways – B31
We Have Sinned, Lord – A30, B208, C167
You Are Light in the Lord – A40, B44, C44
You Are My Hiding-place, O Lord – C48
You Are Rich in Mercy – A176, A208, B43, B207, C178, C209
Your Word Is Life, Lord – A58, B36, B64, C64

Palm Sunday

Hosanna, Hosanna, Hosanna in the Highest – A44, B50, C50
If I Must Drink This Cup – A46, B52, C52
My God, My God – A45, B51, C51

Holy Thursday

A New Commandment I Give to You – A49, B55, C55
Christ Laid Down His Life for Us – A172, B170
Our Cup of Blessing – A48, B54, C54
Our Glory and Pride is the Cross of Jesus Christ – A47, B53, C53, C227
This Is My Body – A50, B56, C56
With Finest Wheat and Finest Wine – A202, B201, C203

Good Friday

Christ Laid Down His Life for Us – A172, B170
Father, into Your Hands – A51, B57, C57

Easter

A New Commandment I Give to You – A49, B55, C55
All the Ends of the Earth – A14, B14, B87, C14, C179
Alleluia, Alleluia, Alleluia! (I) – B75, C75
Alleluia, Alleluia, Alleluia! (II) – A62, B68, C68
At Your Word Our Hearts Are Burning – A75
Christ the Lord Is Risen Again – A65, B71, C71
Christ, Our Pasch – A67, B70, C70
Clothed in Christ, One in Christ – A28, B69, C69
"Come," Says My Heart – B92, C92
Give Thanks to the Lord, Alleluia (I) – A70
God, Let All the Peoples Praise You – C87

I Am the Way: Follow Me – A81
I Know I Shall See the Goodness of the Lord – A90
I Will Praise You, Lord – A56, B62, C62, C78
I Will Praise Your Name For Ever (I) – C84
I Will See You Again – A88, B91, C91
If You Love Me, Feed My Lambs (I) – C79
Joyfully You Will Draw Water – A57, B27, B205, C63
Keep Us in Your Name – C94
Let All the Earth Cry Out Your Praises – A73, B77, C77
Let Your Alone Love Be Upon Us, O Lord – A80
Like a Deer That Longs for Running Streams – A59, B65, C65
Like Newborn Children – A69, B74, C74
Live on in My Love – A85, A91, B88, B94, C88
Lord, Cleanse My Heart – A61, B46, C67
My Portion and My Cup – A54, B60, B193, C60
My Sheep I Will Pasture – C208
My Shepherd Is the Lord – A39, A233, B42, B82, B141, B191,
    B232, C82, C207, C234
People of God, Flock of the Lord – C81
Put Your Hand Here, Thomas – A72, B76, C76
Send Out Your Spirit – A52, B58, C58
Shine Your Face on Us, Lord – B78
Shout to the Ends of the Earth – B86, C86
Sing to God a New Song – A79, B83, C83
Sing to the Lord – A55, B61, C61
The Earth Is Full of the Goodness of God (I) – A76, B80, C80
The Earth Is Full of the Goodness of God (II) – A53, B59, C59
The Lord Is King (I) – C93
The Stone Which the Builders Rejected – B81
This Is the Day – A66, B72, C72
Touch Me and See – A71, B79
You Are My Praise – B84
You Are Rich in Mercy – A68, A176
You Are the Shepherd – A78
You Are the Vine – A82, B85
You Will Show Us the Path of Life – A74
Your Word Is Life, Lord – B36

Ascension
God Goes Up with Shouts of Joy – A87, B90, C90
I Will See You Again – A88, B91, C91
Shout to the Ends of the Earth – A89
The Lord Is King (I) – C93
Why Stare into the Sky? – A86, B89, C89

Pentecost
Alleluia, Send Out Your Spirit – A93, B96, C96
Come to Me and Drink – A94, B97, C97
Send Out Your Spirit – A52, B58, C58
The Love of God – A92, B95, B200, C95

Christ the King
Alleluia, Send Out Your Spirit – B96
Christ Laid Down His Life for Us – A172, B170
Keep Us in Your Name – C94
Let Us Go Rejoicing – C198
Listen, Listen to the Voice of Jesus – A198, B197
Take Hold of Eternal Life – C174
The Lord Is King (I) – C93
The Lord Is King (II) – B196
Worthy Is the Lamb Who Was Slain – A196, B195, C197

Holy Trinity
Happy Are They Whose God Is the Lord – B199, C151
How Wonderful Your Name, O Lord – C201
The Love of God – A92, B200, C95

For Ever, For Ever, We Praise You For Ever – A200
You Have Shown You Love Us – A199, B198, C200

Body and Blood of Christ
A New Commandment I Give to You – A49, B55, C55
At Your Word Our Hearts Are Burning – A75
Come, Come to the Banquet – C43
Eat My Flesh and Drink My Blood – A236, B235, C237
Finest Food! Choicest Wine! – A178
Not on Bread Alone Are We Nourished – A31, C31
Raise the Cup of Salvation – B202
This Is My Body – A50, B56, C56
With Finest Wheat and Finest Wine – A202, B201, C203
You Are a Priest For Ever – C204

Sacred Heart
A New Commandment I Give to You – A49, B55, C55
All Who Labor, Come to Me – B204, C206
Christ Laid Down His Life for Us – A172, B170
Come to Me and Drink – A94, B97, C97
Joyfully You Will Draw Water – B27, B205
My Sheep I Will Pasture – C208
My Shepherd Is the Lord – A39, A233, B42, B82, B141, B191,
    B232, C82, C207, C234
Your Word Is Life, Lord – A58, B64, C64

Christian Initiation / Baptism
A New Commandment I Give to You – A49, B55, C55
A River Flows – A238, B237, C239
As Seed for the Sowing – A136, A139
Ask and Receive (I) – A143
Ask and Receive (II) – A239, B238, C240
At Your Word Our Hearts Are Burning – A75
Because You Are Filled with the Spirit – B173
Bless the Lord, My Soul – C27
Chosen in Christ, Blessed in Christ – B139
Christ Laid Down His Life for Us – A172, B170
Clothed in Christ, One in Christ – A28, B28, B69, C69
Come to Me and Drink – A94, B97, C97
Come, All You Good and Faithful Servants – A195
Come, Come to the Banquet – A146, C43
Come, My Children – B176
"Come," Says My Heart – B92, C92
Do Not Abandon Me, Lord! – B186, C188
Do Not Store Up Earthly Treasures – C149, C171
Finest Food! Choicest Wine! – A178
For You My Soul Is Thirsting – A158, C129
From the East and West, from the North and South – A186, C158
Give Us Living Water – A37, B39, C39
Go to the Ends of the Earth – C120
God Feeds Us, God Saves Us – A115, C183
Happy Are They Who Follow – A108
Happy Are They Whose God Is the Lord – B199, C151
Heaven and Earth Will Fade Away – A109, B194
How I Thirst for You – A235, B234, C236
I Am the Way: Follow Me – A81
I Will Dwell with You – A237, B236, C238
I Will Praise You, I Will Thank You – A215, B214, C216
If You Love Me, Feed My Lambs (I) – C79
If You Love Me, Feed My Lambs (II) – A219, B218, C220
Joyfully You Will Draw Water – A57, B27, B205, C63
Keep These Words in Your Heart and Soul – A118
Let the Word Make a Home in Your Heart – A19, B161
Light of the World – A100, A106
Like Newborn Children – A69, B74, C74

Listen, Listen to the Words of Jesus – A148
Listen: I Stand at the Door and Knock – A140
Live on in My Love – A85, A91, B88, B94, C88
Lord, This Is the People – A230, B229, C231
Lose Your Life and Save It – B167, B227, C130
Love Bears All Things – C106
Love Is My Desire – A121
My Shepherd Is the Lord – A39, A233, B42, B82, B141, B191, B232, C82, C207, C234
Not on Bread Alone Are We Nourished – A31, C31
Our Cup of Blessing – A48, B54, C54
People of God, Flock of the Lord – A123, C81
Speak Your Word, O Lord – C121
Take Hold of Eternal Life – C174
Take Your Place at the Table – C177
The Greatest Among You – B182
The Last Shall Be First – A168
The Love of God – A92, B95, B200, C95
The Seed That Falls on Good Ground – A135
The Word of God at Work in Us – A188
This Is My Body – A50, B56, C56
Those Who Do the Will of God – B124
Walk in My Ways – B31, B103
We Will Follow You, Lord – C133
When You Fill Us with Your Word – B178, C148
With All My Heart I Cry (II) – A142
You Are God's Temple – A247, B246, C248
You Are Light in the Lord – A40, B44, C44
You Are the Shepherd – A78
You Shall Be a Royal Priesthood – A124
Your Word Is Life, Lord – A58, B36, B64, C64

Confirmation

A New Commandment I Give to You – A49, B55, C55
Alleluia, Send Out Your Spirit – A93, B96, C96
As One Body in Your Spirit – C103
Because You Are Filled with the Spirit – B173
Bless the Lord, My Soul – C27
Chosen in Christ, Blessed in Christ – B139
Christ Laid Down His Life for Us – A172, B-170
Come, All You Good and Faithful Servants – A195
Give Us Living Water – A37, B39, C39
Go to the Ends of the Earth – C120
I Loved Wisdom More Than Health or Beauty – B179, C163
I Will Praise You, I Will Thank You – A215, B214, C216
If You Love Me, Feed My Lambs (II) – A219, B218, C220
Light of the World – A100, A-106
Live on in My Love – A85, A91, B88, B94, C88
Lord, This Is the People – A230, B229, C231
Lose Your Life and Save It – A228, B167, B227, C130
Love Bears All Things – C106
People of God, Flock of the Lord – A123, C81
Send Out Your Spirit – A52, B58, C58
Set the Earth on Fire – C155
The Love of God – A92, B95, B200, C95
Walk in My Ways – B103
We Will Follow You, Lord – C133
You Are God's Temple – A247, B246, C248

Marriage

A New Commandment I Give to You – A49, B55, C55
All That Is True – A175
All Things Are from the Lord – A156
As a Bridegroom Rejoices – A240, B239, C100
At Your Word Our Hearts Are Burning – A75

Because You Are Filled with the Spirit – B173
Behold, the Bridegroom Is Here (I) – B118
Finest Food! Choicest Wine! – A178
God Remembers His Covenant For Ever – B18
God's Love is Revealed to Us – A15, B15, C28
Here I Am – A96, B99, C107
How Happy Are You – A194, B175
How Wonderful Your Name, O Lord – C201
I Will Dwell with You – A237, B236, C238
Jesus Christ, the Same Today, Yesterday and Evermore – A22, B22, C22
Keep Us in Your Name – B127
Let the Word Make a Home in Your Heart – A19
Let Us Go Rejoicing – A2, B245, C198
Light of the World – A100, A106
Live on in My Love – A85, A91, B88, B94, C88
Love Bears All Things – C106
Love the Lord Your God – A112, A185, C140
May God Bless Us in Mercy – A21, B21, C21
May God Grant Us Joy of Heart – A250, B249, C251
Merciful and Tender – A111, A164, B117, C36, C114, C187
My Soul Rejoices in God – A225, B8, B224, C12, C226
Our God Has Blessed Us – A249, B248, C250
The Earth Is Full of the Goodness of God (I) – A76, B80, C80
The Earth Is Full of the Goodness of God (II) – A53, B59, C59
The Goodness of the Lord – B150, C41
The Spirit and the Bride Say "Come!" – A231, B230, C232
Those Who Do the Will of God – B124
Those Who Fear the Lord – A105
Walk in My Ways – B103
You Are God's Temple – A247, B246, C248
You Are Rich in Mercy – A176
You Have Given Everything Its Place – A179, B174, C175

Holy Orders / Religious Profession

A New Commandment I Give to You – A49, B55, C55
All Who Labor, Come to Me – A133, C206
Ask and Receive (I) – A143
At Your Word Our Hearts Are Burning – A75
Because You Are Filled with the Spirit – B173
Behold, the Bridegroom Is Here (I) – B118
Blest Are the Poor in Spirit – A103
Cast Out into the Deep – C109
Chosen in Christ, Blessed in Christ – B139
Christ Laid Down His Life for Us – A172, B170
Come, All You Good and Faithful Servants – A195
Do Not Store Up Earthly Treasures – C149, C171
Don't Be Afraid – A150, C152, C196
Go to the Ends of the Earth – C120
God, Come to My Aid – A144, B146, C147, C154
Happy Are They Who Dwell in Your House – A244, B38, C18
Here I Am – A96, B99, C107
How I Thirst for You – A235, B234, C236
I Am the Resurrection – A43, B49, C49
I Am the Way: Follow Me – A81
I Know I Shall See the Goodness of the Lord – A90
I Loved Wisdom More Than Health or Beauty – B179, C163
I Shall Dwell in the House of the Lord – A177
I Will Sing For Ever of Your Love – A129, B11
If You Love Me, Feed My Lambs (I) – C79
If You Love Me, Feed My Lambs (II) – A219, B218, C220
Let the Word Make a Home in Your Heart – A19, B161
Light of the World – A100, A106
Like a Deer That Longs for Running Streams – A59, B65, C65
Listen, Listen to the Words of Jesus – A148
Live on in My Love – A85, A91, B88, B94, C88

I Will Praise You, Lord – A56, B62, C62, C78
If I Must Drink This Cup – A46, B52, C52
In God Alone Is My Soul at Rest – A114
In the Presence of the Angels – C108
In Your Abundant Love – A126
Jesus Christ, the Same Today, Yesterday and Evermore – A22, B22, C22
Lead Me, Guide Me – B110, C110
Let Your Love Be Upon Us, O Lord – A33, A80, B181
Like a Deer That Longs for Running Streams – A59, B65, C65
Lord, You Are Close – A167
Love Bears All Things – C106
Merciful and Tender – A164
My Plans for You Are Peace – A193, B192, C194
My Shepherd Is the Lord – A39, A233, B42, B82, B141, B191, B232, C82, C207, C234
Our Help Shall Come from the Lord – C182
Remember, Lord – A170
Save Me, O Lord – A117
Shine Out, O Lord; You Are My God – B106
Shine Your Face on Us, Lord – B78
Speak Your Word, O Lord – C121
The Lord Is My Light – A99, B122, C33
The Mercy of God Is for All – A153
The Prayer of Our Hearts – C186
This Is My Body – A50, B56, C56
Those Who Love Me, I Will Deliver – A29, B29, C29, C38
To You, O Lord, I Lift My Soul – A1, B1, C2
When the Poor Cry Out – C185
Where Two or Three Are Gathered – A162
You Alone Are My Help – A137, B140, C141
You Are My Hiding-place, O Lord – C48
You Are the Shepherd – A78
Your Mercy Is My Hope – A110, B113, C113

Funerals
All That Is True – A175
All Who Labor, Come to Me – A133, B204, C206
Be Patient, Beloved – A9
"Come," Says My Heart – B92, C92
Come to Me and Drink – A94, B97, C97
Eat My Flesh and Drink My Blood – A236, B235, C237
Everlasting Is Your Love – A155
For You My Soul Is Thirsting – A158, C129
God, Who Raised Jesus from the Dead – A232, B231, C233
How I Thirst for You – A235, B234, C236
I Am the Resurrection – A43, B49, C49
I Am the Way: Follow Me – A81
I Know I Shall See the Goodness of the Lord – A90
I Shall Dwell in the House of the Lord – A177
I Will Dwell with You – A237, B236, C238
I Will See You Again – A88, B91, C91
I Will Walk in the Presence of the Lord – B33, B166
In God Alone Is My Soul at Rest – A114
Jesus Christ, the Same Today, Yesterday and Evermore – A22, B22, C22
Let Us Go Rejoicing – A2, B245
Live on in My Love – A85, A91, B88, B94, C88
Lord, Listen to My Prayer – A234, B233, C235
Lord, You Are Close – A167
Merciful and Tender – A111, A164, B117, C36, C114, C187
My Portion and My Cup – A54, B60, B193, C60, C132
My Shepherd Is the Lord – A39, A233, B42, B82, B141, B191, B232, C82, C207, C234
One Thing I Seek – A122, B125, C125
Our Glory and Pride is the Cross of Jesus Christ – A47, B53, C53, C227
Rejoice, Your Names Are Written in Heaven – C136

The Lord Is My Light – A99, B122, C33
This Is My Body – A50, B56, C56
Those Who Love Me, I Will Deliver – A29, B29, C29, C38
To You, O Lord, I Lift My Soul – A1, B1, C2
Unless a Grain of Wheat – B48
You Will Show Me the Path of Life – B188
You Will Show Us the Path of Life – A74
Your Word Is Life, Lord – A58, B36, B64, B158, C64

Blessed Virgin Mary
A Woman Clothed with the Sun – A223, B222, C224
As a Bridegroom Rejoices – A240, B239, C100
My Soul Rejoices in God – A225, B8, B224, C12, C226
Rise Up, O Lord – A224, B223, C225
Sing to God a New Song – A79, B83, C83
The Spirit and the Bride Say "Come!" – A231, B230, C232

Saints
Come, All You Good and Faithful Servants – A195
Give: Your Father Sees – A210, B209, C211
God's Tender Mercy – A6, B215, C217
I Called in My Distress – A218, B217, C219
I Will Praise You, I Will Thank You – A215, B214, C216
If You Love Me, Feed My Lambs (II) – A219, B218, C220
John Was Sent from God – A214, B213, C215
Lord, This Is the People – A230, B229, C231
Rejoice in the Lord on This Feast of the Saints – A229, B228, C230
Rejoice, Your Names Are Written in Heaven – C136
Take Hold of Eternal Life – C174
Take Your Place at the Table – C177
The Message Goes Forth – A98, B101
The Spirit and the Bride Say "Come!" – A231, B230, C232
You Are Peter – A217, B216, C218

Eucharistic Devotion
As Seed for the Sowing – A136
At Your Word Our Hearts Are Burning – A75
Behold the Lamb of God! – A97, B100
Behold, the Bridegroom Is Here (I) – B118
Christ Laid Down His Life for Us – A172, B170
Come to Me and Drink – A94, B97, C97
Come to Me and You Shall Never Hunger – A147, B148
Come, Come to the Banquet – A146
Eat My Flesh and Drink My Blood – A236, B235, C237
Finest Food! Choicest Wine! – A178
For You My Soul Is Thirsting – A158, C129
Give Us Living Water – A37, B39, C39
God Feeds Us, God Saves Us – A115
God Heals the Broken – B109, C173
Here in Your Presence – B121
How I Thirst for You – A235, B234, C236
I Am the Resurrection – A43, B49, C49
Like a Deer That Longs for Running Streams – A59, B65, C65
Live on in My Love – A85, A91, B88, B94, C88
My Portion and My Cup – A54, B60, B193, C60, C132
O Praise the Lord, Jerusalem – A203, B151
The Goodness of the Lord – B150, C41
This Is My Body – A50, B56, C56
This Is the Bread – B147, B155
Touch Me and See – A71, B79
Venite, Adoremus – A245, B107, C246
With Finest Wheat and Finest Wine – A202, B201, C203
You Are the Shepherd – A78
You Are the Vine – A82
You Open Your Hand – A127
Your Word Is Life, Lord – B158

Almsgiving / Generosity

Ask and Receive (I) – A143
Do Not Store Up Earthly Treasures – C149
Forgive, and You Will Be Forgiven – C115
Give: Your Father Sees – A210, B209, C211
If You Will Love Each Other – A165
Light of the World – A106
Those Who Do Justice – A151, B160, C142
Those Who Fear the Lord – A105
Where Two or Three Are Gathered – A162

Angels

In the Presence of the Angels – C108
Praise the Lord, Alleluia! – B108
Rejoice in the Lord on This Feast of the Saints – A229, B228, C230

Blessing / Benediction

All Things Are from the Lord – A156
Ask and Receive (II) – A239, B238, C240
For Ever, For Ever, We Praise You For Ever – A200
God, Let All the Peoples Praise You – A152, C87
How Happy Are You – A194, B175
May God Bless Us in Mercy – A21, B21, C21
May God Grant Us Joy of Heart – A250, B249, C251
Our Glory and Pride is the Cross of Jesus Christ – A47, B53, C53, C227
Our God Has Blessed Us – A249, B248, C250
The Lord Will Bless His People – A27
You Are God's Temple – A247, B246, C248

Christian Life

A New Commandment I Give to You – A49, B55, C55
All That Is True – A175
Ask and Receive (I) – A143
At Your Word Our Hearts Are Burning – A75
Because You Are Filled with the Spirit – B173
Blest Are the Poor in Spirit – A103
Blest Are You Who Weep – C112
Change Your Heart and Mind – A171
Chosen in Christ, Blessed in Christ – B139
Christ Laid Down His Life for Us – A172, B170
Clothed in Christ, One in Christ – A28, B28, B69, C69
Come, All You Good and Faithful Servants – A195
Do Not Store Up Earthly Treasures – C149, C171
Forgive, and You Will Be Forgiven – C115
Give Us Living Water – A37, B39, C39
Give: Your Father Sees – A210, B209, C211
Happy Are They Who Follow – A108
Heaven and Earth Will Fade Away – A109, B194
Here I Am – A96, B99, C107
How Happy Are You – A194, B175
I Am the Way: Follow Me – A81
If You Love Me, Feed My Lambs (I) – C79
If You Will Love Each Other – A165
Keep These Words in Your Heart and Soul – A118
Light of the World – A100, A106
Like Newborn Children – A69, B74, C74
Listen, Listen to the Words of Jesus – A148
Listen: I Stand at the Door and Knock – A140, C143
Live on in My Love – A85, A91, B88, B94, C88
Lord, This Is the People – A230, B229, C231
Lose Your Life and Save It – A228, B167, B227, C130, C165
Love Bears All Things – C106
Love Is My Desire – A121
Love the Lord Your God – A112, A185, C140
Not on Bread Alone Are We Nourished – A31, C31
Our Glory and Pride is the Cross of Jesus Christ – A47, B53, C53, C227
Planted Like a Tree – C111
Take Hold of Eternal Life – C174

Take Your Place at the Table – C177
Teach Me Your Path – B30
The Last Shall Be First – A168
The Word of God at Work in Us – A188
Those Who Do Justice – A151, B160, C142
Those Who Do the Will of God – B124
Those Who Fear the Lord – A105
Unless a Grain of Wheat – B48
Walk in My Ways – B31, B103
We Will Follow You, Lord – C133
Where Two or Three Are Gathered – A162
You Are God's Temple – A247, B246, C248
You Are Light in the Lord – A40, B44, C44
You Are the Vine – A82, B85
You Shall Be a Royal Priesthood – A124

Christian Unity

As One Body in Your Spirit – C103
Ask and Receive (II) – A239, B238, C240
Clothed in Christ, One in Christ – A28, B28, B69, C69
God, Let All the Peoples Praise You – A152, C87
Keep Us in Your Name – B127, C94
People of God, Flock of the Lord – A123, C81
You Are God's Temple – A247, B246, C248

Church (People of God, House of God)

A River Flows – A238, B237, C239
Come, All You Good and Faithful Servants – A195
From the East and West, from the North and South – A186, C158
God, Let All the Peoples Praise You – A152, C87
Happy Are They Who Dwell in Your House – A244, B38, C18
Happy Are They Whose God Is the Lord – C151
I Will Dwell with You – A237, B236, C238
If You Will Love Each Other – A165
Jesus Christ, the Same Today, Yesterday and Evermore – A22, B22, C22
Let Us Go Rejoicing – A2, B245, C198
Lord, This Is the People – A230, B229, C231
People of God, Flock of the Lord – A123, C81
Rejoice, Rejoice, All You Who Love Jerusalem! – A38, B40, C40
Salvation Has Come to This House – C190
The People of God Are the Vineyard – A174
Those Who Do Justice – A151, B160, C142
Venite, Adoremus – A245, B107, C246
Where Two or Three Are Gathered – A162
Within Your Temple – A131, B134, C134
You Alone Are Lord – A181
You Are God's Temple – A247, B246, C248
You Are Peter – A217, B216, C218

Comfort and Consolation

All Who Labor, Come to Me – A133, B204, C206
Arise, Jerusalem, Look to the East – A23, B23, C23
Arise, Jerusalem, Stand on the Height – A4, B6, C4
Be Patient, Beloved – A9
Be Strong, Our God Has Come to Save Us (I) – B9, C9
Blest Are the Poor in Spirit – A102
"Come," Says My Heart – B92, C92
Every Valley Shall Be Filled – C6
God Heals the Broken – B109, C173
I Am With You – C30
I Am Your Savior, My People – A166, B168, C169
I Know I Shall See the Goodness of the Lord – A90
I Will Praise You, Lord – A56, B62, C62, C78
I Will See You Again – A88, B91, C91
Keep My Soul in Peace – A187
Look on My Toil – A116, B119, C119
Lord, You Are Close – A167

My Shepherd Is the Lord – A39, A233, B42, B82, B141, B191, B232, C82, C207, C234
One Thing I Seek – A122, B125, C125
Rejoice, Rejoice, All You Who Love Jerusalem! – A38, B40, C40
The Lord Is My Light – A99, B122, C33, C122
The Mercy of God Is for All – A153
The Spirit and the Bride Say "Come!" – A231, B230, C232
This Is My Body – A50, B56, C56
You Are My Hiding-place, O Lord – C48
You Are Rich in Mercy – A68, A176, B43
You Will Show Me the Path of Life – B188
You Will Show Us the Path of Life – A74
Your Mercy Is My Hope – A110, B113, C113

Compassion
Heal Me in Your Mercy – B112
I Will Praise Your Name For Ever (I) – C84
If You Love Me, Feed My Lambs (I) – C79
In Your Abundant Love – A126
Light of the World – A106
Lord, You Are Close – A167
Merciful and Tender – A111, A164, B117, C36, C114, C187
Open Your Hand, Lord – B145
Save Us, Lord – B142
The Love of God – A92, B95, C95
The Mercy of God Is for All – A153
Those Who Fear the Lord – A105
You Are Good and Forgiving – A138
You Open Your Hand – A127, B144

Conversion / Repentance
All Your Sins Have Been Forgiven – C127
Behold, the Bridegroom Is Here (I) – B118
Change Your Heart and Mind – A171
Give Us Living Water – A37, B39, C39
God of Hosts, Bring Us Back – B2, C11
Heal Me in Your Mercy – B112
Heal My Soul – B114
Listen! Listen! Open Your Hearts! – A36, B37, C37
Look on My Toil – A116, B119, C119
Lord, Cleanse My Heart – A61, B46, C67
Lose Your Life and Save It – A228, B227, B167, C130, C165
Love Is My Desire – A121
Merciful and Tender – A111, A164, B117, C36, C114, C187
My Grace Is Enough – B136
Remember, Lord – A170
Set the Earth on Fire – C155
Shine Out, O Lord; You Are My God – B106
The Last Shall Be First – A168
The Prayer of Our Hearts – C186
There Is Mercy in the Lord – A42, B47, C47
Turn Our Hearts from Stone to Flesh – A35, B35, C35
Turn to the Lord – B111, C126
We Look to You, O Lord – B135
You Are Light in the Lord – A40, B44, C44
You Are Rich in Mercy – A208, B207, B177, C209, C178
You Are the Vine – A82, B85

Courage and Strength
All Who Labor, Come to Me – A133, B204, C206
Be Patient, Beloved – A9
Be Strong, Our God Has Come to Save Us (I) – B9, C9
Be Strong, Our God Has Come to Save Us (II) – B164
Come, My Children – B176
Courage! Get Up! – B185
Don't Be Afraid – A150, B133, C152, C196
Give Thanks to the Lord, Alleluia (I) – A70
God Heals the Broken – B109, C173

God of Life, God of Hope – C193
I Love You, Lord – A183
I Shall Dwell in the House of the Lord – A177
In Every Age, O Lord, You Have Been Our Refuge – C164
In God Alone Is My Soul at Rest – A114
Lead Me, Guide Me – A107, B110, C110
Let Your Love Be Upon Us, O Lord – A33, A80, B181
Lift Up Your Heads, Stand and Believe – C3
One Thing I Seek – A122, B125, C125
Salvation Has Come to This House – C190
Save Us, Lord – A125, B128, C128
The Lord Is My Light – A99, B122, C33, C122
The Strong Lord Sets Me Free – A184, B116, C116
Those Who Love Me, I Will Deliver – A29, B29, C38, C29
Who Can This Be – B130
You Will Show Me the Path of Life – B188
You Will Show Us the Path of Life – A74

Covenant
A Light Will Shine on Us This Day – A13, B13, C13, C20
All Things Are from the Lord – A156
As a Bridegroom Rejoices – A240, B239, C100
As Seed for the Sowing – A139
Behold, the Bridegroom Is Here (I) – B118
Bless the Lord, My Soul – C27
Blest Are the Poor in Spirit – A102
Christ Is the Light – A211, A213, B210, B212, C212, C214
Come, Come to the Banquet – A146, C43
God Feeds Us, God Saves Us – A115, C183
God Heals the Broken – B109, C173
God of Life, God of Hope – C193
God Remembers His Covenant For Ever – B18
Here in Your Presence – B121
I Thank You, Lord, with All My Heart – C180
I Will Dwell with You – A237, B236, C238
I Will Sing For Ever of Your Love – A129, B11
Let the Word Make a Home in Your Heart – A19, B161
My Sheep I Will Pasture – C208
Our Shelter and Our Help – C124
The People of God Are the Vineyard – A174
This Day Is Holy to the Lord Our God – C101
Turn Our Hearts from Stone to Flesh – A35, B35, C35
You Are Rich in Mercy – A176
Yours Is the Day – B149, C150

Creation
All Things Are from the Lord – A156
Alleluia, Send Out Your Spirit – A93, B96, C96
Bless the Lord, My Soul – C27
From the East and West, from the North and South – A186, C158
How Wonderful Your Name, O Lord – C201
I Will Praise You, I Will Thank You – A215, B214, C216
Our God Has Blessed Us – A249, B248, C250
Send Out Your Spirit – A52, B58, C58
The Earth Is Full of the Goodness of God (I) – A76, B80, C80
The Earth Is Full of the Goodness of God (II) – A53, B59, C59
You Have Given Everything Its Place – A179, B174, C175

Cross
Father, into Your Hands – A51, B57, C57
Lose Your Life and Save It – A228, B227, B167, C130, C165
My God, My God – A45, B51, C51
Our Glory and Pride is the Cross of Jesus Christ – A47, B53, C53, C227
Rise Up and Tell All Your Children – A227, B226, C228
Take Hold of Eternal Life – C174

Death and Eternal Life
Alleluia, Alleluia, Alleluia! (I) – B75, 75

"Come," Says My Heart – B92, C92
Eat My Flesh and Drink My Blood – A236, B235, C237
Give Peace to Those Who Wait – A163, B165, C166
God, Who Raised Jesus from the Dead – A232, B231, C233
I Am the Resurrection – A43, B49, C49
I Am the Way: Follow Me – A81
I Know I Shall See the Goodness of the Lord – A90
I Shall Dwell in the House of the Lord – A177
I Will Dwell with You – A237, B236, C238
I Will See You Again – A88, B91, C91
I Will Walk in the Presence of the Lord – B33, B166
My Portion and My Cup – A54, B60, B193, C60, C132
My Shepherd Is the Lord – A39, A233, B42, B82, B141, B191, B232,
    C82, C207, C234
One Thing I Seek – A122, B125, C125
Our Glory and Pride is the Cross of Jesus Christ – A47, B53, C53, C227
Rejoice, Your Names Are Written in Heaven – C136
Take Hold of Eternal Life – C174
The Lord Is My Light – A99, B122, C33, C122
This Is My Body – A50, B56, C56
Unless a Grain of Wheat – B48
We Shall Be Like You – A222, B221, C223
You Will Show Me the Path of Life – B188
You Will Show Us the Path of Life – A74
Your Mercy Is My Hope – A110, B113, C113
Your Word Is Life, Lord – B158

Discipleship

A New Commandment I Give to You – A49, B55, C55
All That Is True – A175
As One Body in Your Spirit – C103
Ask and Receive (I) – A143
At Your Word Our Hearts Are Burning – A75
Because You Are Filled with the Spirit – B173
Blest Are the Poor in Spirit – A103
Blest Are You Who Weep – C112
Cast Out into the Deep – C109
Change Your Heart and Mind – A171
Chosen in Christ, Blessed in Christ – B139
Christ Laid Down His Life for Us – A172, B170
Clothed in Christ, One in Christ – A28, B28, B69, C69
Come, All You Good and Faithful Servants – A195
Do Not Store Up Earthly Treasures – C149, C171
Forgive, and You Will Be Forgiven – C115
Give Us Living Water – A37, B39, C39
Give: Your Father Sees – A210, B209, C211
Happy Are They Who Follow – A108
Here I Am – A96, B99, C107
I Am the Resurrection – A43, B49, C49
I Am the Way: Follow Me – A81
I Loved Wisdom More Than Health or Beauty – A141, B179, C163
If You Love Me, Feed My Lambs – A219, B218, C79, C220
If You Will Love Each Other – A165
Keep These Words in Your Heart and Soul – A118
Light of the World – A100, A106
Listen! Listen! Open Your Hearts! – A36, A37, C37
Listen, Listen to the Words of Jesus – A148
Listen: I Stand at the Door and Knock – A140, C143
Live on in My Love – A85, A91, B88, B94, C88
Lose Your Life and Save It – A228, B227, B167, C130, C165
Love Bears All Things – C106
Love the Lord Your God – A112, A185, C140
Not on Bread Alone Are We Nourished – A31, C31
Our Glory and Pride is the Cross of Jesus Christ – A47, B53, C53, C227
Planted Like a Tree – C111
Set the Earth on Fire – C155
Take Hold of Eternal Life – C174
Take Your Place at the Table – C177

Teach Me Your Path – B30
The Greatest Among You – B182
The Last Shall Be First – A168
The Love of God – A92, B95, C95
The Word of God at Work in Us – A188
Those Who Do Justice – A151, B160, C142
Those Who Do the Will of God – B124
Those Who Fear the Lord – A105
Turn Our Hearts from Stone to Flesh – A35, B35, C35
Unless a Grain of Wheat – B48
Walk in My Ways – B31, B103
We Will Follow You, Lord – C133
Where Two or Three Are Gathered – A162
With All My Heart I Cry (II) – A142
You Are Light in the Lord – A40, B44, C44
You Are Peter – A217, B216, C218
You Are the Vine – A82, B85
You Shall Be a Royal Priesthood – A124

Encouragement

All That Is True – A175
All Who Labor, Come to Me – A133, B204, C206
Arise, Jerusalem, Look to the East – A23, B23, C23
Arise, Jerusalem, Stand on the Height – A4, B6, C4
Be Patient, Beloved – A9
Be Strong, Our God Has Come to Save Us (I) – B9, C9
Be Strong, Our God Has Come to Save Us (II) – B164
Behold, the Bridegroom Is Here (II) – A192, B3
Cast Out into the Deep – C109
Come, Lord, and Save Us – A8
Come, My Children – B176
Courage! Get Up! – B185
Don't Be Afraid – A150, B133, C152, C196
Every Valley Shall Be Filled – C6
God Heals the Broken – B109, C173
God of Life, God of Hope – C193
Heal Me in Your Mercy – B112
Heaven and Earth Will Fade Away – A109, B194
Home for the Lonely – B143, C144, C161
I Am With You – C30
I Will See You Again – A88, B91, C91
If You Will Love Each Other – A165
In Every Age, O Lord, You Have Been Our Refuge – C164
Justice Shall Flourish – A5
Lift Up Your Heads, Stand and Believe – C3
Light of the World – A100
Look on My Toil – A116, B119, C119
Lord, You Are Close – A167
Merciful and Tender – A111, A164, B117, C36, C114, C187
My Lips Will Tell of Your Justice – C105
My Plans for You Are Peace – A193, B192, C194
My Portion and My Cup – A54, B60, B193, C60, C132
My Sheep I Will Pasture – C208
Now Is the Hour – A3
One Thing I Seek – A122, B125, C125
Our Help Shall Come from the Lord – C182
Our Shelter and Our Help – C124
Rejoice, Rejoice, All You Who Love Jerusalem! – A38, B40, C40
Rejoice, Your Names Are Written in Heaven – C136
Save Us, Lord – B142
Seek the Lord! Long for the Lord! – A32, A101, A182, B32, C32
Sing to the Lord – A55, B61, C61
Teach Me Your Path – B30
The Days Are Coming, Surely Coming – C1
The Last Shall Be First – A168
The Lord Is My Light – A99, B122, C33, C122
The Mercy of God Is for All – A153
The Strong Lord Sets Me Free – A184, B116, C116

Those Who Love Me, I Will Deliver – A29, B29, C38, C29
We Receive from Your Fullness – A16, B16, C16
When the Poor Cry Out – C185
Where Two or Three Are Gathered – A162
You Are Good and Forgiving – A138
You Are Rich in Mercy – A68, A176, A208, B43, B207, C209
You Are the Shepherd – A78
You Open Your Hand – A127, B144
Your Mercy Is My Hope – A110, B113, C113
Your Word Is Life, Lord – B158

Eucharist
As One Body in Your Spirit – C103
As Seed for the Sowing – A136
At Your Word Our Hearts Are Burning – A75
Behold the Lamb of God! – A97, B100
Behold, the Bridegroom Is Here (I) – B118
Blest Are You Who Weep – C112
Christ, Our Pasch – A67, B70, C70
Come to Me and You Shall Never Hunger – A147, B148
Come, All You Good and Faithful Servants – A195
Come, Come to the Banquet – A146, C43
Eat My Flesh and Drink My Blood – A236, B235, C237
Finest Food! Choicest Wine! – A178
From the East and West, from the North and South – A186, C158
Here in Your Presence – B121
How I Thirst for You – A235, B234, C236
I Am the Resurrection – A43, B49, C49
If You Love Me, Feed My Lambs (I) – C79
Listen: I Stand at the Door and Knock – A140, C143
Not on Bread Alone Are We Nourished – A31, C31
O Praise the Lord, Jerusalem – A203, B151
Our Cup of Blessing – A48, B54, C54
Raise the Cup of Salvation – B202
Save Us, Lord – B142
Speak Your Word, O Lord – C121
The Goodness of the Lord – B150, C41
This Is My Body – A50, B56, C56
This Is the Bread – B147, B155
Touch Me and See – A71, B79
Unless a Grain of Wheat – B48
With Finest Wheat and Finest Wine – A202, B201, C203
Your Word Is Life, Lord – B158

Exile
Be Strong, Our God Has Come to Save Us (II) – B164
Give Peace to Those Who Wait – A163, B165, C166
God of Life, God of Hope – C193
Laughter Fills Our Mouths – B184, C5
My Plans for You Are Peace – A193, B192, C194
O Let My Tongue Cleave to My Mouth – B41
Praise the Lord, Alleluia! – B108

Faith
Change Your Heart and Mind – A171
Come to Me and You Shall Never Hunger – A147, B148
Don't Be Afraid – A150, B133, C152, C196
Eat My Flesh and Drink My Blood – A236, B235, C237
I Am the Resurrection – A43, B49, C49
In God Alone Is My Soul at Rest – A114
Lift Up Your Heads, Stand and Believe – C3
Listen, Listen to the Words of Jesus – A148
Love Bears All Things – C106
Planted Like a Tree – C111
Put Your Hand Here, Thomas – A72, B76, C76
Take Hold of Eternal Life – C174
The Word of God at Work in Us – A188

Unless a Grain of Wheat – B48
Who Can This Be – B130
With All My Heart I Cry (II) – A142

Faithfulness of God
All Things Are from the Lord – A156
As a Bridegroom Rejoices – A240, B239, C100
As One Body in Your Spirit – C103
As Seed for the Sowing – A136
Ask and Receive (I) – A143
Ask and Receive (II) – C146
Be Strong, Our God Has Come to Save Us (II) – B164
Behold, the Bridegroom Is Here (I) – B118
Blessed Are You, Lord – A169, B171
Blest Are the Poor in Spirit – A102
Cast Out into the Deep – C109
Christ Is the Light – A211, A213, B210, B212, C212, C214
Come, All You Good and Faithful Servants – A195
Come, Come to the Banquet – A146, C43
Come, Lord, and Save Us – A8
Come, My Children – B176
Do Not Store Up Earthly Treasures – C171
Don't Be Afraid – A150, B133, C152, C196
Everlasting Is Your Love – A155
From the Fullness of Our Hearts – C118
Go to the Ends of the Earth – C120
God Feeds Us, God Saves Us – A115, C183
God Heals the Broken – B109, C173
God of Life, God of Hope – C193
God Remembers His Covenant For Ever – B18
Happy Are They Whose God Is the Lord – B199
Heal Me in Your Mercy – B112
Heaven and Earth Will Fade Away – A109, B194
Here in Your Presence – B121
Home for the Lonely – B143, C144, C161
I Am With You – C30
I Called in My Distress – A218, B217, C219
I Know I Shall See the Goodness of the Lord – A90
I Shall Dwell in the House of the Lord – A177
I Thank You, Lord, with All My Heart – C180
I Will Praise Your Name For Ever (II) – A132, C189
I Will Sing For Ever of Your Love – A129, B11
In the Presence of the Angels – C108
Keep Us in Your Name – B127, C94
Let All the Earth Adore and Praise You – A73, B98, C77
Let All the Earth Cry Out Your Praises – A73, B77, C77
Let Your Love Be Upon Us, O Lord – A33, A80, B181
Listen, Listen to the Words of Jesus – A148
Lord, You Are Close – A167
May God Grant Us Joy of Heart – A250, B249, C251
Merciful and Tender – A111, A164, B117, C36, C114, C187
My Grace Is Enough – B136
My Lips Will Tell of Your Justice – C105
My Sheep I Will Pasture – C208
Open Your Hand, Lord – B145
Our Help Shall Come from the Lord – C182
Our Shelter and Our Help – C124
People of God, Flock of the Lord – A123, C81
Praise the Lord, Alleluia! – B108
Rejoice in the Lord, Again Rejoice! – A7, B7, C7
Save Us, Lord – B142
Sing and Make Music – A248, B247, C249
Speak Your Word, O Lord – C121
The Mercy of God Is for All – A153
Those Who Love Me, I Will Deliver – C29
Who Can This Be – B130
You Alone Are Lord – A181
You Are My Praise – B84

You Are Rich in Mercy – A68, A176, B43
You Have Shown You Love Us – A199, B198, C200
You Open Your Hand – A127, B144
Yours Is the Day – B149, C150

Family Life / Parenthood
How Happy Are You – A194, B175
Let the Word Make a Home in Your Heart – A19, B161
Those Who Fear the Lord – A105
You Are God's Temple – A247, B246, C248

Food / Hunger
As Seed for the Sowing – A136
Blest Are You Who Weep – C112
Come to Me and You Shall Never Hunger – A147, B148
Come, Come to the Banquet – A146, C43
Finest Food! Choicest Wine! – A178
Give: Your Father Sees – A210, B209, C211
God Feeds Us, God Saves Us – A115, C183
If You Love Me, Feed My Lambs (I) – C79
Not on Bread Alone Are We Nourished – A31, C31
Save Us, Lord – B142
This Is the Bread – B147, B155
With Finest Wheat and Finest Wine – A202, B201, C203

Forgiveness / Reconciliation
All Who Labor, Come to Me – A133, B204, C206
All Your Sins Have Been Forgiven – C127
Change Your Heart and Mind – A171
Do Not Abandon Me, Lord! – B186, C188
For You My Soul Is Thirsting – A158, C129
Forgive, and You Will Be Forgiven – C115
Give Us Living Water – A37, B39, C39
God of Hosts, Bring Us Back – B2, C11
Heal Me in Your Mercy – B112
Heal My Soul – B114
If You Will Love Each Other – A165
Jesus, Mighty Lord, Come Save Us – A12
Lord, Cleanse My Heart – A61, B46, C67
Lord, You Are Close – A167
Love Is My Desire – A121
Merciful and Tender – A111, A164, B117, C36, C114, C187
Remember, Lord – A170
The Last Shall Be First – A168
The Love of God – A92, B95, C95
The Mercy of God Is for All – A153
The Prayer of Our Hearts – C186
There Is Mercy in the Lord – A42, B47, C47
Turn Our Hearts from Stone to Flesh – A35, B35, C35
Turn to the Lord – B111, C126
We Have Sinned, Lord – A30, B208, C167
We Look to You, O Lord – B135
Where Two or Three Are Gathered – A162
You Are Good and Forgiving – A138
You Are Light in the Lord – A40, B44, C44
You Are My Hiding-place, O Lord – C48
You Are Rich in Mercy – A68, A176, A208, B43, B177, B207, C178, C209

Freedom
God's Tender Mercy – B215, C217
I Called in My Distress – A218, B217, C219
Jesus, Mighty Lord, Come Save Us – A12
Lead Me, Guide Me – A107, B110, C110
Lift Up Your Heads, Stand and Believe – C3
Ring Out Your Joy – B120
The Strong Lord Sets Me Free – A184, B116, C116

Gathering
All That Is True – A175
All Things Are from the Lord – A156
All You Nations – A128, B131, C131
At Your Word Our Hearts Are Burning – A75
Because You Are Filled with the Spirit – B173
Christ Is the Light – A211, B210, C212
Christ the Lord Is Risen Again – A65, B71, C71
Christ, Our Pasch – A67, B70, C70
Clothed in Christ, One in Christ – A28, B28, B69, C69
"Come," Says My Heart – B92, C92
Come to Me and Drink – A94, B97, C97
Come, All You Good and Faithful Servants – A195
Come, My Children – B176
Do Not Store Up Earthly Treasures – C149, C171
Don't Be Afraid – A150, B133, C152, C196
For Ever, For Ever, We Praise You For Ever – A200
From the East and West, from the North and South – A186, C158
From the Fullness of Our Hearts – C118
Give Peace to Those Who Wait – A163, B165, C166
God of Hosts, Bring Us Back – B2, C11
God's Love Is Revealed to Us – A15, B15, C28
God's Tender Mercy – A6
God, Let All the Peoples Praise You – A152, C87
Heaven and Earth Will Fade Away – A109, B194
I Am the Way: Follow Me – A81
I Am Your Savior, My People – A166, B168, C169
I Loved Wisdom More Than Health or Beauty – A141, B179, C163
I Will Dwell with You – A237, B236, C238
I Will Praise You, I Will Thank You – A215, B214, C216
I Will Praise Your Name For Ever – A132, C84, C189
If You Will Love Each Other – A165
Jesus Christ, the Same Today, Yesterday and Evermore – A22, B22, C22
Jesus, Mighty Lord, Come Save Us – A12
Lead Me, Guide Me – A107, B110, C110
Let All the Earth Adore and Praise You – A73, B98, C77
Let All the Earth Cry Out Your Praises – A73, B77, C77
Let the King of Glory Come In – A11, B211, C213
Let the Word Make a Home in Your Heart – A19, B161
Let Us Go Rejoicing – A2, B245, C198
Light of the World – A100, A106
Listen! Listen! Open Your Hearts! – A36, A37, C37
Listen, Listen to the Voice of Jesus – A198, B197
Listen, Listen to the Words of Jesus – A148
Listen: I Stand at the Door and Knock – A140, C143
May God Bless Us in Mercy – A21, B21, C21
My God, My Strength, Defend My Cause – A41, B45, C45
People of God, Flock of the Lord – A123, C81
Praise to God Who Lifts Up the Poor – C170
Proclaim the Wonders God Has Done – C99
Ring Out Your Joy – B120
Seek the Lord! Long for the Lord! – A32, A101, A182, B32, C32
Shout to the Ends of the Earth – A89, B86, C86
Sing and Make Music – A248, B247, C249
Sing to God a New Song – A79, B83, C83
Speak Your Word, O Lord – C121
Take Your Place at the Table – C177
The Days Are Coming, Surely Coming – C1
The Earth Is Full of the Goodness of God (I) – A76, B80, C80
The Last Shall Be First – A168
This Day Is Holy to the Lord Our God – C101
Those Who Do Justice – A151, B160, C142
Those Who Love Me, I Will Deliver – A29, B29, C38, C29
To You, O Lord, I Lift My Soul – A1, B1, C2
Turn Our Hearts from Stone to Flesh – A35, B35, C35
Turn to the Lord – B111, C126
Venite, Adoremus – A245, B107, C246
Where Two or Three Are Gathered – A162

With All My Heart I Praise You – B115
Within Your Temple – A131, B134, C134
Worthy Is the Lamb Who Was Slain – A196, B195, C197
You Are My Praise – B84
You Have Given Everything Its Place – A179, B174, C175
You Have Shown You Love Us – A199, B198, C200
Yours Is the Day – B149, C150

God the Father (Creator)
Everlasting Is Your Love – A155
I Will Praise You, I Will Thank You – A215, B214, C216
Let All the Earth Adore and Praise You – A73, B98, C77
Let All the Earth Cry Out Your Praises – A73, B77, C77
Shout to the Ends of the Earth – A89, B86, C86
The Lord Will Bless His People – A27
You Have Shown You Love Us – A199, B198, C200

Grace
All Your Sins Have Been Forgiven – C127
Because You Are Filled with the Spirit – B173
"Come," Says My Heart – B92, C92
Courage! Get Up! – B185
Do Not Abandon Me, Lord! – B186, C188
Don't Be Afraid – A150, B133, C152, C196
From the Fullness of Our Hearts – C118
Give Thanks to the Lord, Alleluia (I) – A70
God's Love Is Revealed to Us – A15, B15, C28
God's Tender Mercy – B215, C217
Happy Are They Who Follow – A108
Heal Me in Your Mercy – B112
I Am Your Savior, My People – A166, B168, C169
I Shall Dwell in the House of the Lord – A177
I Will Walk in the Presence of the Lord – B33, B166
In the Presence of the Angels – C108
Lose Your Life and Save It – A228, B227, B167, C130
Love Is My Desire – A121
Merciful and Tender – A111, A164, B117, C36, C114, C187
My Grace Is Enough – B136
My Sheep I Will Pasture – C208
Our Glory and Pride is the Cross of Jesus Christ – A47, B53, C53, C227
Praise to God Who Lifts Up the Poor – C170
Remember, Lord – A170
Shine Out, O Lord; You Are My God – B106
Speak Your Word, O Lord – C121
The Last Shall Be First – A168
The Love of God – A92, B95, C95
The Mercy of God Is for All – A153
The Strong Lord Sets Me Free – A184, B116, C116
Turn Our Hearts from Stone to Flesh – A35, B35, C35
Turn to the Lord – B111, C126
We Receive from Your Fullness – A16, B16, C16
When the Poor Cry Out – C185
You Alone Are My Help – A137, B140, C141
You Are Good and Forgiving – A138
You Are Light in the Lord – A40, B44, C44
You Are My Hiding-place, O Lord – C48
You Are Rich in Mercy – A68, A176, A208, B43, B177, B207, C178, C209

Grieving / Mourning
Do Not Abandon Me, Lord! – B186, C188
How I Thirst for You – A235, B234, C236
Let My Prayer Come Before You, Lord – A189, B189, C191
Lord, Listen to My Prayer – A234, B233, C235
My God, My God – A45, B51, C51
My Shepherd Is the Lord – A39, A233, B42, B82, B141, B191, B232, C82, C207, C234
O Let My Tongue Cleave to My Mouth – B41

Guidance
Ask and Receive (I) – A143
Cast Out into the Deep – C109
Change Your Heart and Mind – A171
"Come," Says My Heart – B92, C92
Do Not Store Up Earthly Treasures – C171
Don't Be Afraid – A150, B133, C152, C196
God of Life, God of Hope – C193
Heaven and Earth Will Fade Away – A109, B194
I Am the Way: Follow Me – A81
I Loved Wisdom More Than Health or Beauty – A141, B179, C163
If You Will Love Each Other – A165
In Every Age, O Lord, You Have Been Our Refuge – C164
Keep These Words in Your Heart and Soul – A118
Lead Me, Guide Me – A107, B110, C110
Light of the World – A100, A106
Listen, Listen to the Words of Jesus – A148
Listen: I Stand at the Door and Knock – A140, C143
Look on My Toil – A116, B119, C119
Lose Your Life and Save It – C165
Love the Lord Your God – A112, A185, C140
My Grace Is Enough – B136
My Sheep I Will Pasture – C208
My Shepherd Is the Lord – A39, A233, B42, B82, B141, B191, B232, C82, C207, C234
Not on Bread Alone Are We Nourished – A31, C31
One Thing I Seek – A122, B125, C125
Remember, Lord – A170
Rise Up and Tell All Your Children – A227, B226, C228
Save Me, O Lord – A117
Speak Your Word, O Lord – C121
Teach Me Your Path – B30
The Lord Is My Light – A99, B122, C33, C122
The Prayer of Our Hearts – C186
The Word of God at Work in Us – A188
Those Who Do Justice – A151, B160, C142
To You, O Lord, I Lift My Soul – A1, B1, C2
Turn Our Hearts from Stone to Flesh – A35, B35, C35
Turn to Me, Answer Me – A154, B156, C156
Walk in My Ways – B31, B103
We Will Follow You, Lord – C133
When You Fill Us with Your Word – B178, C148
Where Two or Three Are Gathered – A162
With All My Heart I Cry (II) – A142
You Are Light in the Lord – A40, B44, C44
You Will Show Me the Path of Life – B188
You Will Show Us the Path of Life – A74
Your Word Is Life, Lord – A58, B36, B64, C64

Healing
All Who Labor, Come to Me – A133, B204, C206
All Your Sins Have Been Forgiven – C127
Be Patient, Beloved – A9
Be Strong, Our God Has Come to Save Us (I) – B9, C9
Be Strong, Our God Has Come to Save Us (II) – B164
Change Your Heart and Mind – A171
Courage! Get Up! – B185
Don't Be Afraid – A150, B133, C152, C196
Give Peace to Those Who Wait – A163, B165, C166
God Heals the Broken – B109, C173
Guard Me as the Apple of Your Eye! – B180, C181
Heal Me in Your Mercy – B112
Heal My Soul – B114
I Called in My Distress – A218, B217, C219
I Will Dwell with You – A237, B236, C238
Let Your Love Be Upon Us, O Lord – A33, A80, B181
Like a Deer That Longs for Running Streams – A59, B65, C65
Lord, Cleanse My Heart – A61, B46, C67

Jesus Christ, the Same Today, Yesterday and Evermore – A22, B22, C22
Jesus, Mighty Lord, Come Save Us – A12
Let the King of Glory Come In – A11, B211, C213
Light of the World – A100, A106
Listen, Listen to the Voice of Jesus – A198, B197
Listen, Listen to the Words of Jesus – A148
Live on in My Love – A85, A91, B88, B94, C88
Lose Your Life and Save It – C165
Our Glory and Pride is the Cross of Jesus Christ – A47, B53, C53, C227
Take Hold of Eternal Life – C174
The Love of God – A92, B95, B200, C95
The Stone Which the Builders Rejected – B81
Worthy Is the Lamb Who Was Slain – A196, B195, C197
You Are the Shepherd – A78
You Shall Be a Royal Priesthood – A124

Journey / Pilgrimage
All That Is True – A175
Be Strong, Our God Has Come to Save Us (I) – B9, C9
Be Strong, Our God Has Come to Save Us (II) – B164
Cast Out into the Deep – C109
Come, All You Good and Faithful Servants – A195
Do Not Store Up Earthly Treasures – C149
God of Life, God of Hope – C193
Home for the Lonely – B143, C144, C161
How I Thirst for You – A235, B234, C236
I Am the Way: Follow Me – A81
I Know I Shall See the Goodness of the Lord – A90
I Shall Dwell in the House of the Lord – A177
Let Us Go Rejoicing – A2, B245, C198
Lord, This Is the People – A230, B229, C231
Lose Your Life and Save It – A228, B227, B167, C130
My Sheep I Will Pasture – C208
Now Is the Hour – A3
One Thing I Seek – A122, B125, C125
Our City Has No Need of Sun or Moon – A25, B25, C25
Rejoice, Rejoice, All You Who Love Jerusalem! – A38, B40, C40
Take Hold of Eternal Life – C174
Teach Me Your Path – B30
Unless a Grain of Wheat – B48
Walk in My Ways – B31, B103
We Will Follow You, Lord – C133
You Are Light in the Lord – A40, B44, C44

Joy / Gladness / Delight
A River Flows – A238, B237, C239
All That Is True – A175
All Things Are from the Lord – A156
All You Nations – A128, B131, C131
As a Bridegroom Rejoices – A240, B239, C100
Come to Me and You Shall Never Hunger – A147, B148
Come, All You Good and Faithful Servants – A195
For Ever, For Ever, We Praise You For Ever – A200
From the East and West, from the North and South – A186, C158
God's Love Is Revealed to Us – A15, B15, C28
Great In Our Midst Is the Holy One – C8
Happy Are They Whose God Is the Lord – C151
How Wonderful Your Name, O Lord – C201
I Will See You Again – A88, B91, C91
In the Presence of the Angels – C108
It Is Good to Give You Thanks – B126, C117
Joyfully You Will Draw Water – A57, B27, B205, C63
Laughter Fills Our Mouths – B184, C5
Let Us Go Rejoicing – A2, B245, C198
Like Newborn Children – A69, B74, C74
Listen: I Stand at the Door and Knock – A140, C143
May God Grant Us Joy of Heart – A250, B249, C251
My Portion and My Cup – A54, B60, B193, C60, C132

People of God, Flock of the Lord – A123, C81
Rejoice in the Lord, Again Rejoice! – A7, B7, C7
Rejoice, Rejoice, All You Who Love Jerusalem! – A38, B40, C40
Rejoice, Your Names Are Written in Heaven – C136
Ring Out Your Joy – B120
Shout to the Ends of the Earth – A89, B86, C86
Sing to the Lord – A55, B61, C61
The Earth Is Full of the Goodness of God (I) – A76, B80, C80
The Earth Is Full of the Goodness of God (II) – A53, B59, C59
This Day Is Holy to the Lord Our God – C101
This Is the Day – A66, B72, C72
Turn to the Lord – B111, C126
Venite, Adoremus – A245, B107, C246
With All My Heart I Praise You – B115
You Are Rich in Mercy – A68, A176, B43
You Have Given Everything Its Place – A179, B174, C175
You Will Show Me the Path of Life – B188
You Will Show Us the Path of Life – A74

Kin(g)dom / Kin(g)ship / Reign of God
All You Nations – A128, B131, C131
At Your Word Our Hearts Are Burning – A75
Be Patient, Beloved – A9
Be Strong, Our God Has Come to Save Us (I) – B9, C9
Be Strong, Our God Has Come to Save Us (II) – B164
Behold, the Bridegroom Is Here (II) – A192, B3
Blest Are the Poor in Spirit – A102, A103
Blest Are You Who Weep – C112
Come, Lord, and Save Us – A8
Do Not Store Up Earthly Treasures – C149
Give: Your Father Sees – A210, B209, C211
God's Tender Mercy – A6
I Will Dwell with You – A237, B236, C238
I Will Praise Your Name For Ever (I) – C84
I Will Praise Your Name For Ever (II) – A132, C189
Jesus Christ, the Same Today, Yesterday and Evermore – A22, B22, C22
Justice Shall Flourish – A5
Let the King of Glory Come In – A11, B211, C213
Lift Up Your Heads, Stand and Believe – C3
Open, You Skies: Rain Down the Just One – A10, B10, C10
Our City Has No Need of Sun or Moon – A25, B25, C25
Praise to God Who Lifts Up the Poor – C170
Proclaim the Wonders God Has Done – C99
Rejoice in the Lord, Again Rejoice! – A7, B7, C7
Rejoice, Your Names Are Written in Heaven – C136
Take Hold of Eternal Life – C174
The Days Are Coming, Surely Coming – C1
The Last Shall Be First – A168
The Lord Is King (I) – A221, B220, C93
The Spirit and the Bride Say "Come!" – A231, B230, C232
They Shall Adore You – A24, B24, C24
Those Who Do Justice – A151, B160, C142
Walk in My Ways – B31, B103
You Are My Praise – B84
You Shall Be a Royal Priesthood – A124

Lament / Suffering
Do Not Abandon Me, Lord! – B186, C188
God, Come to My Aid (II) – A144, B146, C147
How I Thirst for You – A235, B234, C236
I Am Your Savior, My People – A166, B168, C169
In Your Abundant Love – A126
Let My Prayer Come Before You, Lord – A189, B189, C191
Look on My Toil – A116, B119, C119
Lose Your Life and Save It – A228, B227, B167, C130
My God, My God – A45, B51, C51
My God, My Strength, Defend My Cause – A41, B45, C45
O Let My Tongue Cleave to My Mouth – B41

Remember, Lord – A170
Save Us, Lord – A125
Shine Out, O Lord; You Are My God – B106
The Mercy of God Is for All – A153
The People of God Are the Vineyard – A174
Turn to Me, Answer Me – A154, B156, C156
We Have Sinned, Lord – A30, B208, C167
You Are Rich in Mercy – B177, C178
Your Mercy Is My Hope – A110, B113, C113

Life
Eat My Flesh and Drink My Blood – A236, B235, C237
God of Life, God of Hope – C193
God's Love Is Revealed to Us – A15, B15, C28
God, Who Raised Jesus from the Dead – A232, B231, C233
I Am the Way: Follow Me – A81
I Will Praise You, I Will Thank You – A215, B214, C216
In Every Age, O Lord, You Have Been Our Refuge – C164
Let the Word Make a Home in Your Heart – A19, B161
Love the Lord Your God – A112, A185, C140
This Is the Bread – B147, B155
Your Word Is Life, Lord – B158

Light
A Light Will Shine on Us This Day – A13, B13, C13, C20
Christ Is the Light – A211, A213, B210, B212, C212, C214
Light of the World – A100, A106
Our City Has No Need of Sun or Moon – A25, B25, C25
Shine Your Face on Us, Lord – B78
The Lord Is My Light – A99, B122, C33, C122
Those Who Fear the Lord – A105
We Receive from Your Fullness – A16, B16, C16
We Shall Be Like You – A222, B221, C223
You Are Light in the Lord – A40, B44, C44

Loneliness
Do Not Abandon Me, Lord! – B186, C188
Heaven and Earth Will Fade Away – A109, B194
In Your Abundant Love – A126
Let My Prayer Come Before You, Lord – A189, B189, C191
Lord, You Are Close – A167

Longing / Seeking / Thirsting
All Who Labor, Come to Me – A133, B204, C206
All Your Sins Have Been Forgiven – C127
Ask and Receive (I) – A143
Ask and Receive (II) – C146
Be Patient, Beloved – A9
"Come," Says My Heart – B92, C92
Come to Me and Drink – A94, B97, C97
Come to Me and You Shall Never Hunger – A147, B148
Do Not Abandon Me, Lord! – B186, C188
Do Not Store Up Earthly Treasures – C149, C171
Eat My Flesh and Drink My Blood – A236, B235, C237
For You My Soul Is Thirsting – A158, C129
Give Peace to Those Who Wait – A163, B165, C166
Give Us Living Water – A37, B39, C39
God, Come to My Aid (I) – C154
God, Come to My Aid (II) – A144, B146, C147
Happy Are They Who Dwell in Your House – A244, B38, C18
How I Thirst for You – A235, B234, C236
I Know I Shall See the Goodness of the Lord – A90
In Your Abundant Love – A126
Keep My Soul in Peace – A187
Let My Prayer Come Before You, Lord – A189, B189, C191
Let Your Love Be Upon Us, O Lord – A33, A80, B181
Light of the World – A100
Like a Deer That Longs for Running Streams – A59, B65, C65
Like Newborn Children – A69, B74, C74

Lord, Cleanse My Heart – A61, B46, C67
Lord, Listen to My Prayer – A234, B233, C235
Lord, This Is the People – A230, B229, C231
My God, My Strength, Defend My Cause – A41, B45, C45
One Thing I Seek – A122, B125, C125
Open Your Hand, Lord – B145
Remember, Lord – A170
Save Me, O Lord – A117
Save Us, Lord – B142
Seek the Lord! Long for the Lord! – A32, A101, A182, B32, C32
Shine Out, O Lord; You Are My God – B106
Shine Your Face on Us, Lord – B78
Speak Your Word, O Lord – C121
The Lord Is My Light – A99, B122, C33, C122
The Mercy of God Is for All – A153
The Prayer of Our Hearts – C186
To Gaze on Your Glory – A134, B137, C137
Turn to Me, Answer Me – A154, B156, C156
We Have Sinned, Lord – A30, B208, C167
We Look to You, O Lord – B135
We Shall Be Like You – A222, B221, C223
With All My Heart I Cry (I) – A160, B162
You Are Rich in Mercy – B177, C178
You Will Show Me the Path of Life – B188
You Will Show Us the Path of Life – A74

Loss
Do Not Abandon Me, Lord! – B186, C188
How I Thirst for You – A235, B234, C236
In Your Abundant Love – A126
Look on My Toil – A116, B119, C119
Lord, Listen to My Prayer – A234, B233, C235
My God, My God – A45, B51, C51
O Let My Tongue Cleave to My Mouth – B41
Turn to Me, Answer Me – A154, B156, C156

Love for God
A New Commandment I Give to You – A49, B55, C55
Ask and Receive (I) – A143
Don't Be Afraid – A150, B133, C152, C196
For Ever, For Ever, We Praise You For Ever – A200
For You My Soul Is Thirsting – A158, C129
I Love You, Lord – A183
I Will Praise Your Name For Ever (I) – C84
I Will Praise Your Name For Ever (II) – A132, C189
I Will Sing For Ever of Your Love – A129, B11
In God Alone Is My Soul at Rest – A114
In the Presence of the Angels – C108
Love Bears All Things – C106
Love the Lord Your God – A112, A185, C140
Proclaim the Wonders God Has Done – C99
Those Who Do the Will of God – B124
Those Who Love Me, I Will Deliver – C29
To You, O Lord, I Lift My Soul – A1, B1, C2
With All My Heart I Cry (II) – A142
With All My Heart I Praise You – B115
You Alone Are Lord – A181

Love for Others
A New Commandment I Give to You – A49, B55, C55
All That Is True – A175
Ask and Receive (II) – A239, B238, C240
Christ Laid Down His Life for Us – A172, B170
Forgive, and You Will Be Forgiven – C115
If You Love Me, Feed My Lambs (I) – C79
If You Love Me, Feed My Lambs (II) – A219, B218, C220
If You Will Love Each Other – A165
Light of the World – A106
Live on in My Love – A85, A91, B88, B94, C88

Remember, Lord – A170
Shine Out, O Lord; You Are My God – B106
Shine Your Face on Us, Lord – B78
Show Us, Lord, Your Kindness – A149, B5
The Love of God – A92, B95, C95
The Mercy of God Is for All – A153
The Prayer of Our Hearts – C186
There Is Mercy in the Lord – A42, B47, C47
We Have Sinned, Lord – A30, B208, C167
We Look to You, O Lord – B135
You Are Good and Forgiving – A138
You Are Rich in Mercy – A68, A176, A208, B43, B177, B207,
    C178, C209
Your Mercy Is My Hope – A110, B113, C113

Mission / Ministry
A New Commandment I Give to You – A49, B55, C55
As One Body in Your Spirit – C103
Because You Are Filled with the Spirit – B173
Cast Out into the Deep – C109
Chosen in Christ, Blessed in Christ – B139
Christ Laid Down His Life for Us – A172, B170
Give: Your Father Sees – A210, B209, C211
Go to the Ends of the Earth – C120
If You Love Me, Feed My Lambs (I) – C79
If You Love Me, Feed My Lambs (II) – A219, B218, C220
If You Will Love Each Other – A165
Light of the World – A100, A106
Live on in My Love – A85, A91, B88, B94, C88
Love Bears All Things – C106
Proclaim the Wonders God Has Done – C99
The Greatest Among You – B182
The Message Goes Forth – A98, B101
Those Who Do Justice – A151, B160, C142
Those Who Fear the Lord – A105
Unless a Grain of Wheat – B48
Where Two or Three Are Gathered – A162
You Are Light in the Lord – A40, B44, C44
You Are the Vine – A82, B85
You Shall Be a Royal Priesthood – A124

Morning / Evening / Night
All That Is True – A175
All Things Are from the Lord – A156
Arise, Jerusalem, Look to the East – A23, B23, C23
Arise, Jerusalem, Stand on the Height – A4, B6, C4
Christ Is the Light – A211, B210, C212
Clothed in Christ, One in Christ – A28, B28, B69, C69
Come, All You Good and Faithful Servants – A195
Everlasting Is Your Love – A155
For Ever, For Ever, We Praise You For Ever – A200
Give Peace to Those Who Wait – A163, B165, C166
Give Us Living Water – A37, B39, C39
God's Tender Mercy – B215, C217
How Wonderful Your Name, O Lord – C201
I Am Your Savior, My People – A166, B168, C169
If You Will Love Each Other – A165
In Every Age, O Lord, You Have Been Our Refuge – C164
It Is Good to Give You Thanks – B126, C117
Jesus, Mighty Lord, Come Save Us – A12
Keep My Soul in Peace – A187
Let My Prayer Come Before You, Lord – A189, B189, C191
Listen! Listen! Open Your Hearts! – A36, B37, C37
Listen, Listen to the Words of Jesus – A148
May God Bless Us in Mercy – A21, B21, C21
One Thing I Seek – A122, B125, C125
Our City Has No Need of Sun or Moon – A25, B25, C25
Our Help Shall Come from the Lord – C182

Shine Your Face on Us, Lord – B78
The Lord Is My Light – A99, B122, C33, C122
This Day Is Holy to the Lord Our God – C101
Those Who Love Me, I Will Deliver – A29, B29, C38, C29
To You, O Lord, I Lift My Soul – A1, B1, C2
Venite, Adoremus – A245, B107, C246
When You Fill Us with Your Word – B178, C148
Where Two or Three Are Gathered – A162
With All My Heart I Cry (I) – A160, B162
With All My Heart I Praise You – B115
You Have Given Everything Its Place – A179, B174, C175
Your Word Is Life, Lord – A58, B36, B64, C64
Yours Is the Day – B149, C150

Music
All the Ends of the Earth – A14, B14, B87, C14, C179
All You Nations – A128, B131, C131
From the Fullness of Our Hearts – C118
God's Love Is Revealed to Us – A15, B15, C28
It Is Good to Give You Thanks – B126, C117
Let All the Earth Adore and Praise You – A73, B98, C77
Let the Word Make a Home in Your Heart – A19, B161
People of God, Flock of the Lord – A123, C81
Ring Out Your Joy – B120
Sing and Make Music – A248, B247, C249
Sing to God a New Song – A79, B83, C83
The Earth Is Full of the Goodness of God (I) – A76, B80, C80
The Earth Is Full of the Goodness of God (II) – A53, B59, C59
When You Fill Us with Your Word – B178, C148
With All My Heart I Praise You – B115

Mystery of God
Because You Are Filled with the Spirit – B173
Blessed Are You, Lord – A169, B171
Chosen in Christ, Blessed in Christ – B139
Clothed in Christ, One in Christ – A28, B28, B69, C69
For Ever, For Ever, We Praise You For Ever – A200
God's Love Is Revealed to Us – A15, B15, C28
I Loved Wisdom More Than Health or Beauty – A141, B179, C163
I Will Praise You, I Will Thank You – A215, B214, C216
I Will See You Again – A88, B91, C91
In Every Age, O Lord, You Have Been Our Refuge – C164
Jesus Christ, the Same Today, Yesterday and Evermore – A22, B22,
    C22
Lord, You Are Close – A167
The Love of God – B200
The Word of God at Work in Us – A188

New Year
All That Is True – A175
All Things Are from the Lord – A156
Come, All You Good and Faithful Servants – A195
In Every Age, O Lord, You Have Been Our Refuge – C164
Jesus Christ, the Same Today, Yesterday and Evermore – A22, B22, C22
Listen, Listen to the Voice of Jesus – A198, B197
May God Bless Us in Mercy – A21, B21, C21

Obedience
A New Commandment I Give to You – A49, B55, C55
Behold, the Bridegroom Is Here (II) – A192, B3
Change Your Heart and Mind – A171
Christ Laid Down His Life for Us – A172, B170
Do Not Store Up Earthly Treasures – C149, C171
Father, into Your Hands – A51, B57, C57
Forgive, and You Will Be Forgiven – C115
Give: Your Father Sees – A210, B209, C211
Happy Are They Who Follow – A108
Heaven and Earth Will Fade Away – A109, B194

Here I Am – A96, B99, C107
I Loved Wisdom More Than Health or Beauty – A141, B179, C163
If I Must Drink This Cup – A46, B52, C52
Keep These Words in Your Heart and Soul – A118
Listen! Listen! Open Your Hearts! – A36, B37, C37
Listen, Listen to the Voice of Jesus – A198, B197
Listen, Listen to the Words of Jesus – A148
Live on in My Love – A85, A91, B88, B94, C88
Love Is My Desire – A121
Love the Lord Your God – A112, A185, C140
Planted Like a Tree – C111
Take Your Place at the Table – C177
Teach Me Your Path – B30
The Greatest Among You – B182
This Day Is Holy to the Lord Our God – C101
Those Who Do Justice – A151, B160, C142
Those Who Do the Will of God – B124
Walk in My Ways – B31
We Will Follow You, Lord – C133
With All My Heart I Cry (II) – A142

Offering / Sacrifice
Father, into Your Hands – A51, B57, C57
Give: Your Father Sees – A210, B209, C211
Here I Am – A96, B99, C107
I Will Show God's Salvation – A120
If I Must Drink This Cup – A46, B52, C52
Lose Your Life and Save It – A228, B227, B167, C130
Love Is My Desire – A121
The Last Shall Be First – A168
You Alone Are My Help – A137, B140, C141

Paschal Mystery
A New Commandment I Give to You – A49, B55, C55
Alleluia, Alleluia, Alleluia! (I) – B75, C75
At Your Word Our Hearts Are Burning – A75
Christ Laid Down His Life for Us – A172, B170
Christ the Lord Is Risen Again – A65, B71, C71
Clothed in Christ, One in Christ – A28, B28, B69, C69
Eat My Flesh and Drink My Blood – A236, B235, C237
I Am the Resurrection – A43, A49, C49
I Am the Way: Follow Me – A81
I Will See You Again – A88, B91, C91
If I Must Drink This Cup – A46, B52, C52
If You Will Love Each Other – A165
Jesus Christ, the Same Today, Yesterday and Evermore – A22, B22, C22
Live on in My Love – A85, A91, B88, B94, C88
Lose Your Life and Save It – A228, B227, B167, C130
Love Is My Desire – A121
Our Cup of Blessing – A48, B54, C54
Our Glory and Pride is the Cross of Jesus Christ – A47, B53, C53, C227
Take Hold of Eternal Life – C174
The Greatest Among You – B182
The Last Shall Be First – A168
The Love of God – A92, B95, B200, C95
The Stone Which the Builders Rejected – B81
This Is My Body – A50, B56, C56
Unless a Grain of Wheat – B48
Where Two or Three Are Gathered – A162
Worthy Is the Lamb Who Was Slain – A196, B195, C197
You Are the Shepherd – A78

Patience
Ask and Receive (II) – C146
Be Patient, Beloved – A9
Be Strong, Our God Has Come to Save Us (II) – B164
Behold, the Bridegroom Is Here (II) – A192, B3
Courage! Get Up! – B185

Give Peace to Those Who Wait – A163, B165, C166
Guard Me as the Apple of Your Eye! – B180, C181
Keep These Words in Your Heart and Soul – A118
Let My Prayer Come Before You, Lord – A189, B189, C191
Let Your Love Be Upon Us, O Lord – A33, A80, B181
Lift Up Your Heads, Stand and Believe – C3
Love Bears All Things – C106
My God, My Strength, Defend My Cause – A41, B45, C45
O Let My Tongue Cleave to My Mouth – B41
Seek the Lord! Long for the Lord! – A32, A101, A182, B32, C32
The Days Are Coming, Surely Coming – C1
The Mercy of God Is for All – A153
With All My Heart I Cry (I) – A160, B162

Peace
All That Is True – A175
Be Patient, Beloved – A9
Christ Is the Light – A211, B210, C212
Give Peace to Those Who Wait – A163, B165, C166
Justice Shall Flourish – A5
Keep My Soul in Peace – A187
Let Us Go Rejoicing – A2, B245, C198
May God Grant Us Joy of Heart – A250, B249, C251
My Plans for You Are Peace – A193, B192, C194
Now Is the Hour – A3
Rejoice, Rejoice, All You Who Love Jerusalem! – A38, B40, C40
Show Us, Lord, Your Kindness – A149, B5

Perseverance
Ask and Receive (II) – C146
Be Strong, Our God Has Come to Save Us (II) – B164
Behold, the Bridegroom Is Here (II) – A192, B3
Courage! Get Up! – B185
Give Peace to Those Who Wait – A163, B165, C166
God's Tender Mercy – B215, C217
Guard Me as the Apple of Your Eye! – B180, C181
Heaven and Earth Will Fade Away – A109, B194
I Am Your Savior, My People – A166, B168, C169
Keep These Words in Your Heart and Soul – A118
Let My Prayer Come Before You, Lord – A189, B189, C191
Let Your Love Be Upon Us, O Lord – A33, A80, B181
Lift Up Your Heads, Stand and Believe – C3
Light of the World – A100, A106
Lord, This Is the People – A230, B229, C231
Love Bears All Things – C106
My God, My Strength, Defend My Cause – A41, B45, C45
My Plans for You Are Peace – A193, B192, C194
O Let My Tongue Cleave to My Mouth – B41
Rise Up and Tell All Your Children – A227, B226, C228
Seek the Lord! Long for the Lord! – A32, A101, A182, B32, C32
The Days Are Coming, Surely Coming – C1
The Mercy of God Is for All – A153
To Gaze on Your Glory – A134, B137, C137
Turn to Me, Answer Me – A154, B156, C156
With All My Heart I Cry (I) – A160, B162

Petition / Prayer
All Your Sins Have Been Forgiven – C127
Ask and Receive (I) – A143
Ask and Receive (II) – A239, B238, C146, C240
Do Not Abandon Me, Lord! – B186, C188
Don't Be Afraid – A150, B133, C152, C196
From the Fullness of Our Hearts – C118
Give Peace to Those Who Wait – A163, B165, C166
Give Us Living Water – A37, A39, C39
Give: Your Father Sees – A210, B209, C211
God, Come to My Aid (I) – C154
God, Come to My Aid (II) – A144, B146, C147

Guard Me as the Apple of Your Eye! – B180, C181
Heal Me in Your Mercy – B112
Heal My Soul – B114
How I Thirst for You – A235, B234, C236
I Am Your Savior, My People – A166, B168, C169
I Called in My Distress – A218, B217, C219
I Will Walk in the Presence of the Lord – B33, B166
If I Must Drink This Cup – A46, B52, C52
In Your Abundant Love – A126
Keep My Soul in Peace – A187
Lead Me, Guide Me – A107, B110, C110
Let My Prayer Come Before You, Lord – A189, B189, C191
Let Your Love Be Upon Us, O Lord – A33, A80, B181
Like a Deer That Longs for Running Streams – A59, B65, C65
Look on My Toil – A116, B119, C119
Lord, Cleanse My Heart – A61, B46, C67
Lord, Listen to My Prayer – A234, B233, C235
Lord, You Are Close – A167
May God Grant Us Joy of Heart – A250, B249, C251
My Plans for You Are Peace – A193, B192, C194
One Thing I Seek – A122, B125, C125
Open Your Hand, Lord – B145
Remember, Lord – A170
Save Me, O Lord – A117
Save Us, Lord – A125, B128, B142, C128
Shine Out, O Lord; You Are My God – B106
Shine Your Face on Us, Lord – B78
Show Us, Lord, Your Kindness – A149, B5
The Goodness of the Lord – B150, C41
The Mercy of God Is for All – A153
The Prayer of Our Hearts – C186
There Is Mercy in the Lord – A42, B47, C47
To Gaze on Your Glory – A134, B137, C137
To You, O Lord, I Lift My Soul – A1, B1, C2
Turn Our Hearts from Stone to Flesh – A35, B35, C35
Turn to Me, Answer Me – A154, B156, C156
We Have Sinned, Lord – A30, B208, C167
We Look to You, O Lord – B135
We Will Follow You, Lord – C133
With All My Heart I Cry (I) – A160, B162
You Alone Are My Help – A137, B140, C141
You Are Rich in Mercy – B177, C178
Your Mercy Is My Hope – A110, B113, C113

Poverty / Poverty of Spirit
Blest Are the Poor in Spirit – A102, A103
Blest Are You Who Weep – C112
Do Not Store Up Earthly Treasures – C149, C171
Father, into Your Hands – A51, B57, C57
From the Fullness of Our Hearts – C118
Give: Your Father Sees – A210, B209, C211
Here I Am – A96, B99, C107
I Know I Shall See the Goodness of the Lord – A90
I Loved Wisdom More Than Health or Beauty – A141, B179, C163
If I Must Drink This Cup – A46, B52, C52
Keep My Soul in Peace – A187
Let My Prayer Come Before You, Lord – A189, B189, C191
Like a Deer That Longs for Running Streams – A59, B65, C65
Lord, Cleanse My Heart – A61, B46, C67
Love Is My Desire – A121
Praise to God Who Lifts Up the Poor – C170
Take Hold of Eternal Life – C174
Teach Me Your Path – B30
The Greatest Among You – B182
The Last Shall Be First – A168
The Spirit and the Bride Say "Come!" – A231, B230, C232
When the Poor Cry Out – C185
You Alone Are My Help – A137, B140, C141

Praise / Worship / Adoration
All the Ends of the Earth – A14, B14, B87, C14, C179
All Things Are from the Lord – A156
All You Nations – A128, B131, C131
As Seed for the Sowing – A139
Ask and Receive (II) – A239, B238, C240
At Your Word Our Hearts Are Burning – A75
Bless the Lord, My Soul – C27
Blessed Are You, Lord – A169, B171
Clothed in Christ, One in Christ – A28, B28, B69, C69
Come to Me and You Shall Never Hunger – A147, B148
Everlasting Is Your Love – A155
For Ever, For Ever, We Praise You For Ever – A200
From the Fullness of Our Hearts – C118
Give Thanks to the Lord, Alleluia (I) – A70
Give Thanks to the Lord, Alleluia (II) – B129
Give the Lord Power – A180
Go to the Ends of the Earth – C120
God Feeds Us, God Saves Us – A115, C183
God Goes Up with Shouts of Joy – A87, B90, C90
God Heals the Broken – B109, C173
God Remembers His Covenant For Ever – B18
God's Love Is Revealed to Us – A15, B15, C28
God's Tender Mercy – A6
God, Let All the Peoples Praise You – A152, C87
Great In Our Midst Is the Holy One – C8
Home for the Lonely – B143, C144, C161
How Wonderful Your Name, O Lord – C201
I Called in My Distress – A218, B217, C219
I Love You, Lord – A183
I Thank You, Lord, with All My Heart – C180
I Will Praise You, I Will Thank You – A215, B214, C216
I Will Praise You, Lord – A56, B62, C62, C78
I Will Praise Your Name For Ever (I) – C84
I Will Praise Your Name For Ever (II) – A132, C189
I Will Sing For Ever of Your Love – A129, B11
In the Presence of the Angels – C108
It Is Good to Give You Thanks – B126, C117
Joyfully You Will Draw Water – A57, B27, B205, C63
Let All the Earth Adore and Praise You – A73, B98, C77
Let All the Earth Cry Out Your Praises – A73, B77, C77
Let the King of Glory Come In – A11, B211, C213
Let the Word Make a Home in Your Heart – A19, B161
Listen! Listen! Open Your Hearts! – A36, B37, C37
May God Bless Us in Mercy – A21, B21, C21
May God Grant Us Joy of Heart – A250, B249, C251
Merciful and Tender – A111, A164, B117, C36, C114, C187
My Soul Rejoices in God – A225, B8, B224, C12, C226
O Praise the Lord, Jerusalem – A203, B151
Our City Has No Need of Sun or Moon – A25, B25, C25
People of God, Flock of the Lord – A123, C81
Praise the Lord, Alleluia! – B108
Praise to God Who Lifts Up the Poor – C170
Proclaim the Wonders God Has Done – C99
Rejoice in the Lord, Again Rejoice! – A7, B7, C7
Ring Out Your Joy – B120
Seek the Lord! Long for the Lord! – A32, A101, A182, B32, C32
Shout to the Ends of the Earth – A89, B86, C86
Sing and Make Music – A248, B247, C249
Sing to God a New Song – A79, B83, C83
The Earth Is Full of the Goodness of God (I) – A76, B80, C80
The Earth Is Full of the Goodness of God (II) – A53, B59, C59
The Goodness of the Lord – B150, C41
The Lord Is King (I) – A221, B220, C93
The Lord Will Bless His People – A27
The Love of God – A92, B95, C95
The Strong Lord Sets Me Free – A184, B116, C116

They Shall Adore You – A24, B24, C24
This Day Is Holy to the Lord Our God – C101
This Is the Day – A66, B72, C72
To Gaze on Your Glory – A134, B137, C137
Venite, Adoremus – A245, B107, C246
We Receive from Your Fullness – A16, B16, C16
With All My Heart I Praise You – B115
Within Your Temple – A131, B134, C134
Worthy Is the Lamb Who Was Slain – A196, B195, C197
You Alone Are Lord – A181
You Are God's Temple – A247, B246, C248
You Are My Hiding-place, O Lord – C48
You Are My Praise – B84
You Are the Shepherd – A78
You Have Given Everything Its Place – A179, B174, C175
You Have Shown You Love Us – A199, B198, C200
You Open Your Hand – A127, B144
You Shall Be a Royal Priesthood – A124
Yours Is the Day – B149, C150

Presence of God
A River Flows – A238, B237, C239
At Your Word Our Hearts Are Burning – A75
Here in Your Presence – B121
I Am With You – C30
I Will See You Again – A88, B91, C91
If You Will Love Each Other – A165
In Every Age, O Lord, You Have Been Our Refuge – C164
Keep My Soul in Peace – A187
Let the Word Make a Home in Your Heart – A19, B161
Listen, Listen to the Words of Jesus – A148
Listen: I Stand at the Door and Knock – A140, C143
Lord, You Are Close – A167
Our Help Shall Come from the Lord – C182
Our Shelter and Our Help – C124
Salvation Has Come to This House – C190
The Love of God – B200
Those Who Love Me, I Will Deliver – A29, B29, C38, C29
Where Two or Three Are Gathered – A162
You Will Show Me the Path of Life – B188
You Will Show Us the Path of Life – A74

Promise
Ask and Receive (II) – C146
Be Patient, Beloved – A9
Blest Are the Poor in Spirit – A103
Come, Lord, and Save Us – A8
Courage! Get Up! – B185
Every Valley Shall Be Filled – C6
God Heals the Broken – B109, C173
God of Life, God of Hope – C193
God Remembers His Covenant For Ever – B18
Heaven and Earth Will Fade Away – A109, B194
Keep Us in Your Name – B127, C94
Lift Up Your Heads, Stand and Believe – C3
My Portion and My Cup – A54, B60, B193, C60, C132
My Sheep I Will Pasture – C208
Our Shelter and Our Help – C124
Rejoice, Your Names Are Written in Heaven – C136
Remember, Lord – A170
Speak Your Word, O Lord – C121
The Days Are Coming, Surely Coming – C1
The Goodness of the Lord – B150, C41
The Spirit and the Bride Say "Come!" – A231, B230, C232
Those Who Love Me, I Will Deliver – A29, B29, C38, C29
You Are Rich in Mercy – A176
Your Mercy Is My Hope – A110, B113, C113
Yours Is the Day – B149, C150

Protection / Providence of God
All Things Are from the Lord – A156
All Who Labor, Come to Me – A133, B204, C206
As Seed for the Sowing – A136, A139
Ask and Receive (I) – A143
Ask and Receive (II) – C146
Be Patient, Beloved – A9
Be Strong, Our God Has Come to Save Us (I) – B9, C9
Be Strong, Our God Has Come to Save Us (II) – B164
Bless the Lord, My Soul – C27
Blest Are the Poor in Spirit – A102
Cast Out into the Deep – C109
Chosen in Christ, Blessed in Christ – B139
Christ Is the Light – A211, A213, B210, B212, C212, C214
Come, All You Good and Faithful Servants – A195
Come, Come to the Banquet – A146, C43
Come, Lord, and Save Us – A8
Come, My Children – B176
Come to Me and You Shall Never Hunger – A147, B148
Do Not Store Up Earthly Treasures – C149, C171
Don't Be Afraid – A150, B133, C152, C196
Give Thanks to the Lord, Alleluia (II) – B129
Give: Your Father Sees – A210, B209, C211
God Feeds Us, God Saves Us – A115, C183
God Heals the Broken – B109, C173
God of Life, God of Hope – C193
God's Tender Mercy – B215, C217
God, Come to My Aid (II) – A144, B146, C147
Guard Me as the Apple of Your Eye! – B180, C181
Happy Are They Who Dwell in Your House – A244, B38, C18
Happy Are They Whose God Is the Lord – B199, C151
Heal My Soul – B114
Home for the Lonely – B143, C144, C161
I Am the Resurrection – A43, B49, C49
I Am With You – C30
I Am Your Savior, My People – A166, B168, C169
I Called in My Distress – A218, B217, C219
I Know I Shall See the Goodness of the Lord – A90
I Love You, Lord – A183
I Shall Dwell in the House of the Lord – A177
I Thank You, Lord, with All My Heart – C180
I Will Praise You, Lord – A56, B62, C62, C78
I Will Praise Your Name For Ever (I) – C84
I Will Praise Your Name For Ever (II) – A132, C189
I Will Walk in the Presence of the Lord – B33, B166
In Every Age, O Lord, You Have Been Our Refuge – C164
In God Alone Is My Soul at Rest – A114
In Your Abundant Love – A126
It Is Good to Give You Thanks – B126, C117
Jesus Christ, the Same Today, Yesterday and Evermore – A22, B22, C22
Keep Us in Your Name – B127, C94
Laughter Fills Our Mouths – B184, C5
Lead Me, Guide Me – A107, B110, C110
Let All the Earth Adore and Praise You – A73, B98, C77
Let All the Earth Cry Out Your Praises – A73, B77, C77
Let Your Love Be Upon Us, O Lord – A33, A80, B181
Listen! Listen! Open Your Hearts! – A36, B37, C37
My Grace Is Enough – B136
My Plans for You Are Peace – A193, B192, C194
My Portion and My Cup – A54, B60, B193, C60, C132
My Sheep I Will Pasture – C208
My Shepherd Is the Lord – A39, A233, B42, B82, B141, B191, B232, C82, C207, C234
My Soul Rejoices in God – A225, B8, B224, C12, C226
O Praise the Lord, Jerusalem – A203, B151
Open Your Hand, Lord – B145
Our Help Shall Come from the Lord – C182

Our Shelter and Our Help – C124
Praise the Lord, Alleluia! – B108
Praise to God Who Lifts Up the Poor – C170
Save Me, O Lord – A117
Save Us, Lord – A125, B128, B142, C128
Shine Out, O Lord; You Are My God – B106
Shine Your Face on Us, Lord – B78
Shout to the Ends of the Earth – A89, B86, C86
Show Us, Lord, Your Kindness – A149, B5
Sing and Make Music – A248, B247, C249
The Goodness of the Lord – B150, C41
The Lord Is My Light – A99, B122, C33, C122
The Lord Will Bless His People – A27
The Love of God – A92, B95, B200, C95
The Strong Lord Sets Me Free – A184, B116, C116
Those Who Love Me, I Will Deliver – A29, B29, C38, C29
To Gaze on Your Glory – A134, B137, C137
To You, O Lord, I Lift My Soul – A1, B1, C2
When the Poor Cry Out – C185
Who Can This Be – B130
With All My Heart I Praise You – B115
You Alone Are Lord – A181
You Alone Are My Help – A137, B140, C141
You Are Rich in Mercy – A68, B43
You Are the Shepherd – A78
You Open Your Hand – A127, B144
Your Mercy Is My Hope – A110, B113, C113
Yours Is the Day – B149, C150

Redemption
All Your Sins Have Been Forgiven – C127
Be Strong, Our God Has Come to Save Us (I) – B9, C9
Be Strong, Our God Has Come to Save Us (II) – B164
Behold, the Bridegroom Is Here (I) – B118
Blest Are the Poor in Spirit – A102
Blest Are You Who Weep – C112
Change Your Heart and Mind – A171
Chosen in Christ, Blessed in Christ – B139
Christ Laid Down His Life for Us – A172, B170
Clothed in Christ, One in Christ – A28, B28
Come, Lord, and Save Us – A8
Come, My Children – B176
Don't Be Afraid – A150, B133, C152, C196
Every Valley Shall Be Filled – C6
God's Tender Mercy – B215, C217
God, Come to My Aid (II) – A144, B146, C147
Heal Me in Your Mercy – B112
Heal My Soul – B114
I Am the Way: Follow Me – A81
I Called in My Distress – A218, B217, C219
I Will Praise You, Lord – A56, B62, C62, C78
Keep Us in Your Name – B127, C94
Laughter Fills Our Mouths – B184, C5
Lead Me, Guide Me – A107, B110, C110
Let All the Earth Adore and Praise You – A73, B98, C77
Let All the Earth Cry Out Your Praises – A73, B77, C77
Love Is My Desire – A121
Merciful and Tender – A111, A164, B117, C36, C114, C187
My Plans for You Are Peace – A193, B192, C194
My Sheep I Will Pasture – C208
My Soul Rejoices in God – A225, B8, B224, C12, C226
Open Your Hand, Lord – B145
Our Shelter and Our Help – C124
Praise the Lord, Alleluia! – B108
Rejoice, Your Names Are Written in Heaven – C136
Remember, Lord – A170
Shine Out, O Lord; You Are My God – B106
Shout to the Ends of the Earth – A89, B86, C86

Take Hold of Eternal Life – C174
The Days Are Coming, Surely Coming – C1
The Love of God – B200
The Mercy of God Is for All – A153
The Spirit and the Bride Say "Come!" – A231, B230, C232
There Is Mercy in the Lord – A42, B47, C47
Those Who Love Me, I Will Deliver – C29
Turn Our Hearts from Stone to Flesh – A35, B35, C35
Turn to the Lord – B111, C126
Who Can This Be – B130
With All My Heart I Praise You – B115
You Alone Are My Help – A137, B140, C141
You Are My Hiding-place, O Lord – C48
You Are Rich in Mercy – A176, A208, B177, B207, C178,
    C209
You Are the Shepherd – A78

Refuge
A River Flows – A238, B237, C239
All Who Labor, Come to Me – A133, B204, C206
Blest Are the Poor in Spirit – A102
Cast Out into the Deep – C109
"Come," Says My Heart – B92, C92
Come to Me and You Shall Never Hunger – A147, B148
Do Not Store Up Earthly Treasures – C149, C171
Don't Be Afraid – A150, B133, C152, C196
God, Come to My Aid (I) – C154
God, Come to My Aid (II) – A144, B146, C147
God, Who Raised Jesus from the Dead – A232, B231, C233
Happy Are They Who Dwell in Your House – A244, B38, C18
Home for the Lonely – B143, C144, C161
I Am Your Savior, My People – A166, B168, C169
I Know I Shall See the Goodness of the Lord – A90
I Love You, Lord – A183
I Shall Dwell in the House of the Lord – A177
In Every Age, O Lord, You Have Been Our Refuge – C164
In God Alone Is My Soul at Rest – A114
Keep My Soul in Peace – A187
Lead Me, Guide Me – A107, B110, C110
Let Your Love Be Upon Us, O Lord – A33, A80, B181
My Lips Will Tell of Your Justice – C105
My Portion and My Cup – A54, B60, B193, C60, C132
One Thing I Seek – A122, B125, C125
Our Help Shall Come from the Lord – C182
Our Shelter and Our Help – C124
Save Me, O Lord – A117
Save Us, Lord – A125
Shine Out, O Lord; You Are My God – B106
The Lord Is My Light – A99, B122, C33, C122
The Strong Lord Sets Me Free – A184, B116, C116
To Gaze on Your Glory – A134, B137, C137
We Will Follow You, Lord – C133
When the Poor Cry Out – C185
Who Can This Be – B130
You Alone Are My Help – A137, B140, C141
You Are My Hiding-place, O Lord – C48
You Open Your Hand – A127, B144
You Will Show Me the Path of Life – B188
You Will Show Us the Path of Life – A74

Rest
Here in Your Presence – B121
I Shall Dwell in the House of the Lord – A177
In God Alone Is My Soul at Rest – A114
My Portion and My Cup – A54, B60, B193, C60, C132
My Sheep I Will Pasture – C208
My Shepherd Is the Lord – A39, A233, B42, B82, B141, B191,
    B232, C82, C207, C234
Sing to the Lord – A55, B61, C61

Salvation

All the Ends of the Earth – A14, B14, B87, C14, C179
All Who Labor, Come to Me – A133, B204, C206
As a Bridegroom Rejoices – A240, B239, C100
Ask and Receive (II) – C146
Be Patient, Beloved – A9
Be Strong, Our God Has Come to Save Us (I) – B9, C9
Be Strong, Our God Has Come to Save Us (II) – B164
Behold the Lamb of God! – A97, B100
Behold, the Bridegroom Is Here (I) – B118
Blest Are the Poor in Spirit – A102
Cast Out into the Deep – C109
Chosen in Christ, Blessed in Christ – B139
Come, All You Good and Faithful Servants – A195
Come, Lord, and Save Us – A8
Do Not Abandon Me, Lord! – B186, C188
Don't Be Afraid – A150, B133, C152, C196
Give Us Living Water – A37, B39, C39
God Feeds Us, God Saves Us – A115, C183
God Heals the Broken – B109, C173
God of Hosts, Bring Us Back – B2, C11
God of Life, God of Hope – C193
God's Love Is Revealed to Us – A15, B15, C28
God, Come to My Aid (II) – A144, B146, C147
God, Who Raised Jesus from the Dead – A232, B231, C233
Great In Our Midst Is the Holy One – C8
Happy Are They Whose God Is the Lord – C151
Heal Me in Your Mercy – B112
Heal My Soul – B114
Home for the Lonely – B143, C144, C161
I Am the Way: Follow Me – A81
I Am With You – C30
I Am Your Savior, My People – A166, B168, C169
I Love You, Lord – A183
I Thank You, Lord, with All My Heart – C180
I Will Dwell with You – A237, B236, C238
I Will Praise You, Lord – A56, B62, C62, C78
I Will Show God's Salvation – A120
In the Presence of the Angels – C108
Jesus, Mighty Lord, Come Save Us – A12
Joyfully You Will Draw Water – A57, B27, B205, C63
Keep My Soul in Peace – A187
Keep Us in Your Name – B127, C94
Laughter Fills Our Mouths – B184, C5
Lead Me, Guide Me – A107, B110, C110
Lose Your Life and Save It – A228, B227, B167, C130
Love Is My Desire – A121
May God Grant Us Joy of Heart – A250, B249, C251
My God, My Strength, Defend My Cause – A41, B45, C45
My Lips Will Tell of Your Justice – C105
My Plans for You Are Peace – A193, B192, C194
My Portion and My Cup – A54, B60, B193, C60, C132
My Sheep I Will Pasture – C208
My Shepherd Is the Lord – A39, A233, B42, B82, B141, B191, B232, C82, C207, C234
Our Help Shall Come from the Lord – C182
Praise to God Who Lifts Up the Poor – C170
Raise the Cup of Salvation – B202
Rise Up and Tell All Your Children – A227, B226, C228
Salvation Has Come to This House – C190
Save Me, O Lord – A117
Save Us, Lord – A125, B128, B142, C128
Shine Out, O Lord; You Are My God – B106
Show Us, Lord, Your Kindness – A149, B5
Sing to God a New Song – A79, B83, C83
Speak Your Word, O Lord – C121
Take Hold of Eternal Life – C174
The Love of God – B200

The Mercy of God Is for All – A153
The Spirit and the Bride Say "Come!" – A231, B230, C232
The Strong Lord Sets Me Free – A184, B116, C116
Those Who Love Me, I Will Deliver – A29, B29, C38, C29
Turn Our Hearts from Stone to Flesh – A35, B35, C35
We Receive from Your Fullness – A16, B16, C16
We Shall Be Like You – A222, B221, C223
When the Poor Cry Out – C185
You Alone Are Lord – A181
You Alone Are My Help – A137, B140, C141
You Are Rich in Mercy – A176
You Will Show Me the Path of Life – B188
You Will Show Us the Path of Life – A74
Your Mercy Is My Hope – A110, B113, C113

Second Coming

Arise, Jerusalem, Look to the East – A23, B23, C23
Arise, Jerusalem, Stand on the Height – A4, B6, C4
At Your Word Our Hearts Are Burning – A75
Be Patient, Beloved – A9
Be Strong, Our God Has Come to Save Us (I) – B9, C9
Be Strong, Our God Has Come to Save Us (II) – B164
Behold, the Bridegroom Is Here (II) – A192, B3
Clothed in Christ, One in Christ – A28, B28, B69, C69
Come, Lord, and Save Us – A8
Every Valley Shall Be Filled – C6
Heaven and Earth Will Fade Away – A109, B194
I Am the Resurrection – A43, B49, C49
I Will Dwell with You – A237, B236, C238
I Will See You Again – A88, B91, C91
Jesus, Mighty Lord, Come Save Us – A12
Let the King of Glory Come In – A11, B211, C213
Lift Up Your Heads, Stand and Believe – C3
My Plans for You Are Peace – A193, B192, C194
My Portion and My Cup – A54, B60, B193, C60, C132
Our City Has No Need of Sun or Moon – A25, B25, C25
Sing to the Lord – A55, B61, C61
Take Hold of Eternal Life – C174
The Days Are Coming, Surely Coming – C1
They Shall Adore You – A24, B24, C24
We Receive from Your Fullness – A16, B16, C16
Why Stare into the Sky? – A86, B89, C89
Worthy Is the Lamb Who Was Slain – A196, B195, C197

Sin and Temptation

All Your Sins Have Been Forgiven – C127
Change Your Heart and Mind – A171
Do Not Abandon Me, Lord! – B186, C188
Heal My Soul – B114
Like a Deer That Longs for Running Streams – A59, B65, C65
Lord, Cleanse My Heart – A61, B46, C67
Remember, Lord – A170
Those Who Love Me, I Will Deliver – A29, B29, C38, C29
Turn Our Hearts from Stone to Flesh – A35, B35, C35
Turn to the Lord – B111, C126
We Have Sinned, Lord – A30, B208, C167
You Are My Hiding-place, O Lord – C48
You Are Rich in Mercy – B177, C178

Social Concern and Justice

A New Commandment I Give to You – A49, B55, C55
Be Patient, Beloved – A9
Blest Are the Poor in Spirit – A102
Blest Are You Who Weep – C112
Forgive, and You Will Be Forgiven – C115
Give: Your Father Sees – A210, B209, C211
God Heals the Broken – B109, C173